JOURNEYS

JOURNEYS

The Impact of Personal Experience on Religious Thought

edited by
GREGORY BAUM

PAULIST PRESS
New York, N.Y. / Paramus, N.J.

Library of Congress
Catalog Card Number: 75-31401

ISBN: 0-8091-0204-8 (cloth)

ISBN: 0-8091-1909-9 (paper)

Published by Paulist Press
Editorial Office: 1865 Broadway, N.Y., N.Y. 10023
Business Office: 400 Sette Drive, Paramus, N.J. 07652

Printed and bound in the
United States of America.

Contents

Introduction

A few years ago, in the summer of 1972 to be precise, I participated in a theological workshop on biography and styles of theology. Several speakers had been invited to present papers relating their theological orientation to the story of their lives. The lectures and the subsequent discussion convinced the participants that there is an important relation, not always clearly recognized, between personal life and theological interest and methodology. As there is a "sociology of knowledge" relating concepts and truth to the social background in which they emerge and prosper, so there ought to be a "psychology of knowledge" connecting people's intellectual approach to the significant events of their biographies.

Research and thinking are always based on personal concerns. This is also true in theology. Even when the issues that preoccupy us are mainly social and political or affect humanity in general, there are always highly personal reasons why these more universal issues mean so much to us. More than that, why do we trust certain methods of research while others fail to convince us? Theologians used to say, possibly partially in jest, that a person was either a Platonist or an Aristotelian and that the difference between them was a matter of temperament rather than rationality. What is certainly true is that we trust certain methods of research and reflection because they have made sense to us, because they have shed light on issues that are personally important to us, possibly even because they are related to important events of childhood. Why not? In childhood the foundations are laid for the disposition of the mind. Why do we think the way we do? It is not all due to adult experience and university training. Our early biography surely has something to do with it.

1

The proceedings of the theological workshop were never published. When, at a later time, I showed my written contribution to Father Kevin Lynch, editor of Paulist Press, he felt that the relationship between biography and styles of theology would make an excellent topic for a book. He suggested to me that I write to Catholic theologians in North America, known to the public through their books and articles, and ask them whether they would be interested in writing a paper on their personal life and its relationship to their work as theologians. Why do we think the way we do? How has our personal experience influenced our style of thought? Since we have lived through the same dramatic changes in the Catholic Church and the conflicts engendered by them, we might find that we have had many important experiences in common and even share in a certain common theological orientation. Who knows? Should we not find out? Several theologians gave a positive reply to my request, some with enthusiasm, others with certain hesitations. Some theologians were involved in projects of their own and unable at this time to write a biographical article. Ten articles, including my own piece, are collected in this volume and offered to the public.

Since the topic of biography and theology is inevitably open and undefined, the contributors to this volume understood their tasks in different ways. Some were almost exclusively concerned with their intellectual history and paid attention to personal experiences only to the extent that these influenced their thought. Others felt that a more inclusive biography would be necessary to explain the way they think, and hence they summarized for the reader the significant events of their lives. Others again adopted an even more personal style. It was important for them to be known by the reader: for only through such a personal acquaintance could the reader understand what they are up to in their theology. Because of these different responses, the collected articles are of very different styles.

Despite the differences, all the articles are useful and interesting. They prove that much more is hidden in our lives than we at first realize. We have to be taught to take our own experience seriously. This book persuades us that hidden in our lives are resources for reflection. A contact with our own life story is for us a way to self-knowledge and, beyond that, an entry into wisdom. While the collected articles demonstrate the profound effect that personal experiences have on the way we think, they also prove that it is impossible to make many generalizations on this topic. The same experience can give rise to a variety of meanings and interpretations. There remains something wholly unaccountable in the life of the mind. There are moments of discontinuity in our mental histories when we create an intellectual orientation as the unfolding of insights mediated by life experience, or as a defense against them. While the way we think is determined by biography, our thoughts remain free, which here means dependent on the unaccountable moments when we are being addressed by God's word.

GREGORY BAUM

Personal Experience and Styles of Thought

GREGORY BAUM

The style adopted in theological reflection depends in large measure on personal biography. Students of theology, depending on the school they attend, are trained in a particular theological approach. Later they may find that the method they have learned will not solve the intellectual problems that confront them. They try new approaches, and when they find a manner of treating the issue that gives them new insight, new sensitivity, a deeper understanding of hidden connections, and an intellectual experience that assures them they are in touch with truth, they will adopt the new method and try to apply it to other subjects. The style of theology acquired by theologians, then, is largely fashioned out of the methods that have guided them in the important turning points of their personal and intellectual history.

When I say that the style of theological thinking depends on personal biography, I include in this, of course, the cultural sphere to which theologians belong and the social and political conditions that form the coordinates of their personal lives. Thinking is never a purely private affair. It is always linked to the experience of a community, a people, or a class, which is the bearer of an intellectual style. As this group moves through a crisis and reorients its purpose and meaning, the style proper to the group will also undergo signifcant changes. It is possible, therefore, to analyze the changes in theological thinking taking place in the Christian Churches during the twentieth century by relating them to the cultural crisis of the West and new social and political pressures under which the Churches were forced to live.

There are, then, several ways of telling the same story. What I want to do in this paper is to describe the important intellectual experiences, connected to turning points in my life, that have determined my style of theological reflection. I realize, of course, that in these personal experiences, the tensions and pressures of society were operative. But this is not the aspect I wish to pursue. I prefer at this time to remain more personal in my remarks.

At the outset I should say that I became a Christian at the age of twenty-three. I come from a German Jewish family (from Berlin, to be exact) that, following the nineteenth-century trend of assimilation, had abandoned Jewish practices and lost all interest in religion. The values to which I was initiated as a child were the secular ideals of culture, meaning, and beauty, typical of the German bourgeoisie. The Germans called this *Bildung*. The great cultural hero of this educated class was Goethe. Goethe, the poet, the artist, the searcher, the wise man, the genius, who had yet been comfortable in the courtly life at Weimar, had been the guiding light of many generations. When Hitler destroyed the good life for the Germans and, in particular, for the German Jews (before he destroyed their life altogether), the values cherished for so long fell apart. As Hitler tore asunder the web of our life, nothing remained of the ideals that inspired us. When, as a boy of sixteen, I was able to leave Germany for England in 1939, I felt that my world had gone under. The people I knew, my family and friends, had become mute. They had nothing to say. None of the inherited values shed light on the new situation. Life had lost all meaning. I well remember how amazed I was at the silence of my elders. It was soon afterward that I began to search for a view of life and a source of wisdom that could outlast catastrophe. In Canada, in 1946, I became a Christian in the Catholic Church.

This is not the story I want to tell at this point. My topic is not faith, but styles of theology. At the University of Fribourg, Switzerland, in the years from 1950 to 1956, I received an excellent training in Thomistic theology, understood not as a narrow system, as this sometimes happens, but as a coherent vehicle of the universal Christian tradition. We studied St.

Thomas not simply as a thinker who adopted Aristotle to the Christian Middle Ages: we regarded him as a shining witness of the Pauline-Augustinian tradition with its stress on the primacy of grace and faith and a brilliant heir of Platonic and neo-Platonist wisdom with its stress on participation in, and yet the unknowability of, the divine mystery. When I studied the great Thomistic synthesis in the early fifties, I was firmly convinced that I was acquiring the concepts and the method I would use in theological research and reflection for the rest of my life. This delighted me at the time. Since so much of Catholic thought had become somewhat narrow after the conflict with Protestantism and the Enlightenment, the adoption of a fresh Thomison, nourished by Scripture and the fathers, was an act critical of contemporary Catholicism and seeming to hold much promise for the future.

Catholic theologians of my generation tend to find themselves in similar circumstances: we were trained in a style of thought we expected to last us a lifetime; yet as we took hold of the ecclesiastical renewal, or as this renewal took hold of us, we found that the methods in which we had been trained were no longer adequate. Under the pressure of new experiences, we set out to find new approaches to theological reflection, and we kept on moving ever since, opening ourselves to various lines of thought and methods of inquiry, keeping our thinking tentative and provisional. The older generation of Catholic theologians were able to build their theological reflection on the foundation laid when they were young. In one way or another, they sought to perfect a theological system. They were able to present their theology with an air of certainty; they had fully assimilated the methods they used, and they were convinced that these methods produced adequate results. The Catholic theologians of my generation had to change their minds many times. We kept on modifying our style. It seemed to us that in a Church in transition, the style of theology must remain provisional.

A historical event that profoundly affected my theological thinking was the ecumenical movement. From the beginning of my theological studies I had been interested in Protestant thought. This was due in part to my close association with Protestants in my upbringing and later at the university in

Canada. More than that, I have always been deeply concerned about how people look upon "the others," "the outsiders," "the minority." To this day, I regard this as one of the crucial tests of morality: how do we look upon and treat "the others"? I suppose that belonging to a Jewish family I was particularly sensitive to this point, for Jews had always been "the others" in the so-called Christian nations and often suffered from the cruel, unreflected, paranoid behavior of the established majority toward the dissident group. It was not surprising, therefore, that from the beginning of my theological studies, I was saddened by the Catholic attitude toward Protestants and the ignorance, lack of understanding, and outright prejudice that characterized Catholic theological treatments of Protestant issues. Later, I came to realize that the ignorance and the prejudice were mutual. In this situation, I found the ecumenical movement an exciting event with the power to deliver men from ignorance, distortions, and fear. I was allowed to experience the force of dialogue and the changes that dialogue induces in the participants. At that time, in the middle fifties, when few Catholics paid attention to the movement, I devoted myself to the study and the practice of ecumenism. It was probably because I had written my doctoral dissertation on an ecumenical subject that, several years later, I was appointed by Pope John as a member of the newly founded Secretariat for Promoting Christian Unity, then a preparatory body for the coming Vatican Council.

The ecumenical movement introduced me to dialogue as a way of truth. Dialogue, I discovered, has the power to change the self-awareness of both partners. First, dialogue revealed to us that our own view of the partner had been false. We discovered our prejudices in regard to the other. In trying to understand his viewpoint and approach, we developed new sensitivities. We opened ourselves to perspectives hidden from us before. And as our theological awareness expanded, we often discovered that our own traditional manner of understanding divine revelation had suffered from one-sidedness. The defensive and prejudicial stance against others, we then discovered, was not only unjust in regard to these others, it was also positively harmful to ourselves since it narrowed our own assimilation of the Christian tradition. Gaining a more truthful understanding of the partner made us want to change ourselves. In this way, the discovery of prejudice led to a deeper conversion to the truth we held.

Secondly, dialogue enabled us to listen to what the partner had to say to us. Instead of adopting a defensive position, instead of pushing aside his objections and critical remarks as so many expressions of hostility, we were willing to listen seriously to how other people, in this case Protestants, looked on us. We realized that we cannot come to self-knowledge by looking at ourselves: only as we are engaged in conversation with others, and reflect on their reactions to us, are we able to gain greater insight into who we are. In dialogue, then, we were willing to let ourselves be addressed by Protestant Christians. We began to see forms of infidelity and elements foreign to the Gospel that were deeply inscribed in our past and that, as a result of the dialogue, we desired to overcome. Dialogue inevitably summons to renewal. Dialogue, then, is a powerful instrument of the divine Word, transforming the self-awareness of both partners and thus leading them into greater truth.

Ecumenical dialogue, moreover, extended the common ground between Catholics and Protestants. As the ongoing conversation changed our self-awareness, we discovered that we shared the central convictions of the Gospel. Since we abandoned the narrow interpretation of our dogmatic traditions and made room in them for complementary aspects we had neglected, we found that the central themes of the Gospel were held by us in common. The points on which we differed were hardly Church-dividing. We found, in fact, that there was usually more doctrinal disagreement within a single Church than there was among ecumenical theologians gathered from various Churches. At the same time we learned to appreciate that Protestants and Catholics look upon the Gospel from different perspectives, and while we wanted to be united as brothers, we cherished this difference of perspective and shied away from any vision of Christian unity that demanded uniformity. We felt united in the Gospel, but committed to pluralism within that unity. For a vast number of Christians, the great discovery of the ecumenical movement and the dialogue associated with it was the realization that fidelity and openness can and must go together. It is possible, we found out, to be faithful to our deep convictions and, at the same time, open to the message addressed to us by others. Dialogue does not lead to compromise nor to the conversion from one side to the other. Dialogue leads to the convergence of the Christian traditions while protecting the plurality of approaches.

Today all of us take this dialogue for granted. But there was a time, not so long ago, when few Christians were interested in dialogue between Catholics and Protestants. At that time the ecclesiastical institutions were, on the whole, opposed to this dialogue, and if not opposed, then at least cautious in regard to it. And they had reason to be apprehensive, for ecumenical dialogue was a powerful and explosive activity with far-reaching effects on the self-understanding of the Churches and the possibility of Christian renewal. Today this sort of dialogue is readily accepted. Vatican Council II released a great amount of energy in the Catholic Church, setting Catholics free to explore the new friendship with other Christians and learn from traditions they had long neglected. But while this sort of conversation has come to determine the style of theological reflection at most seminaries and universities, the organized ecumenical movement has become so dominated by institutional interests that its power has been greatly reduced. It is hardly a movement any more. The Churches officially represented in the new "committee ecumenism" often prevent the really embarrassing questions from being raised. It often appears as if the Churches come together to guarantee one another their inherited structures and vested interests.

Yet for me the ecumenical movement of the fifties was the context in which I discovered dialogue as a powerful theological method. This method reached much further than Catholic-Protestant relations. It was applicable to the whole of theology and to any branch of knowledge. Since we are always limited in our own perspective, theologians or any other researchers must remain learners. They must realize that their own viewpoint is inevitably incomplete and hence seek conversation with other branches of knowledge or other intellectual traditions. Because Christian theologians believe that in Christ they have access to the truth that shall never be surpassed, they may be more reluctant than philosophers and other thinkers to recognize the need for dialogue. At least this used to be the case prior to the ecumenical movement. Since then, dialogue has led Christian theologians to open conversations with many new partners, religious and secular.

How does this dialogue affect the style of theological thinking? It gives theological reflection a certain provisional character. Since we wish to remain learners and do not know beforehand what the effect of a new conversation will be, we hold our intellectual elaboration of the Christian message with a certain tentativeness. We are quite willing to acknowledge that a prolonged dialogue with sociology or, to give another example, Hinduism, will have a profound effect on our thinking, and while we trust that we shall remain faithful to God's revelation in Jesus Christ, we are quite unable to foresee how our theological understanding will be affected by this conversation.

Dialogue as method in theology, then, keeps us open to new perspectives. More must be said. My own experience of dialogue and its power convinced me that greater insight is not always reached by adding new truth to what we already know: dialogue on significant issues transforms our self-awareness and hence makes us see ourselves and our history in a new light. The passage from being a traditional Catholic to being an ecumenical one is not a process of learning new truths; it is a conversion. The quest for truth in theology then (and probably in any other branch of knowledge) is never a purely intellectual exercise. The ecumenical movement convinced me that dialogue, personal involvement, and the subsequent transformation of consciousness were indispensible elements of the theological enterprise. Scholarship alone will not do. I could think of many great scholars who had studied Christian history and the great Christian authors and made significant contributions to specialized theological research and who, at the same time, were quite insensitive to crucial insights that less-learned theologians, more open to dialogue and the viewpoint of others, had gained in their personal lives. It became quite clear to me at that time, through the ecumenical movement, that the highly intellectual understanding of truth in the academic tradition and in scientific theology had obscured a significant factor in the search for truth, namely the expansion of awareness through dialogue, sympathy, and personal involvement. Often academic theology created a cast of mind that was insensitive to authentic conversation. The reliance on purely intellectual criteria tended to make theologians incapable of understanding experiences and interpretations that did not fit their own categories. I became convinced that theology could only be done fruitfully if a theologian were engaged in some non-academic activities, i.e., if he were willing to interrupt the conversation with his colleagues and engage in dialogue and cooperation with other people, other schools of thought, or other groups, be they secular or religious. In order to do theology, it is necessary to transcend the boundaries of one's own limited world.

The profound impression that dialogue as a way of truth made on me prepared me for the theological position I was to discover later, namely that present in all truly human conversations is the divine Word. God is Word, summons, critique, new truth, operative in human conversation. Every truly human conversation is, therefore, redemptive. As people grow and come to be through dialogue and interaction, the divine mystery is graciously present in their ongoing and never ending self-making. This is good news.

At the time when I discovered the power of dialogue and adopted it as theological method, I did not clearly see the limits of dialogue. While I was quite certain, because of my personal fate as a German Jew, that religious people and value-oriented humanists could not and should not have been in dialogue with the Nazis, I did not reflect on the conditions that prohibit dialogue and demand conflict as the responsible stance. Later theological experiences raised this question for me with greater urgency.

II

The second personal event that had a profound effect on my theological reflection was the painful discovery of the anti-Jewish trend present in Christian preaching almost from the beginning. At the end of the fifties, I was asked to prepare several lectures on the relationship of the Church to the Jewish people. Though I come from a Jewish family, I had never reflected on this topic. I have no childhood memory of Jewish religion or Jewish ceremony. To be Jewish had only a secular meaning to me. When asked to give these lectures, I had to acquaint myself with the literature on the topic. It was only after giving the lectures that I hit upon Jules Isaac's book *Jésus et Israel* (only recently translated into English), which brought out as no book had done before the manner in which the preaching of the Gospel had vilified the Jewish people and sought to create contempt for them among Christians. The book shattered me. It was imperative that I spend the next years studying the history of Christian anti-Semitism and its roots in the New Testament. When I wrote *The Jews and the Gospel* (later revised as *Is the New Testament Anti-Semitic?*), I clearly acknowledged the anti-Jewish trends in the Christian tradition, yet strongly defended the New Testament against the accusation of containing anti-Semitic material. At that time, I thought that a Christian theological understanding of the New Testament demanded this sort of defense from me. Today I have come to realize, thanks to the research of scholars like Rosemary Ruether, that despite its privileged character as God's Word in the Church, the New Testament bears the marks of the sinfulness of the human condition and, in particular, reflects in its polemics the bitter conflict between the Synagogue and the young Christian community. The New Testament contains a bias against Jewish religion.

Let me briefly summarize the anti-Jewish trends in the biblical record and the Church's subsequent preaching. They may be classified according to their references to the people of Israel before, during, and after the time of Christ. This classification, if I remember correctly, was introduced by John Oesterreicher and adopted as the basic structure of the preparatory draft, *De Judaeis*, of Vatican Council II. It is still recognizable in the Council's final declaration correcting traditional errors.

First, there was the tendency to glorify the new covenant made in Christ by belittling the ancient covenant made with Israel in the desert. Forgetting the divine mercy at the heart of

Israel's liberation from Egypt and the covenant that sealed their peoplehood, some New Testament authors contrasted the Christian economy of love with the old economy of justice and obedience. Some raised the question whether God had really been with Israel on its pilgrimage. At best the people of Israel had access to a shadow, to a faint anticipation of the triumphant grace available in Christ and his Church. In some passages, St. Paul contrasted the old and the new Jerusalem as a regime of slavery over against a realm of freedom. While St. Paul corrected this polemical imagery by more positive symbols, such as Israel as noble olive tree, the Church's subsequent preaching concentrated on the negative evaluation of Israel's past. Jewish religion was under the law and hence a way of spiritual death. Some Christians went so far as to regard the deity of the Hebrew Scriptures as a god of justice and revenge and acknowledged as true God only the divine Father revealed in the New Testament. In this extreme form, the anti-Jewish trend was condemned by the Church as heretical.

A second trend present in the New Testament was to denigrate the religion of Israel contemporary to Christ. The New Testament account of the scribes and Pharisees is not a historically accurate picture but a polemical presentation to bring out the power of the Gospel. Modern scholarship has established the integrity and creativity of various Jewish groups in the Israel of Jesus' time. The image of contemporary religion drawn by the New Testament has influenced Christian preaching throughout the ages. In the Christian imagination, the Jews were religiously corrupt. They were hypocritical, compulsive, selfish, and proud. Christians hardly retained any consciousness that Jesus, Mary, the Apostles, and most of the people with whom Jesus spoke were Jews. In the Christian imagination, Judas was more Jewish than Jesus. Connected with this trend was the common interpretation, advocated by Christian preachers, that Jesus was crucified by "the Jews." Historically the entire drama of Jesus' mission in Israel involved mainly Jews: some were for him, and some against him. But by regarding the temple clique as the representative of Israel and overlooking the role of the Romans in Jerusalem, Christian preachers have claimed that it was the Jews, the Jewish people, who crucified Christ. We have here the source of malevolent legends of Israel's deicide and unending divine punishment.

The third anti-Jewish trend in the New Testament, with influence in later Christian preaching, concerns the future of the Jewish people. Some New Testament writers record the view that because of Israel's infidelity, the ancient covenant has been abrogated, that Israel is no longer God's people; and while St. Paul occasionally makes special claims for Israel in the present economy and believes that she remains dear to God as his first-loved people, other biblical texts suggest that Israel has been replaced by the Gentiles, foretell the divine punishment appointed for the evil generation of Jerusalem, and hint that the entire future of Israel stands under the shadow of its infidelity like under a curse. Even the continuing election of Israel acknowledged by St. Paul in Romans 11 was not a source of present grace for Jews but a promise they will eventually be restored to the Church. In the meantime Israel has fallen into blindness. The subsequent preaching of the Church produced ever more dreadful scenarios for the future of the Jewish people. All in all there can be no doubt that in the Church's preaching, Jewish religion has been presented as a corrupt and empty worship, the Jewish people as unfaithful, legalistic, hostile to virtue and wisdom, and Jewish history as an ever-visible demonstration of divine wrath.

Since World War II and the extermination of six million Jews by the Nazis, Christians have begun to be aware of the anti-Semitic trend in their own history. Many of the Churches have reviewed and corrected their liturgy, their catechetical instructions, and their manner of preaching. In the Catholic Church, the declaration on Jewish-Christian relations, promulgated by Vatican II, was a significant eccleciastical act that—despite its inadequacies—rectified and continues to rectify the Christian attitude toward Jews and the Jewish religion.

What effect did this discovery have on my own theological reflection? I became deeply involved in the movement that sought to correct the Christian roots of anti-Semitism, and during the Vatican Council, I was fortunate enough to be associated with the composing of the declaration mentioned above. There was, however, a still deeper effect of this startling discovery on my theology. What my studies of Christian anti-Semitism taught me was that the dreadful things people do to one another are hidden from them. It would be quite unjust to suppose that the Christian preachers, in biblical times or in subsequent ages, entertained a conscious hatred of Jews. Some of them may indeed have hated them, but the vast majority of preachers were willing to adopt and embellish the anti-Jewish myth without being fully aware of what they were doing. The process that produced the devastating mythology was largely unconscious. As the Church set itself off first from the Jewish community in which it was born and later from the Jewish religion and other religions that surrounded it as rivals, Christians proclaimed the Gospel as a wall protecting the Church from outside influence and giving the Christian community the assurance of victory. What took place in the Church was the formation of ideology.

Ideology, according to the Marxian use of the term, refers to the largely unconscious production of ideas that protect the power of a group or class. Ideology is the deformation of truth for the sake of social interest. Without being fully aware of it, the Christian Church proclaimed the Christian message with strong ideological overtones. The Christian message built a wall around the Church, reserved the light of grace to its members, and depicted outsiders as blind and hard-hearted. By dividing the world into "we" and "they," the Church generated a rhetoric of exclusion, i.e., a manner of speaking that elevated itself and its members and vilified the others, the outsiders, and more especially the Jews, who were its very ancestors. This rhetoric of exclusion subtly entered the language we spoke, the ideas we entertained, the institutions we created, and eventually the very heart of the Christian civilization. So deeply was the anti-Jewish trend inscribed in Christian culture that ordinary men and women of intelligence and good will were unable to discover it. It was woven right into their consciousness. Only a profound shock, only a crime as vast as Nazi anti-Semitism and the Jewish holocaust, was able to make the Christian West discover the anti-Jewish ideology built into its heritage.

My study of Jewish-Christian relations brought me in contact with the social unconscious. In a highly individualistic culture, we tend to pay attention only to the personal unconscious discovered by Freud. But the sociologists, from the nineteenth century on, discovered that there was a social unconscious: operative in society were processes hidden from personal consciousness that had a powerful effect on the creation of culture and religion. The deepest purposes at work in a society are hidden from the individuals who constitute it: they are woven into their very being. These purposes find expression in the symbols, cultural or religious, which the society cherishes and celebrates. It was Karl Marx who analyzed the destructive function of this social unconscious. He tried to show how the basic economic conflict and the largely unconscious effort of the ruling class to preserve and strengthen its privileges created sets of symbols, cultural or religious, through which people interpreted their lives and accepted as a natural or divine necessity the division of society into rich and poor, powerful and powerless, owners and workers. For Marx, all of philosophy and religion was ideological, was mystification of the real situation, was a largely unconscious power play to defend the present social order. Since Marx's time, sociologists have taken the notion of ideology out of the specifically Marxist context. Non-Marxist sociologists regard Marx's use of this term as one-sided. Marx tried to reduce the whole of culture and religion to ideology; at the same time he denied that the working-class movement produced an ideology of its own. Later sociologists, while rejecting Marx's reductionism, have learned to apply the notion of ideology to the analysis of all movements and groups, including the Communist parties. Every community of men is subject to ideology-producing trends. Every movement is in need of an ideological critique.

Today it is essential for the theologian to realize the possibility of an ideological deformation of the truth. Today it has become impossible to engage in theological reflection without raising the question of false consciousness. The discovery of ideology always produces a profound shock. To discover it means to become converted in some measure. Some people discover what ideology is through the struggle of the blacks in the U.S.: they suddenly see that built into the institutions and values of the society they love, fashioned by good intentions, are elements of conquest and oppression. This can be seen only if one is willing to redefine for oneself what it means to be an American (or a white Western Christian). The recognition of ideology is always costly. Other people discover the power of ideology through the struggle of women for liberation. They are able to discern in the ideals and institutions that have created us and that we cherish the structures that in fact oppress women and keep them in a subservient role in society. Male domination over women is so deeply marked in the fibers of our culture and religion that intelligence and good will alone are not enough to discover it. These fibers are so much part of our own self-understanding that our very consciousness is falsified. Only through shock and conversion are we able to see things as they are. For me, this shock and this conversion came through the discovery of the anti-Semitic trends in Christian preaching.

Before I describe the effects of this discovery on theological reflection, I wish to say that having learned what ideology is from the critical analysis of religion and not from the Marxist analysis of society, I have never been able to accept the view that social injustices are reducible to a single form of oppression, i.e., to the oppression inflicted by a single class on all other sections of society. For Marx, as heir of the Hegelian dialectic, the conflict in society occurred according to a definite law: there were two and only two conflicting economic classes, and out of this conflict, the new society would arise. While I admit that there have been and there are some societies where it is in fact a single conflict between the powerful and the exploited that dominates the whole of life and hence determines the ideological character of all cultural manifestations, there is nothing necessary about this. There are other societies where the conflicts are different, where more than two parties are involved, where the economic factor is overshadowed by the ethnic, the linguistic, or the religious factor, and where it would be false reductionism to interpret cultural expressions in terms of a single ideology. To take for granted that the conflicts in any society are reducible to a single oppressor/oppressed category is, to my mind, a dogmatism that may do violence to the facts of the situation. It may be important, for strategic purposes, to restrict oneself for a time to a single category of oppressor/oppressed, such as the black power people have done, but if this is understood as a necessary principle of interpretation rather than an emergency measure to assure survival and recovery, it mystifies the complexity of human society and hence promotes injustices. American society must be analyzed in terms of several interest groups struggling for power and recognition.

How does the discovery of ideology affect the style adopted in the theological thinking? Theologians must examine the possibility of false consciousness in themselves and the Christian community whose experience they interpret. Theologians must ask themselves to what extent the Church is involved in the power struggles of society and to what extent its message is an expression of ecclesiastical dominance and privilege acquired throughout the ages. The discovery of ideology introduces a new, critical perspective into theology: the tradition must be reexamined. The religious experience of people and the ecclesiastical consensus achieved in past and present are not immune from unconscious ideological deformation. Theologians committed to this critique will regard it as their task to situate themselves in regard to various institutions, including the ecclesiastical, in such a way that they become free to discern the ideological trends; and while they realize that none may ever fully free themselves from the taint of hidden group-interest, they are determined to embark on a road of self-criticism and repeated transformations of consciousness.

The Jewish-Christian encounter and the discovery of ideology have raised in my mind very difficult dogmatic questions. To what extent is a hidden imperialism built into the common understanding of the Christian message? Are we quite certain that Jesus wanted to affirm himself as the unique and universal mediator? Did he desire the disappearance of all religions and their replacement by his own? Or is there another way of reading the New Testament witness? The ordinary preaching of the Gospel and the central theological tradition do create a consciousness in which non-Christians are inferior beings, whose main dignity consists in their destiny to become Christians. Theologians reexamining the Christian doctrine in regard to hidden ideologies become aware of many aspects they over-looked in the past. Was it really necessary to introduce monar-chical elements in the notion of God? Could we not have pre-ferred to speak of the divine, as does the Fourth Gospel, in terms of Love, Light, and Life? Could we not have followed, as Rosemary Ruether has suggested, the Pauline hint to make the divine kenosis in Jesus the key for the understanding of God's lordship? To what extent is the divine majesty of Christian the-ology the hidden, ideological defense of earthly powers? Surely the Christian message did not necessitate interpreting God as supreme authority. He could have been spoken of, as some theologians have done, as piercing truth and tender love opera-tive, victoriously operative, in the universe.

Christian theologians must ask themselves to what extent the exclusivist form of Christian preaching and the conscious-ness it created are responsible for the suspicion, injustice, and cruelty Christians have often shown toward outsiders. Is there a connection between a narrow understanding of Jesus as uni-versal saviour and the Western world's conquest of the globe? Is there a link between our claim to be holy Church and thus better than others and the paranoidal trend in our behavior toward members of other religions and dissident Christian groups? The Christian theologian can no longer study the Church's teaching without questioning the consciousness of re-ality expressed in this teaching or even created by it. What the discovery of ideology demands of theologians is that they ask themselves what is the weight and power of a doctrinal state-ment in the consciousness of the Church and hence in the histo-ry of the society in which it is situated. At first I was aware only of the historical effects of the Church's language about the Jews. I detected the many ways in which contempt for Jews and for other groups was built into Christian teaching. It was many years later that I turned to a wider ideological critique of the Church's teaching.

I hasten to add that it would be one-sided and distorting if we sought only the ideological components of the Christian tradition. We must also make ourselves sensitive to the posi-tive, redeeming thrust of the Christian message. The Gospel humanizes and socializes. While we admit that the Church has created contempt for the Jewish people, provided religious legitimation for authoritarian governments, often protected various regimes of privilege, and so forth, Christians are also aware that the Church has created the dream of a reconciled and liberated community, introduced people to interpersonal relations of fellowship and trust, and laid the foundation for a never-waning hope that the present order disguises the true nature of human life and that humankind is still moving toward its true destiny. Religion is an ambiguous reality. It contains ideological elements, but it also provides a matrix for social and cultural developments beyond the status quo. Religion exhibits conservative as well as radical trends.

The social impact of religion became a special area of interest in my life at a later period—I anticipate in my story here. From 1969 to 1971 I studied sociology at the New School for Social Research in New York City, and from that time on my theological research and reflection have focused on the social dimension of the Gospel and the Christian Church, including the ideological and the radical components.

III

The study of the Church's relationship to the Jews, as I indicated, raised a question mark in my mind in regard to the Church's unique role in mediating divine grace. Was it really possible to suppose that God's redemptive action was principally present in the Christian Church and only occasionally, by way of exception, operative in other religions and secular communities? During the late fifties I was involved in a good deal of pastoral ministry and came close to the lives of many people. The conviction grew in me at that time that there was not much difference between Christians and non-Christians. The same inner and outer drama seemed to go on in all the people I met. What I observed in myself and in others were the same fears, the same hopes, the same struggles, the same loves. There were the crushing defeats and the surprising and marvelous victories.There was the wrestling between trust and despair, the choice between moving into the future and clinging to the past, the quest for peace and inner strength. Since I was unable at that time to square this conviction with the Church's teaching, I was wondering if I could remain a Christian myself. It was then that I studied Karl Rahner; thanks to his writings, at least as I understood them, I gained a new perspective on the Christian faith.

I learned from Karl Rahner that it was possible to affirm at one and the same time the universality of divine grace and the uniqueness of Christ and the Christian Church. God's gift of himself was operative in the lives of all men, whether they realized it or not. They made the important options in regard to the divine as they worked out their engagement with life itself. The decision about God is made in a man's relationship to his neighbor. Faith, openness, trust is not confined to Christians who explicitly acknowledge divine revelation in Jesus Christ: faith is a dimension of every person's life. Every person, in other words, is summoned by life itself to open himself/herself to newness, to trust that one is alive by a power that transcends him/her, and to acknowledge oneself as caught up in a total web of meaning that is life-giving and gracious. According to Rahner's theology, the mystery that in a hidden, partial, and provisional manner is operative in the whole of human life has become visibly, fully, and definitively manifest in the person of Jesus Christ. In him, then, we discover what human life is about. Christ reveals to us the grace operative in every human being. What Christian believers encounter in Christ is, therefore, their own depth: they discover in Christ the mystery at work in their lives from the beginning, and because they are now able to name it, they are able to relate themselves more consciously to it and thus reorient their own personal history. Jesus Christ is unique because he raises man's consciousness about what really goes on in their lives and thereby initiates them into a new relationship to one another and to the divine ground out of which they come to be. Christ is not the beginning of God's gracious plan for mankind: he is rather the pivotal point of salvational history where partial and provisional dispensations of grace are brought together, elevated to a new level and moved toward convergence in a reconciled humanity.

The study of this "new" theology was extraordinarily liberating for me. I readily followed the new theological perspective, even though it took me many years to work out for myself the many implications of the new viewpoint. What was demanded of me was a total rethinking of the theology I had studied: there was not a single topic that remained unaffected by the new perspective. Eventually the very doctrine of God would have to be rethought, for if the divine mystery is present in man's discovery of herself as situated in the human world, and is operative in man's ongoing creation of her future, then God is not extrinsic to human life but the gracious presupposition of man's humanity and hence in no way, however qualified, a possible object of the human mind.

In later years I discovered that the turning point in Catholic theology had been the thought of Maurice Blondel who, at the end of the last century, rejected theological extrinsicism, affirmed God's redemptive presence to the whole of sinful humanity, and regarded God's revelation in Christ as the specification and clarification of the divine mystery operative in the lives of every human being. In Protestant theology the same theme had already been developed in the nineteenth century.

This new perspective, which in my writings I often called the Blondelian shift, had a profound effect on my style of theological reflection. I gladly admit that I attached much more importance to Blondel's and Rahner's radical humanism than I did to their respective metaphysical systems. They had brought out as no Catholic theologian before them that theology and anthropology were inseparably intertwined. Thanks to the new theological perspective I was able to interpret the Gospel as a divinely revealed humanism and look upon theology as humanist in orientation.

In itself the term "humanism" is quite undefined. There are many different kinds of humanisms that have little to do with one another. Marxism is a humanism; so is behaviorism. It is possible, however, to distinguish between closed and open humanisms. Closed humanism is proper to thinkers who believe that they have seen through man, can define a human being, outline the principles according to which a human being must be understood, and hence refuse to admit the possibility of newness and surprise. Closed humanism is always reductionist. It reduces the astonishing creativity in human life to

known categories. Here man is locked into her own self-definition. Dogmatic Marxist humanism is closed; so is the beha-
viorist understanding of man. Open humanism, on the other
hand, is a philosophy of life (or possibly a religion) that understands man in terms of an unpredictable creativity operative in
her history. Thinkers who adopt this viewpoint are open to the
new; they refuse to lock human beings into the categories in
which they understood themselves at one time; they acknowledge the need of man to listen to the call addressed to her in
new situations and admit the possibility of new, expanding,
unheard-of potentialities breaking open for her. Open humanism acknowledges a limitless horizon for the ongoing transformation of human consciousness. In the perspective of Blondel
and Rahner, this open-ended humanism is actually, consciously
or unconsciously, a form of theistic faith. What characterizes
this sort of humanism is a trust in the unpredictable, unlimited,
and hence undefinable goodness operative in human life.

Christian faith is an open-ended humanism: the Gospel
proclaims that the truth and love operative in the transformation of a human being is the divine mystery that has been fully
revealed in Jesus Christ. In this perspective it becomes clear
that divine grace humanizes man. God's own self-gift makes
men and women more truly human. It should be possible,
therefore, to study the various aspects of the Christian religion,
doctrine, sacraments, ministry, from the viewpoint of their humanizing effects. The theologians who do not adopt the new
perspective feel that this approach neglects the supernatural
character of the Gospel. In answer to them, it must be pointed
out that human life itself, thanks to God's gratuitous presence
to it, is supernatural. The surprising, unmerited, marvelous,
gracious does take place in human life and is co-constitutive of
human history. It is, therefore, possible to affirm that divine
grace humanizes man. God's grace—to revert to traditional
theological language—recreates the believer in the image of the
perfect humanity revealed in Christ. According to the Gospel,
then, God's self-communication creates redeemed humanity.

What follows from the new perspective, moreover, is that
the gifts of Christ in the Church are not totally new and exclusive: they are the explicit offering of gifts that in a more implic-

it and hidden manner are offered to all men and women in their history. Theology, therefore, not only studies the divine gifts in the Church, it also studies the gift-dimension of the whole of human life. What Scripture tells us about the Word of God addressing us in Christ and his message is, in a sense, also applicable to the summons addressing people in the significant situations of their lives. What is revealed to us in the Christian sacraments is not only the grace they mediate in the Church but also the grace offered to all people in the human gestures by which they relate to another in trust and love. The doctrine of ministry does not exhaust its meaning within the ecclesiastical community: it brings out the truth about leadership in the wider human family. Here God's revelation in Jesus becomes the key for the understanding of the whole of human life. This sort of thinking became part of my theological methodology.

Let it be said at this point that Blondel was not sensitive to the problem of ideology raised above. His view of the self was highly personalistic. He did not fully appreciate that a person comes to be in a process in which language, culture, and society are involved and that her consciousness, therefore, is largely though by no means fully created by her participation in wider social processes. Blondel was innocent of sociology. He did not fully appreciate that man cannot be delivered from ideological deformations altogether until the very structure of society is changed.

The strength of the new perspective, one I greatly appreciated, was the recovery of the ancient agnostic tradition in Christian theology and Christian spirituality. Since God is not extrinsic to human life, since God is not an object of the mind, since the divine is present in man as presupposition, as orientation, as vitality, as call, as horizon, it makes sense again to stress the unknowability of this divine mystery. The traditional *via negativa* had to be assigned a more central place in Catholic theology. We do not know God: he/she/it is different from everything with which we compare God. God is not a being among other beings, nor a person among other persons. What we proclaim of God refers to his/her/its gracious presence in human life and hence to the transformation of man's consciousness. God may not be thought of, therefore, as a fully constituted subject situated outside of history: God is not a reality that may univocally be referred to by the pronoun "he" or any noun or pronoun. What we know about God, thanks to the divine self-revelation in Jesus, is God's redemptive presence in human life. It is possible, therefore, to speak of the divine mystery without mentioning the name.

IV

In telling the story of the important experiences that have influenced my style of theological reflection I must mention, finally, my association with a psychotherapeutic movement in Toronto called Therafields, which lasted over many years in the sixties and had a profound influence on my understanding of human life. Long before the movement assumed the name of Therafields, we often called it communication therapy. What the movement tried to do was to apply the principles of psychotherapy to the communication taking place in groups. In addition to the private sessions traditional in psychotherapy, we also explored our own personal history and the layers of the unconscious in group sessions. The multiple transferences possible in groups enabled the participants to work through more effectively their unresolved conflicts of the past. In this process all participants became patients and therapists at different moments: they experienced healing and communicated it to others. This group process released unexpected creativity. Many of the participants began to devote themselves to communication therapy on a full-time basis. After a few years, when the movement had reached out to greater numbers of men and women, some decided to use the principles of group communication to create a new style of life in community and to set up their own living environment in the city and later in the country as well.

The immediate effect of communication therapy is the initiation into greater self-knowledge. What is brought about in this process is a greater awareness of the unconscious dimension of life and a clearer recognition of the deep wishes operative in human action. What counts in this therapy is to enter the often painful process of facing the negativity within us, of confronting the destructive patterns of action to which we unconsciously cling, of acknowledging the many forms under which we prefer death to life. Whatever the particular psychotherapeutic theory may be regarding this negativity—whether one accepts the Freudian trend of assigning an independent role to it, or the Reichian trend of deriving the destructive powers in us from the frustration and repression of life-giving energies—what actually counts in the therapeutic process is the trust that as this negativity is confronted, we do not find ourselves empty or fall apart altogether, but that beneath it is a ground on which growth is possible, especially if this ground is nourished by the sympathy and affection of the group. In a group, people may gain the trust that enables them to acknowledge their own deep feelings. There they may be able to face the hurts of childhood, the angers and frustrations long repressed; there they may detect how these are still unconsciously operative in their present relationships to others and to the group as a whole. They may discover that even their strongest and most creative side is still marked by some destructiveness which prevents them from further growth and causes damage to other people. Communication therapy brings people in touch with their illness, which is the universal condition for being well.

At the same time communication therapy also creates a better understanding of what takes place in groups. Unconscious processes are also at work in human communities. Groups of people can be centers of healing as well as places that draw humans into illness and depression. Communication therapy reveals to the participants some of these sick-making processes. We discover how we invest some people with authority over us while we try to make others subservient to us. The tensions, divisions, and rivalries in groups are to some extent due to unconscious factors. At the same time the generosity and warmth of a group support its members in their personal growth. Since people always live in groups, in families, schools, offices, churches, universities, nations, etc., the exploration of the unconscious factors in social life has important political consequences. Communication therapy generates ideals of social life that provide an effective critique of the existing institutions belonging to our culture. While traditional psychotherapy leads to a highly individualistic view of man and often withdraws people's energies from concern with society, communication therapy brings out the social consequences of personal conflicts and reveals the pathology proper to institutions.

This is a brief summary of what Therafields has meant to me. Of interest for this paper is the effects that my association with Therafields has had on the style of my theological reflection.

In the first place I gained a better understanding of the human condition. The brokenness in which we are born inevitably marks our history. Life is never a neutral affair: it is always a struggle between the powers of life and death. The pathological trends that produce illness in persons and in society are universal. At the same time a man is not wholly delivered over to these forces: healing too is universal. In conversation and friendship with others, new growth and new directions become available to us. In association with others we gain some insight, become more aware of what goes on in our lives, and through the love and confidence offered us we are freed, at least partially, to create our own future and restructure the pattern of our lives in community. Looked upon with the sensitivity created by the psychotherapeutic process, the lives of ordinary people, which on the surface may appear eventless, reveal themselves as a great drama, a struggle between life and death, between growth and regression, between vision and blindness, a struggle that, in my view, is symbolized and disclosed by the paschal mystery, the death and resurrection of Jesus. May not the language describing man's inner life, then, become useful for speaking of divine redemption?

The majority of theologians who have adopted the Blondelian-Rahnerian shift and regard God as the transcendent mystery present in human life, have retained a highly philosophical and systematic terminology when dealing with this divine presence. Their writings tended to remain abstract. Though their theology dealt with the concrete present, they were still satisfied with a highly theoretic language. But if it is true that the divine mystery is present in man's becoming, if it is true that divine grace initiates people more deeply into their humanity, then it should be possible to talk about this mystery in terms drawn from the ordinary language people actually use when they speak of the deep things that preoccupy them. As soon as people get away from this language, they are one step removed from where the divine Word is present in human conversation. What I have tried to do, therefore—how successfully I do not know—is to use the language in which people describe the threats to their lives, and the transformations that occasionally occur to them, to render an account of God's gracious presence in human life. In my book, *Man Becoming*, I have tried to translate every sentence of the creed dealing with God into a promise for new possibilities of human life.

Secondly, my association with Therafields has taught me that there is not only a political but also a therapeutic critique of Christian doctrine. The formulations of the Gospel and the concrete forms of Church institutions have political effects that must be studied and evaluated; but they also have effects on man's personal growth, retarding or promoting it, that deserve careful scrutiny. The manner in which the Church speaks of God, of man, of sin and grace provides the basic symbolism in which the faithful interpret life and as such has great power over them. The doctrine of God, for instance, may be presented in various ways with correspondingly different psychological effects. It is possible to speak of God in such a way as to encourage man's passive dependence on a parent figure or to facilitate the unconscious projection of superego on the divinity. It is equally possible to present the doctrine of God as the transcendent mystery operative within human life and thus to help Christians free themselves from any superior authority totally external to them and assume responsibility for their own future.

The doctrine of God, of man, of Church must be studied from this point of view. There are not only political ideologies that may taint the Christian theology, there is also something that may be called personal ideology, i.e., ideas or mental trends that help persons to disguise their illness from themselves or to create an alternate, but illusory world for themselves. Personal ideologies may also be operative in our reflection on the Gospel. Doctrine and theology themselves are therefore in need of further redemption, for they may have been created, in part at least, out of humanity's estrangement from its own vitality and hence serve as a defense against truth and a screen protecting it from reality. Theologians must recognize that otherworldliness not only has problematic political consequences, it also provides possibilities for schizoid trends in personal life and the estrangement from one's own bodily and sexual existence.

This leads me, thirdly, to the most significant effect that, in my view, the psychotherapeutic process has on the work of theologians. It enables theologians (as well as other intellectuals, of course) to raise the question in regard to the inner, psychological sources of their own intellectual quest and effort. What generates the energy for their search? What determines the direction in which they look? Unless theologians (and intellectuals, politicians, or others devoted to a task) examine their own emotional life, they cannot discover to what extent their work may be an unconscious defense against facing the truth or a secret rationalization of their own estrangement from life. False consciousness is not only a political category. The most perfect intellectual system and the greatest scholarship may still be used to promote blindness and insensitivity to the realities of life. Intellectual effort may make people more obedient servants of the destructive trends in themselves and in society. There is a psychic phenomenon among intellectuals, theologians not excluded, that might be called "flight into intelligence." Because we cannot deal with life, because we cannot face the summons present in our history and the involvement to which we are called, we rush off into the mental world of knowledge and attach ourselves to ideas as if they were more important than life itself. This is quite different from a sincere passion for thinking. Theologians must ask themselves out of what inner resources they produce their theological reflections and out of what levels of the mind they create their language. Unless they engage in a critical approach of this kind, they may not trust that their theological work will further the liberation or redemption of Christian consciousness. The personal ground of the theological enterprise must be the conversion of the mind, i.e., the readiness to be converted again and again to greater truth.

Here I will stop telling my story. There are many other experiences I could mention, including the social and political pressures to which my generation has been exposed. I could also mention what my dedication to the ministry has meant in my life or what I learned in the two years I spent studying sociology. I could write about thinkers with whom I am linked in personal friendship—Aarne Siirala, Rosemary Ruether, Philip McKenna, Emil Fackenheim, Leslie Dewart—and whose thought both challenges and supports me. But, then, every story is incomplete. What I wanted to do in this paper is present significant experiences of my life as the personal foundation for my style of theological reflection.

While this has been a personal account, some readers may find that it describes, in part at least, the territory through which they have moved. Intellectual experiences are hardly ever as private as they seem: they usually express what is taking place in a wider social group. From my association with Catholic theologians of my generation I have the distinct impression that in some way we have all had equivalent experiences and passed through similar personal and intellectual transformations. Perhaps it is because I am a Catholic theologian, with the stress on Catholic in this context, that I am so conscious of belonging to a community of faith, of sharing in the spiritual and intellectual experiences of this community, and of interpreting in my theological work not only what the Gospel means to me personally but also and especially what it means to the wider community to which I belong, and in which I experience the significant conflicts.

By way of summary I wish to contrast, briefly, the style of theological reflection I have adopted with the theological method I learned at the university.

In traditional theology the theologian himself as well as the material studied by him were regarded as unproblematic. (In this context I can say without hesitation he, not she, the theologian.) The notion of false consciousness was not recognized. It was taken for granted that the theologian had faith and a certain sensitivity acquired by his life in the Church, but no questions were asked about the limits of his awareness and the blindspots resulting from hidden ideology. The great theological authors, it is true, always demanded that the theologian be engaged in a personal quest for holiness and in this way distinguished theological wisdom from the more aloof and objective search proper to purely academic endeavors, but they did not realize the degree to which unconscious resistance to truth falsifies awareness and knowledge. It was not supposed that in his theological research and reflection the theologian pass through many transformations.

Equally unproblematic was the traditional approach to the material studied in theology, whether it be biblical, doctrinal, liturgical, or whatever. Once its historical authenticity was established, the theologian accepted the material at its face value. Today theologians cannot avoid altogether the Marxian and Freudian questions. They must ask themselves to what extent the religious documents they study are expressions of ideology. They must pay attention to the actual weight and power of these documents in history, to the political life they promoted, and the kind of people they created or helped to create. The raising of these questions demands that theologians clarify for themselves their own political commitment and seek greater awareness of the sources of their emotional life. For whether thinkers realize it or not, the understanding of the past and the interpretation of documents and events are always in some sense a function of their political and personal involvement. While this insight has produced a crisis in the social sciences and history, the same insight is, to my mind, more truly at home in theology. For in Scripture we had been told that truth and love are intimately connected and that it is only through a certain commitment and orientation of life that the truth becomes available to us.

A second difference between traditional theology and the style of theological reflection I have adopted is the greater realization that the Church needs the world to become Church. In order to understand the Good News and know who Jesus Christ was, we have to be in conversation with the whole of humankind. At a time when theologians supposed that God's Word addressed the Church primarily and almost exclusively in the special history of salvation, their task was to clarify the meaning of the divine message from the scriptural record and the witness of tradition. Only afterward were they ready to turn to the world, give witness to the Christian message, and possibly compare and contrast it with the wisdom of others. But if the same divine Word is simultaneously uttered in the world, and if we cannot be faithful to this Word unless we also listen to what this Word says in the present generation, then theologians are unable to clarify the meaning of biblical revelation for the Church unless they engage in conversation with the world. The meaning of the Gospel cannot be deciphered in separation from the experience of history. We need others to understand the Christian message! In order to grasp what Jesus Christ signifies to the Church and how we are to interpret his message, we must listen to Scripture and tradition as well as to the Word addressing us in history, our own and that of others. This does not mean, of course, that theologians dispense themselves from studying the Bible and the normative Christian witness of the past; we need this memory of Christ to detect and decipher the divine voice addressing us in the conversation with others. But theologians, it seems to me, must always cross some boundaries. They must be in conversation with a wisdom that is not their own. What dialogue with other religions, with other world interpretations, with other branches of knowledge, will do to theology and influence the understanding of the Gospel is impossible to say beforehand. We trust that God's Word will address us through these conversations and that the Spirit will guide the Christian community to greater truth. But since theologians cannot be faithful to the Gospel if they limit themselves to intra-ecclesiastical conversations, they must take the risk of new conversations. Perhaps we are still only beginning to understand what Jesus Christ is all about.

Beginnings:
An Intellectual Autobiography

ROSEMARY RADFORD RUETHER

It is difficult to be objective about one's personal biography. There is so much that one chooses to forget or to interpret with the wisdom of hindsight in that selective vision that we bring to our own pasts. It is by no means easy for me to describe how I came to move down a path that has made me a stranger to much of the climate of my childhood. Yet I did so with little sense of making violent breaks or definitive repudiations of the various aspects of that heritage. It seemed, rather, that every step was foreordained as a necessary development of an inner rationale that constantly drew from the storehouse of my inherited riches.

Through my mother, nee Rebecca Cresap Ord, I grew up with an exacting sense of family history and a consciousness of being rooted in the stories of many generations. In religion she was the descendent of an English Catholic family that came to this country in the early nineteenth century. Although a Catholic, the ethnic experience of most American Catholics was foreign to me. James Ord, my mother's family's American founder, arrived here as a ward of Archbishop Carroll of Maryland under somewhat mysterious circumstances (according to family legend, the son of Mrs. Fitzherbert and George IV) and graduated in one of the first classes at Georgetown University. He married Rebecca Cresap, daughter of a notable clan of Revolutionary War fame. The Cresaps still today are so ancestor-proud that they maintain the Cresap Historical Society to record their own family.

My father was from Virginia and Mississippi gentry, the Radfords and the Armstrongs. The letters that were sent between my maternal and paternal great-grandfathers, Admiral William Radford and General Edward Otho Cresap Ord, during the Civil War were framed on our dining-room wall, along with assorted dress swords. The pride and sadness of this tradition hung like incense over such memories. However alien this history to me, I cannot walk the Virginia hills today without being shaken with deep emotion, tears starting to my eyes. Deep under the earth I feel the heaving bones of slave and slavemaster, their broken bodies entwined together. The ghosts of aristocratic gentlemen rise on gently rolling slopes, seated between the pillars of their Greek mansions, holding in their hands bold declarations of Human Rights, while behind them dusky slaves, some their own denied offspring, give the lie to their words.

As a child I went with my father to Fotheringay, his family place near Radford, Virginia. His elderly cousins still lived there then. Progressively impoverished, shooing chickens from the wicker chairs on the porch, they lived among their family portraits with perfect assurance of inborn worth. Cousin Anne was a medium of some local reputation. I remember her darting up the curving staircase to put on her golden slippers and turban when a visitor arrived to learn his fortune. Cousin Eskridge, once a talented actor, was told by the family that "we don't become actors" and lived out his eighty years in idleness, churning butter slowly in the big, cool kitchen. A great marble tomb on the hillside marked the burial place of the "Colonel," according to legend seated bolt upright so he could watch his slaves eternally cultivating his acres.

My father was an Anglican of the twice-a-year variety. He retained the family pew at Christ Church, Georgetown. When I was small I went with him to services on Christmas Eve. My mother was a devout Catholic, but of independant mind, with little trace of ecclesiastical subservience. We usually attended the Jesuit parish near Georgetown University, which had a habit of supplementing its staff with alcoholic theologians from the university. My childhood picture of the typical priest was one of an eloquent, silver-haired Jesuit around whom hung an indefinable air of tragic depression and who occasionally stumbled as he descended the altar stairs.

I spent much time playing around the ample grounds of a home for the elder run by the Carmelites down the street from where we lived. My mother served on the board of trustees for this home and we went there for daily Mass. Largely through my mother's selectivity, my memories of childhood Catholicism were generally pleasant. Climbing the apple trees of the convent and teaching some of the young nuns how to ride a bicycle; quiet moments of depth and mystery in the daily liturgy; little sense of constraint by petty authoritarianism. My mother dismissed most of the *dicta* of the Irish priests and nuns at school or in the parish as boorish and ill-educated, with an impatience that I now recognize to be drawn as much from class bias as from liberalism. I grew up assuming that Catholicism was the cloak of a *mysterium tremendum*. When it exhibited a vulgar or narrowly doctrinaire style, I felt assured that it could usually be safely ignored. I realize now that this is an uncommon experience. American Catholics received mostly the fear of the second, little resiliency in the first.

I am, as far as I know, the first professional scholar in my family. But both sides of my family had a high tradition of lay education. The first James Ord was trained in a classical education and gave his sons Latin-sounding names, like Pacificus Ord. A great aunt on my father's side married an aristocrat of French and Russian ancestry and lived in Petersburg before the fall of the Czar. I knew her as a grand old woman with white hair piled elegantly on her head. She published a biography of her father, the Admiral, and wrote many other books, as well as translations from Russian, most of which did not find their way into print. Like most of my family, she believed in the occult and wrote about her experiences at a time when this was not very fashionable with publishers. The women of the family took for granted the European tour and a polite fluency in French. My mother's family helped explore California and married into the Spanish ranching families there. She grew up speaking Spanish, and developed a fair fluency in French and some German in European trips. Many bookshelves filled with dark-bound volumes lined my family home. From them I absorbed the romance and tragedy of Lee's Lieutenants and the old South in an education that had little to do with what I was being taught in school.

My own bent for scholarship, it seems to me, must have come partly from the lively historical consciousness that I developed from these surroundings, plus a childhood spent mostly as a loner. I was thrown back much of the time on my own inner resources. I am not sure that I consciously felt "different." But on the tree-lined street in old Georgetown, there were not many girls my age. At the Catholic girl's seminary I attended there were few kindred spirits. I was not without friends in grade and high school. It seemed natural, however, to spend more time with adults than with other children, and to have many hours by myself, reading, thinking, walking alone, or painting. From the age of twelve until I was eighteen I had ambitions to be an artist. But this interest atrophied when I turned to scholarship in college. My aunt, Sophie Radford, had somewhat mysteriously stepped outside family tradition by marrying a Jew from New York (in all other respects, she was totally conventional). Her husband, David Sandow, was our favorite uncle and surrogate father. A gifted man, whose cheerfulness concealed a melancholy disposition, he nurtured us in knowledge and love of the great masters of art and music. His own father had committed suicide and he himself seemed to have a death wish of the spirit. Through a strange inability to muster self-confidence, his extraordinary talents in art, music, and architecture remained a light hidden under a bushel.

I also developed an independant flair for writing, although I did not visualize myself becoming a writer. When I was eleven and twelve we lived for a time in Greece, where my father was director of the engineering program to rebuild the roads and bridges destroyed by the departing Nazis. I made many sketches of the ruined temples of antiquity, and also started a weekly newspaper, with several friends, filled mostly with articles of a satiric type. I attended a French Ursuline convent but turned my linguistic abilities more to Greek street slang. The scars of the Nazi occupation were still strong in the memories of the Greek people at that time, even as the American fleet lay in the harbor to ward off the encroaching Communists in the

North. In 1952, several years after my father's death in Greece (from pneumonia contracted during his years in France during the war), we moved to La Jolla, near my mother's childhood home in San Diego. She followed in the footsteps of her own mother and grandmother in returning, as a widow, to this area. In La Jolla I broke out of Catholic education to attend the public high school, where I became the editor of the school paper. Our paper developed a surprising reputation for creative journalism under my direction, even being honored by an attack by the local anti-Communist vigilantes as a "subversive" publication. A sensible principal fortunately ignored their outcries and encouraged our efforts.

I can't remember any special interest in religious ideas at this time, although my critical editorials on the vulgarization of Christmas and other such matters must have won me some esteem in this field, since I was selected to give the address on a religious theme at the graduation. It was in the first year of college that my rather elitist but fairly secure Catholicism collapsed rapidly under the scrutiny of historical study. It very soon appeared to me that very little that I had been taught had the sort of historical foundations that I had been led to assume. Turning my newly critical eye upon the credal doctrines, I found that these too seemed to fall apart, like an ancient fabric, preserved in a dark mansion, that turns to dust when suddenly exposed to daylight.

I had had doubts and questions before. I recall a cringing sense of shame when the mother of a high-school friend made withering remarks about the intellectual repressiveness of the Catholic Church. Sometime around the age of sixteen I remember standing on a street corner watching a passing crowd and engaging myself in theological disputation. I reflected that it did not make sense for God to send some of these people to heaven and others to hell since they obviously did not fall into such neat moral opposites. Therefore to assign them such contrary fates corresponded to no reasonable justice on the part of God. *Ergo* either God was unjust or heaven and hell did not exist. In an intense dorm discussion in the early weeks of college I found myself agreeing with a freshman savant who declared that she "didn't believe in life after death" and believed

that her own Jewish tradition did not teach this doctrine. Yet I
experienced a certain wonder at the ease with which this central
tenet of Christian doctrine fell away from me. Did it really
have so little roots in my own inner convictions? In earlier
years intimations of mortality had been revealed to me. At the
age of twelve I was alone in Greece when my father suddenly
fell ill and died. During the grief-torn scenes that followed my
mother's tardy return, I remember feeling a strange detach-
ment. I was haunted by a vivid image of my father in his grave,
sinking down into the earth. Both then and in subsequent
brushes with death, I have experienced a strong sense of human
mortality, the finitude of the individual self. In college when I
read the passage from Homer where Glaukos greets Diomedes
in battle with the words

High hearted son of Tydeus, why ask of my generation? As is
the generation of leaves, so that of men. The wind scatters the
leaves on the ground, but the live timber burgeons with leaves
again in the season of spring returning. So one generation of
men grows while another dies. (*Iliad* 6.145-50)

I put it down in my notebook as an expression of my own perception. Religious visions of angelic souls flying off to heaven
contrasted starkly with this vision of mortality and perpetua-
tion only through the species. Yet the latter seemed to me to
have the sobering ring of truth that was preferable to vain
illusions.

The doctrine of the personal immortality of the soul
slipped away from me as an idea without real roots in my own
better intuitions. Nature clearly cared only for the species, not
the individual. If there is meaning in ongoing human life, it
must be sought somehow in solidarity with the race, with the
earth, with the matrix that binds us all together, not in the
isolated self. This was the perception that took shape in my
mind gradually. Such a critical discarding of the central doctrine of Catholic popular faith, the very nub upon which all discipline and doctrine are hinged, could only mean that, in an ir-
revocable sense, I had crossed over from heteronomous to
autonomous selfhood. Whatever else I made up my mind to
believe in thereafter would be because I personally found it be-

lievable, not because "the Church" taught it. Without knowing it I had also detached the keystone of any relation to the traditional mode of Catholic authority. Years later my Benedictine guru would point out to me the unCatholic character of my method, saying that, like Cardinal Merry del Val, who disputed the faith with Lord Halifax in the nineteenth century, he might not personally believe half so much as I, but he believed everything the Church taught, *because she taught it*. Such fideism was totally alien to me. Upon contact with it I could only shudder, as if encountering a macabre self-emasculation.

My development was, nevertheless, strongly influenced by a series of charismatic adults. I had a tendency to seek out teachers who expressed, through their strength of personality, not merely intellectual attainment, but that fusion of mind and personality that embodied "wisdom." The first of these was a history teacher in the Catholic high school I attended in Washington, D.C. She was a maverick in the fifties, cultivating black friends and teaching, by word and example, the evils of American racism. I did not realize at the time how deeply racist my father's family was, masked as it was with southern gentility. My mother, with her upbringing in Mexico, was more tolerant, but this remained undeveloped through her attachment to my father. The attitudes of my teacher planted new seeds that were not to flower for a decade. In high school in California I was close to several teachers. My student friends were a dissident crew that drew together around the school paper. As a precocious artist I spent much of my time out of school in adult drawing and painting classes where I was close to several older women. This interest led me to Scripps College in Claremont, with its emphasis on the fine arts and humanities.

In college, however, my interest shifted dramatically to classics and ancient history, through the influence of a charismatic teacher, Robert Palmer. Palmer was more than a classicist. He was a man who lived the ancient world view. He believed in the ancient gods as living *daimons*. He was also more than faintly contemptuous of Christianity, which he considered a graveyard religion. Like Achilles in Hades in Lucian's Dialogue, he sighed for a lost world, holding up the skull of Helen of Troy and exclaiming, "Ah, Patroklos, once these dead bones were things of beauty." Before our eyes he reassembled that vanished world for us and made it reappear. Like Libanius in the autumn of antiquity he regarded Christianity with disgust as a cult of dead man's bones that had destroyed the religion of life of ancient humanism and replaced it with a religion of death.

The world of antiquity fascinated me for several reasons. One reason might be called the "secret garden" quest, the attraction to hidden and vanished worlds. This was not just a fairy-tale world of childhood reading, but the real vanished worlds of history that still existed as the buried substratum of our culture. Like an archeologist, one could travel down layer upon layer, lifting off the accumulated debris, as I had once seen them do as a child in the excavations of the Athenian *agora*, opening new doors, discovering inside the still discernable shapes of older existences. Secondly, it was Palmer, the believing pagan, who first taught me to think theologically or, as he would have called it, "mythopoetically." Through him I discovered the meaning of religious symbols, not as extrinsic doctrines, but as living metaphors of human existence. I still remember the great excitement I felt in freshman Humanities when he said something that made me realize that "death and resurrection" was not just some peculiar statement about something that was supposed to have happened to someone 2,000 years ago, with no particular connection to anyone else's life. Rather it was a metaphor for inner transformation and rebirth, the mystery of renewed life. He happened to be talking about Attis or Dionysos, not about Jesus. For the first time I understood a new orientation to Christian symbols that eleven years of Catholic education had never suggested to me. That was the beginning of being interested in religious ideas in a new way.

These two interests, the quest for historical origins and the meaning of religious symbols, converged in that first year in college in a paper that I wrote on "the mystery religions and the origins of Christian sacraments," and have, in one way or another, shaped much of my intellectual élan ever since. Under Palmer, and also Drs. Harry Carroll and Philip Merlan, much of my undergraduate and graduate study was directed toward classical culture and philosophy. The religious worlds I explored with them were mostly those of Homer and Aeschylus, Plato and Plotinus. My first theologian was Palmer's mentor, Walter Otto, author of *The Homeric Gods* and *Dionysos, Myth and Cult*. Philip Merlan described for us the pathway of the soul's ascent to the heavens, divesting itself of its passions as it passed each astral station, until finally it entered into the eighth sphere of transcendent bliss. "I shouldn't be surprised if it happens to me," he declared. Through Walter Otto we learned the formula, "first the God, then the dance, and finally the story." Every religion begins with the concrete experience of the god; not the "one God," but of a particular god. This experience may come to one person, an inspired prophet or seer, or be a collective experience. But, through the seers and poets, it is given form, so that the people can dance it, and relive the experience of the theophany of the god in ritual and drama. Out of the liturgy arises the story, the *mythos*, from which comes, as the last stage, formulated creed and doctrine. Palmer suggested to us a way into the belief of every religion, but not as "religion in general," nor as the projection of baser emotions of fear and need, but rather, first of all, as the concrete revelation of the divine in that time and place.

It was from this background that I turned to the study of the Bible, Christian origins, and theology. I wanted to know how this particular religion has arisen within the framework of the ancient world. How had it somehow managed to fall heir to the entire legacy of the ancient Near Eastern and Graeco-Roman world, the legacies of Egypt, Babylonia and Persia, as well as Palestine, and then Greece and Rome? Yet it had survived the demise of these worlds and gone on to shape a new world, claiming a "virgin birth" from heaven emancipated from its historical paternity. In the quest for origins I sought the key to the meaning of Christianity—a religion that was, on the one hand, the product and synthesis of the heritage of ancient Mediterranian culture, and yet, in another sense, alien to its matrix, a mutant. Seeking the key to this mystery, I began to absorb the work of liberal Protestant scholarship. I had little use for Catholic biblical scholarship that I came across. I once jokingly remarked that an *imprimatur* was useful because it was a good sign that the book wasn't worth reading. With few exceptions, Catholic scholarship appeared to me doctrinally apriorist, lacking what I had come to value as historical consciousness.

But Protestant scholarship also had a defect that would gradually become more apparent to me, although I was able to bracket this for a while in order to learn that tradition of thought. Less doctrinally apriorist than Catholic work, it still remained limited by a fundamental biblical intolerance. For it too "Ba'al" was a symbol of a false god and some kind of "dirty doings," not a real god. When the prophet knocked down the altars and smashed the symbols of other people's religions, we were all supposed to let out a bloodthirsty cheer. I did not cheer. Having dwelt in the households of the suppressed faiths for a time, I felt I was on more sympathetic terms with the Ba'al worshipers. I knew that Ba'al was a real god, the revelation of the mystery of life, the expression of the depths of Being which had broken through into the lives of people and gave them a key to the mystery of death and rebirth. He may not have always lifted them up to the highest levels of virtue and science, but there was more to him than "sex," or to put it another way, there was more to sex than sex. On the other hand, Yahweh had deplorably violent ways, and a lot of evil had been done in the name of Christ. One needed to seek out and understand the truth people had known through the mediation of the god. As for the defects of Ba'al, were they more spectacular than the defects of the biblical God or Messiah, or perhaps less so? No crusades or pogroms had been sent in the name of Ba'al, Isis, or Apollo.

As I had been taught to do, I tried to transpose myself into the mental world of the ancient Hebrews and the early Church, to experience again the world as it appeared to them, not as it is interpreted in modern categories. I wanted to understand what it would feel like to believe in the resurrection of the body and the coming Reign of God in the first century, just as I wanted to know what it felt like to think that the ascent of the soul through the seven planetary spheres "would happen to me." To do this I had to bracket temporarily what I knew about Athena and Artemis, but I would not forget that I had once glimpsed the appearance of their theophanies. Eventually I would have to make a critical transcendence of the biblical world view at the point where it needed to declare all other gods to be idols, mere sticks and stone, or even worse, in Christianity, to be "devils." But I could not do this by a mere eclectic synthesis. One had to respect the particularity of each cultural world view and language, to experience, rather than gloss over, the gaps between the different worlds of perception. But this meant that, finally, I could not give allegiance to any "jealous god" on the level of historical particularity. The ultimate God must be far beyond these particular jealousies that set one people's insight against another's. The true God could be zealous only to lead us out of these antagonisms to higher and higher truths whose final compass is incomplete—the final compass that can embrace all people's histories without having to negate the identities of any of them.

A fundamental tendency toward dialectical thinking became built into my method by this clash between the worlds of antiquity and biblical faith, before I read the Hegelians. I became inherently suspicious of an idea that appeared to be one side of a dualism. Such an idea demanded a critical transcendence, an exploration of the repressed "other side," in order to move beyond both poles to a new synthesis that could include them both. Whenever someone shouted "Yahweh, not Ba'al," or "Christ, not Moses," or even "Wittenberg, not Rome," I would have to take up residence in the other location to find out what was being negated. This was not merely from a desire to be "contrary," I think, for I was also suspicious of the mere grasping of the repressed "other side" that fanatically negated the original thesis. I wanted to resurrect the repressed, so that I could also put the dominant position in a larger context and make sense out of them both in a new way. I was not prepared to repudiate Yahweh, Christ, or even Rome. In that sense I also had to move beyond my classicist teachers, because in learning to love the ancient gods, they had also had to repress their own Jewish and Christian identities. Palmer, who grew up singing Lutheran hymns in a German household, and Merlan, who fled from Warsaw across Russia from Hitler's legions, were not quite revealing about who they really were when they stepped forth in the garb of ancient rhetors and philosophers.

Who am I? I would have to discover that by seeking new conversation with intellectuals from the Catholic tradition, people who had continued to pursue their religious experience within that context. They presumably would also know the historical material that I had learned and so would have some ideas about how these were to be put together. It was a long time before I found anyone who approximated that demand. Indeed I have never discovered that person, but have had to try to become that person myself. But I kept searching and talking to people and reassessing things as I encountered what turned out to be many disappointments. My first shock was to discover how ignorant most priests and even seminary professors in the Catholic tradition were, something I had not expected. For many years I could not find anyone who seemed to have even learned the various traditions of thought that I knew, much less to have reflected on how to put them together with their own heritage. Most were unable even to discuss it, advising me grimly to "stop reading books without imprimaturs," or exhorting me to "pray more often" and "come away to a good Catholic school." One nun at a Catholic university, where I took a summer course in medieval philosophy, insisted on engaging me in counseling sessions where she enquired earnestly after "my devotion to Mary." I could hardly tell her that my devotion to Mary was somewhat less than my devotion to some far more powerful divine females that I knew: Isis, Athena, and Artemis! However, she horrified me in turn by exclaiming, as I departed her school, that she "was so glad that I was getting married that fall," since I "would soon be too busy to read any more of *those* books." Her image of normative marriage was evidently that of a procreative orgy, wherein the mind once possessed by the wife sank rapidly down into the diaper pail and was extinguished forever. I resolved then and there never to let that happen to me! Such a view was not only a betrayal of me as a human being, but an unconscionable betrayal of her profession as a teacher of university women. I was to discover, however, that my non-Catholic teachers had not reflected very much more deeply on why it was that they were so carefully cultivating the minds of young women whom they generally expected to have no destiny beyond that of marriage and motherhood. Most of them seemed to notice that we were women only when we graduated. Then they suddenly made clear what they really thought of us, either by declining really to help us get jobs or graduate fellowships in the same way that they would help a male student, or else suggesting that we might serve for the rest of our lives as their graduate assistants!

However, back to the subject of my new encounter with Catholicism: my experience with Catholicism as a child had been one of some beauty and authenticity, seldom vulgar or stupid. This probably sustained me through a decade of experience in which most of the historical knowledge that I learned about that Church was highly unfavorable to its pretensions of infallibility and moral guidance. Even worse, its eminent representatives that I sought out appeared disappointingly ignorant and closed-minded. If the Second Vatican Council had not happened about this time I probably would have severed any effort to think in the context of this identity at all. But that Council suddenly unbolted the door, within that house itself, on all the repressed questions that I had been asking, and so drew me back into the discussion.

Part of the reason that I could enter the discussion on a new level was that I had come gradually to see nuns, priests, theology professors, with whom I had talked so futilely over the previous years, not as "authorities," but as "people with problems"; people whose narrow base of certainty and identity did not permit them to ask the questions I was asking or to come to terms with the things that I was trying to understand. I came to locate this as "their problem," not mine. Once I had discovered this, the guilt-transference, which Catholics are supposed to feel at dissident ideas and which should leave them with only two options: capitulation or "leaving the Church," could no longer operate. I cannot say that I surmounted this guilt all at once. There was a long time when my interest in further conversation with Catholic thinkers was still motivated partly by the child's desire for "reconciliation with the parent" (archetypal-ecclesial parent, not biological parents). But my relative lack of conditioning in this type of guilt as a child and my early discovery of intellectual independence made it possible for me, I think, to cross a threshold beyond the alternatives of "childhood-dependency capitulation" or "adolescent revolt." I began gradually to take up what I would today call an "adult" stance toward institutional Catholicism. I began to see myself as responsible for it, rather than it as responsible for me. Its problems were things to which I might minister, or which I might not be able to change, but not "norms" that could transfer to me a guilt-and-dependency trip. This also meant that the Catholic world itself ceased to be confined to its own past and discovered the possibility of a new future.

But this third position was clarified only after I had, to some extent, explored existentially the options of "reconversion" or "departure." My interest in religion could not be satisfied with a "head trip." It needed to be nourished by religious experience in worship and prayer in community and this took me back to the good experience of the liturgy that I had known in my childhood. A Benedictine monastery in the high desert area of San Bernadino, with monks who had come from Belgium, via a missionary era in China, promised an environment of worship that would not insult my intellect. St. Andrew's Priory in Valyermo was, for about four years, a spiritual home. I was even, for a while, a third-order lay member. A dimension of the Benedictine spirit was very satisfying to me. It was a monastery stripped of the high medieval trappings, and returned to the spirit of its founder, not closed to "the world," but understanding itself as a spiritual center to which people could come for shorter or longer periods. Vincent Martin, O.S.B., once described Benedictine life as like a "ballet," meaning a harmony in which all parts make up a rhythmic whole. It had a fusion of the Hebrew prophetic spirit with classical balance that I appreciated. Vincent Martin was the most provocative of the charismatic spirits of that community, an extraordinary man with the face of a Savonarola, and the sophistication of a mind trained successively in Louvain, Harvard (as a student of sociology under Talcott Parsons), China (Zen and medicine), and Hebrew studies in Jerusalem.

In the late 1950s St. Andrew's represented the best in theology and liturgical renewal that had been developing in Europe. The monks worked in the spirit of the liturgical and biblical renewal of Maria Laach, translated to St. John's Collegeville by Dom Virgil Michel. They were on top of the best trends in the new theology from France that would flower in the Second Vatican Council. St. Andrew's also became a kind of center for the people who were beginning to organize around civil rights and peace issues and to demand that the Church take a stand on these issues, that group which was to be called the "underground Church" (I believe the term, as used in recent Catholic media, was coined first in relation to this group). The Commonweal Club in Los Angeles, the Catholic Human Relations Council, and the oblates of St. Andrew's were three corners of a network of people that were exchanging ideas and, in time, planning action and protest. We were one beginning of the explosion that was to take place in both the American Catholic Church and American society in the sixties.

Vincent Martin was to fall victim to that explosion somewhat unjustly. Being too closely associated with the sort of ferment represented by these groups, he was pressured out of the monastery by Cardinal MacIntyre and left for a time for Jerusalem. He was, of course, only one of many victims to fall before that Eminence. Most of the young priests that we knew in this era in Los Angeles would also find their ministry destroyed by the Cardinal and his "carpet club," most of them leaving the priesthood. Vincent Martin was too much a veteran to leave the order or the priesthood, but the sort of leadership and movement that he had represented was broken with his ouster. The oblate group protested this action to Belgium, and the mother community was to set some action in motion that would eventually bring Martin back to St. Andrew's. However, in that hiatus between the early and late sixties, much blood had passed under the bridge in the American Church and society. A community that might have grown was dispersed in a way that could not be reconstituted on the earlier groundings. St. Andrew's is still a creative place, but for a while, in the late fifties and early sixties, it was on the cutting edge of creative Catholic life in the Los Angeles area.

For me, Valyermo remains forever fixed in memory in a

golden moment where time intersects with eternity. I am staying in a small rose-covered cottage at the side of the main compound. Rising just before dawn, I walk the small hills at the foot of the San Bernadino Mountains, reading Martin Buber, as the sun slowly turns the desert to a rosy glow. It does not get too hot here. The high desert in spring boasts a carpet of exotic flowers. In the shade lies an occasional desert pond. Converted farm buildings serve as the monastic compound, with the chapel fashioned from the former stable. Walking over the hill as the sun bursts across the horizon, I hear the bell for morning prayers. A flock of ducks from the pond accompany me to the chapel, standing with heads tucked piously into their necks in front of the altar window, swaying from side to side, in seeming imitation of the cowled monks swaying in chant inside. After prayers a simple breakfast of homemade bread, honey, coffee, and a walk back to my cottage to continue writing my dissertation on Gregory Nazianzen, the fourth-century Greek Church Father.

St. Andrew's has changed, I hear from friends in California. There is a big new guest house. I could no longer stay there on the informal terms that partially ignored the rules of cloister. The intellectual openness that once made me feel at home there would not be the same from either side. The leaders have grown more defensive after years of persecution. So I will probably never go back there again to walk the foothills at dawn as a temporary "monk." But a rhythm, a knowledge of a place of inner repose, was instilled at that time which I still carry with me and can find if I wish.

St. Andrew's, while it nourished my spirit, could not fully satisfy my mind. Its liberalism remained bounded by limits of authority and tradition that could not account for many things which I knew. I once showed a friend there several texts from the second century which showed clearly that the early Church understood the brothers and sisters of Jesus in the New Testament to mean siblings, natural children of Mary. He could respond finally only by saying that the texts had to be ignored because "otherwise the tradition would be wrong." That the tradition might be wrong was quite possible to me, unthinkable to him. It became evident that this whole concept of authority made honesty about mistakes impossible. After a period of thinking about and working with this concept of authority, and the way it functioned institutionally, I came to believe that it was an irresolvable impasse, making a clear decision against the Catholic Church, so defined, inevitable.

At this time I had been drawn into a liturgical group of Episcopalians at the university, who were also my community for civil-rights work. It seemed to make sense to move over into this tradition, close to my own in history as well as personal biography. One Friday near Easter I went with the Episcopal chaplain to make this transition at the Anglican monastery at Santa Barbara. About two hours after I arrived, I walked out into a light rain and went down to the Santa Barbara mission, which happened to lie just below, where I caught a ride back to Los Angeles with a carload of poor Mexicans who were emerging from the church.

Why this *volte-face*? To say that I found the Anglican monastery incredibly stifling and somehow inauthentic, like those creepy castles that rich Americans steal from Europe and re-erect along the Pacific, is only part of it. It just became very clear to me that this turn into my father's Church was a blind alley for me, a side-chapel of atavistic piety that had nothing to do with the questions I was asking. I was a little angry at the Episcopal chaplain who had somewhat forced my hand to come. But, basically, this was a door that I needed to open, and having opened it, leave it behind. I was not going to be "reconverted" to a traditional concept of authority, but I was not going to "leave the Church" either. Instead I would have to define my own relation to the Church, rather than letting it define me in relation to norms that were unacceptable. The bad state into which it had gotten itself in the course of a not altogether admirable history was humanly understandable. I am personally convinced that believing that you are infallible is the surest way to become excessively accident-prone. Even this one could get past with some humor and a large dose of repentance. But these mistakes could no longer masquerade as "norms" that could define me as "outside the Church," or on the other hand, force me to contort my mind into strange shapes to fit into Procrustean beds. The Church, like myself, was an unfinished possibility. Therein lies hope for us both. We need to grow by learning from our own mistakes. These mistakes must not be erected into a small doghouse, falsely called "the Church," forcing people to decide "to squeeze or not to squeeze." That is not the question.

Until I was about twenty-five my life was severely academic. Indeed, for much of this time I barely lifted my eyes beyond the fifth century, with an occasional foray into the Renaissance or the Enlightenment. I was a classical humanist through and through, perusing texts in Greek and Latin, garnering the tools of German and French, much of which I have now forgotten. I married the year before college graduation to another scholar who enjoyed getting lost in a library stack as much as I. Together we worked on our Ph.Ds. Our three children, born while we were both in graduate school, did not change the pattern of a day devoted primarily to study. Once when my two-year-old daughter was visiting her grandmother, she contrived a form of play that consisted of taking two books, sitting down very seriously, looking first at one book and then flipping the pages of the other. My mother watched her curiously, wondering what she was doing. Then, with great amusement, she realized that she was imitating "Mommy." Instead of her model for imitation being cooking and housekeeping, her idea of "what Mommy does" was translating texts with a dictionary!

Only after I had crossed the quarter-century mark did I begin to become a social activist. This was partly through my husband, whose field of political science made it more necessary for him to read the newspapers than I had been accustomed to do, and partly through the press of events of the sixties that began to catch up the university and religious worlds that I occupied. I do not regret that long academic seclusion before I joined "the world." My sojourns in the worlds of history and theory have given me a perspective into which I can place various problems and crises in the contemporary Church and society. Most of my friends in the "movement," who became caught up in political life as undergraduates, have not been able to develop this. I think I have a foundation and methodology for understanding the crises of our times that is

important. Nevertheless, it would be impossible for me today
to return to the kind of "pure scholarship" in which I was
trained and which is still, in many places, considered the hallmark of academic "excellence."

In 1972-73 I spent a year teaching at the Harvard Divinity
School. There I found the type of German classical scholar still
going about the sort of philological science that I had been
taught to emulate (although with considerably less flair for interpretation than my teachers!). These scholars had kept their
eyes determinedly averted from the collapse of the society
around them, never allowing it to impinge upon or question
their segregated mental world. Such scholarship seems to me
an apostasy from the mission of the intellectual in society or in
the Church. At the same time, however, I reject the rootless
immediacy of that demand for "relevancy" that insists on
knowing only what the individual self has directly experienced,
which cannot bother to learn what anyone has thought or done
before our times. Here again I find myself seeking a synthesis
between the ivory tower and experiential education. I want to
bring historical consciousness to bear upon contemporary
crises and to make those involved in these crises aware of the
larger cultural and historical roots.

In my experience with seminary education, especially
today, there seems to be a growing division into two hostile and
noncommunicating camps: the classical scholars and the action-reflection people. Moreover, it seems to me that the classical scholars are anxious to burn the bridges and make the
division uncrossable. They are comfortable with the "relevancy" people only if they can define them totally outside their
academic turf. Their wrath falls on the person, like myself, who
is trying to bridge the two. The action-reflection people, in
turn, can scarcely be persuaded to read a book. They seem to
think that human experience began with themselves. Another
false dualism to add to the list! It is impossible for me to return to the world of detached scholarship. But I cannot deny
the perspective and methods that it taught me. I suspect that
we have to give up the Germanic classicist myth of absolute
mastery, purchased at the expense of carefully limiting one's
"field." We must turn to the kind of work that can be done

only by a true community of thinkers, who draw their sources of reflection from theory and history, and also from contemporary practice. Such a community would pool their different skills to work as a team, rather than seeking individual self-glorification. That such an idea of community is entirely alien to not only our universities but also our seminaries today is the measure of the extent to which even religious scholarship has become penetrated by the spirit of competitive capitalism. One of my students jokingly remarked that "when a Harvard professor gets an idea, he does not share it with other people, but runs to the bank and puts it in the vault." In the women's studies courses, we tried to develop a different style, a style that was consciously cooperative rather than competitive. In my courses at Harvard I had the students write the exam jointly, take the exam in groups or on tapes, write papers for each other and exchange them and develop bibliographies for each other. But such practices (which yielded far more work than students did in other courses!) go against the grain of the entire organization of our society. To build a human way of operating, even in the framework of a classroom, finally demands a revolution in our value system, our personality structures, and our socio-economic organization. The radical dimensions of such questions are only beginning to become apparent to me, after ten years of looking at the crisis in American society on expanding levels of relations.

The 1960s seem to have been the decade of consciousness-raising for a certain sector of white middle-class Americans. We discovered that the issue was not merely Jim Crow in the South, but institutional racism in the North. It was not merely a question of racism at home, but racist neo-colonialism and militarism in the relation of rich and poor nations. Intervention abroad bred police repression and bureaucratic paranoia at home. One began to connect the historic structures of oppression: race, class, sex, colonialism, finally the destructive patterns of human society toward nature, in an integrated vision of social contradictions and demands for social revolution.

Like many Americans I traveled the route from civil rights to peace activism to revolutionary analysis in the era between the Mississippi Summer and Kent State. In the summer of 1966 I worked with the Delta Ministry in Mississippi. I did some work in Watts after the explosion there. I experienced what it means to look at America from the "other side." Unlike many white activists, I did not turn away from the black movement with Stokley Carmichael's cry of "black power." I understood this cry as just and necessary. Black power entailed an adjustment of the role of the white person in the black community. If my work was primarily to communicate an understanding of racism to the white community, as the black movement said, then two things seemed to follow that didn't appear to be understood either by white radicals or black nationalists; first, the white person could not seek the "politics of purity" by divorcing oneself from responsibility for the ordinary white American community. One had to remain realistically political and able to communicate with people in institutional life. But one also had to continue to situate oneself in the black and poor communities, not in order to "lead the black community," but in order to unmask one's own false consciousness, to be able to discern the concealed underside of America by looking at it from that underside. So when my husband and I came to Washington, D.C., in 1967 for new teaching appointments, I was determined to live and teach in the black community, so I would not forget what I had seen.

Yet this location primarily in the crises of America did not make me discard what I had learned by a long dalliance somewhere between the fifth century B.C. and the fifth century A.D. Indeed the symbols and history drawn from this era more than ever continued to provide archetypes for our own time. This is particularly true of the black community, which understands intuitively what it means to use biblical metaphor for contemporary America. All the material I had worked on continued to provide both vital analogies and keys to the origins of the present. As a college senior I had done my honors thesis on the transition from futurism to apocalypticism in the Inter-testamental apocalypses. In so doing I had discovered the pattern for radical political theology and the critique of the privatization of Christian theology. I had also discovered a key to the misunderstanding between Judaism and Christianity over the "coming of the Messiah" that was to bear such evil fruit up to the Nazi holocaust and beyond. In my studies on Roman history, and my thesis on a fourth-century Greek Church Father, I had felt what it meant to live "at the end of an era" and to see the entire shape of a great civilization collapse. In asceticism and the rise of monastic life, I had encountered both an institution for survival of social collapse and also an important key to the strange history of women. All this work was to bear endless new insights in writings on political theology, communalism, messianism, anti-Semitism and women. The women's movement particularly demanded a consciousness that reached back to the period of the rise of the urban revolution from tribal society and drew into it everything that I had done on Greek religion, as well as the Bible. What is relevant? Anything you know is relevant, if you use it to bring together larger configurations of experience, sparking new insight into who we are.

Today I find myself variously described as a "Catholic theologian," the exact status of the word "Catholic" uncertain, a feminist, and a social activist. For some people I am an *enfant terrible*, with an inexplicable lust for saying unpleasant things about the Church. For others I am a once-promising patristic scholar who has gone astray with contemporary-mindedness. My concerns have little to do with the presuppositions of either of these schools of thought. I am concerned to remain faithful to the truth, not simply as an intellectual abstraction, but as a *status viatoris*. The roots of the dilemma were planted in the beginnings of civilization. Its final meaning remains still to be determined by human freedom.

Why, however vaguely, remain tied to the identity and history of Catholic Christianity at all? Certainly most thinkers of my kind find the first impossible and some feminists today would demand that women repudiate the second as well. Catholicism, for me, is my paradigm for the human dilemma. I relate to it, not as a repository of truth by which to make a fixed identity, but as a terrible example of what we all are. It is in much the same way that I am passionately an American. It is impossible for me to do otherwise. This is my history, my people. It might be more pleasant to be a Quaker or a Canadian, with less time, less opportunity, less power for evil, but perhaps also more dull. In my histories the magnitude of the human contradiction is writ large on a vast canvas through which one can contemplate the archeological layers of consciousness and grapple with the world-wide implications of an imperial history that today encounters its final contradiction. In this history one can not stand aside, blaming others. One must take responsibility for a long sweep of historical evil, but also draw out many memories of insight when that redeeming alternative, which still eludes us in its fullness, touched the earth. I have no other place to begin.

The Historian as Believer,

or

Looking Back over Your Shoulder Can Give You a Pain in the Neck

DAVID J. O'BRIEN

A friend in Texas reports a recent bumper-sticker that reads "Ambiguity is B.S.," and another "Eschew Obfuscation." A nice way of telling us, I suppose, that there is a world around, with a lot of people in it, who need, in Warren Harding's immortal words, "not nostrums but normalcy." The simple truths of Gerry Ford's religion look good after the contrived self-affirmation of Richard Nixon or the apocalyptic credos of Nixon's enemies. Hard times have a way of puncturing pretensions and creating a demand for understandable, usable ideas; if the danger of oversimplification exists, it is balanced by the benefit of calling the experts to account. When the government falls and the unemployment rate rises, explanations to guide action seem more important than explanations as Ph.D. theses. In the 1930s the "lost generation" put aside frivolity and irresponsibility to work for New Deal agencies or join left-wing cells. The inescapable presence of people in need sobered the righteous aloofness of the national intelligentsia. It may not be too much to expect that homely economic problems, perhaps combined with the crisis of the end of the era of growth, may force the exposure of obfuscation and the reconsideration of ambiguity.

Even if Americans experience a rebirth of social imagination comparable to the New Deal years, they will still confront the recurrent prevalence of popular nostalgia. Today, many Americans who look beyond the complexities of the present moment look not to a new future alive with possibility but to a mythological past when things were more like they ought to be. As Richard Hofstadter once noticed, American reformers always stand on the rear platform of a railroad car, gazing back at the neat homes, straight streets, and clean white spires of the town where they think they lived, hoping that things can again be as clear as they once were. In America, nostalgia often replaces utopia. Eden and not the righteous Kingdom, or is it Egypt rather than Canaan, becomes the object of our hope.

But today there is a difference, of course, for we pay the price of our sophistication. We know what we are doing; and thus we know that the images projected by our minds and spirits are not, after all, the world; history, our story, is not the same thing as History, mankind's story. Our consciousness of our own consciousness is our primal fall from innocence, and from faith. We doubt and are aware of our doubts; we believe and know that we believe; we strive to know and know that we strive, and that the source of our striving often distorts its object. "One is, I take it, on the brink of impotence and nihilism when one begins to be aware of one's own awareness of what one is doing, saying, thinking," John Courtney Murray wrote in 1960. We Catholics liked that; we nodded our heads in agreement. Determined to protect the inner citadels of faith from the corrosive acid of the historical temper, Murray, Christopher Dawson, even Jacques Maritain, extended Catholicism's fellowship to the beleaguered friends of Western civilization. They led us in a last-ditch resistance to the post-modern discovery of consciousness.

Of course the denial of consciousness didn't work. Pope John XXIII opened the windows of the Catholic citadel because he honestly believed that "history is, after all, the teacher of life." But James Joyce and Merry del Val had known better. For Joyce, history was "a nightmare from which I am trying to awaken." His experience of living history as oppression—personal, cultural, social—led to a rebelliousness against outmoded forms, none more omnipresent than the Church. The cardinal and his antimodernist cohorts of the turn of the century regarded such rebelliousness, and the self-awareness that nurtured it, as the root of modern chaos and disorder. Far better to keep such awareness at bay, suppress critical scholarship, and enforce the rituals of certainty than to risk the loss of all that two millennia of struggle had constructed. The denial of historicity was the denial of present and future; though its defenders might be labeled "prophets of doom," they well knew the potential disasters that await those who tamper lightly with the human need for secure hope, sustained precisely by not being grounded in existential reality. The Grand Inquisitor, was not, when we think about it, a bad guy.

We should know now, a decade after Vatican II, the wisdom, however perverted, of such Catholic conservatism. When theology becomes the history of theology, when "the substance of things not evident to the senses" becomes a set of symbols, when the Church "never in need of reform or development" becomes a human construct shaped by the imperatives of monarchist politics and triumphalist ecclesiology, the moorings give way, conscience is set adrift, "the teacher of life" becomes a vast, incomprehensible sea of stuff in which we are sucked and pulled and thrown about. "Whirl is king." Nothing is left to grasp hold of, it seems, but our own consciousness, the ongoing story of ourselves. When life has lost its self-evident meaning, when its goals or laws or mechanics are not accessible to our minds and hearts, then value must lie in the process, the experience of life itself. We tend our garden once again, even if it is no more than the garden of our own sensibility. Unless we can find new foundations for faith and reason within the midst of history, then faith and reason and history itself will become, quite truly, the graveyard of hopes and dreams, our own and those of humankind.

II

In a very real sense the Catholic and the American experience of the years of my maturity converge around the problem of consciousness. In both cases, the fruit of our new awareness of ourselves is our knowledge that there is no return. We can turn aside if we wish, but we can no more recapture the certainty and assurance that we once knew than the child can return to the womb. As Christians and as human beings, we have launched on the search for truth because we believe it right to do so. It is good for us occasionally to reconsider our life and the life of our Church and our society, not to justify ourselves, but to clarify once again, as concretely as possible, the goals and the ethical imperatives, personal and collective, that should provide our governing context. We can, I think, derive considerable benefit, not the least of which will be some sense of the need to continue, from reflection on what has happened to us and our communities in our lifetime.

For most of us, reflection about such matters necessarily involves two levels, the personal and the political. We ask ourselves: *what should I do with my life*? But we also ask: *what should be done with my world*? The Christian task is to answer both the questions, one regarding personal life and the other regarding collective life, in some relationship with each other. Thus the Gospel proclamation of the Kingdom encompasses the goal of *my* life and of *our* life, for it is both our personal destiny and the destiny of man-in-history. While the exact shape and contours of the Kingdom of God are shrouded from our view, we do know that it is God's Kingdom, and that the only power there will be his. People will be free from coercion and restraint not to live as isolated individuals but to experience that love for God and one another that will realize the promise of our common origin and our common redemption. In this view, what we do with our lives personally is intimately bound up with what should be done with our world; both are answered on the basis of God's will for us and for the world, and that will is the Kingdom of God. The experience of aloneness, individuality, and personhood, and the experience of oneness, unity, and love are dimensions of the human experience to be incorporated and integrated in life, not alternatives between which we must choose. Christ knew himself through the experience of alienation, in the desert and in the garden, and in the experience of community, with his family, the disciples, the crowds, the children. Similarly, the lonely tasks of introspection, prayer, contemplation, and reflection go hand in hand with the public tasks of liturgy, community, society. The conclusion is, I think, that our effort to discover what we must do with our lives must reflect our experience of responsibility for our world, and our effort to shape our world must reflect the experience of trying to know ourselves. Some years ago, C. Wright Mills spoke of "the sociological imagination" as the ability to see personal troubles (a man out of work) in terms of social issues (structural unemployment) and social issues (war) in terms of personal troubles (the exile, the victim). Only an ability to do both, in personal decision as much as in social analysis, can allow us to avoid the twin dangers of self-righteousness fanaticism and romantic irrelevance.

Just as American society badly needs the resources that only a socially responsible intelligentsia can supply, so the Church badly needs the guidance of scholars and intellectuals who can assist the community to regain its bearings and realize the promise of new energy and hope raised by the Vatican Council. Thomas O'Dea has argued that the role of the Catholic intellectual has been "completely transformed" by Vatican II. Freed from the defensive "counterpositions" of the post-Reformation era, the Church is learning today "how to act rather than react." The result is rapid change of the kind noted by all observers, changes that involve "a vast expansion of opportunity and a new freedom, but by that very token introduce new problems inherent in the loss of established structures." Thus the present situation is characterized by open-endedness and uncertainty:

Who can say where all this will end? Has the church started upon a course of deinstitutionalization that will lead to a new, more flexible, more adaptable, more creative, and more vital Catholicism? Is this deinstitutionalization the prelude to a new, more appropriate institutionalization? Or has Catholicism entered upon a process of self-liquidation? The present disarray in Catholic ranks shows signs pointing in both directions. In the midst of this risk and uncertainty, we see the tenuousness of faith exposed without the support of a traditional civilizational context. How will the Catholic intellectuals meet these new challenges? Will they prove themselves both creative and responsible? The answer to that question only they can give. Should they prove up to it, they will be able, in the words of

Pope Paul VI, to make their contribution to the creation of a "new humanism which will enable modern man to find himself anew by embracing the higher values of love and friendship, of prayer and contemplation."

No longer bound by ecclesiastical fetters to regard the world as an adversary, and no longer required by the commitment to truth to wage an underground war with Church authorities, the Catholic intellectual is, nevertheless, not freed simply to float as a self-contained and self-justifying gadfly. Rather he must assist his religious community in the arduous and difficult process of reform and renewal, not simply for its own sake, not simply to assist in preserving the institutions of the Church, but in order to allow the light of the Gospel to be a more effective force in the liberation of men and women from bondage to ignorance, oppression, and death.

The Catholic scholar should not adopt an adversary relationship either with his non-Catholic colleagues or with his own tradition. On the contrary, his efforts must be directed toward the enriching of both by the appropriation of their central element and values. What Noam Chomsky has called "the menace of liberal scholarship" represents not the essence but the betrayal of the secular, humanist tradition, while the subordination of intellectual endeavor to ecclesiastical interests so characteristic of much of modern Catholic culture similarly contradicted the essential integrity of Christian scholarship. The values of freedom and reason are endangered today, but the source of the threat lies not in the Church's intellectual parochialism but in what Conor Cruise O'Brien calls the "counter-revolutionary subordination" of truth to power. For the intellectual, "the only abiding loyalty is one to mankind as a whole," Northrop Frye writes. The post-conciliar Catholic affirms that loyalty unequivocally and enthusiastically, but he should know that that very loyalty is a demanding one for which he must pay a price. For loyalty to mankind requires, as O'Brien points out, "the realization of moral responsibility in relation to these regimes over which our society has power— open economic and partly concealed political power. . . . On postulates of morality and responsibility, imaginations should be haunted by these regions and their people." The responsibility that rests upon those who affirm Frye's "loyalty to mankind" joins for the Catholic with the Council's call to "do in love what the truth requires" to pose serious demands on the mind and the spirit. The commitment to truth has naively been accepted as painless, but the fact is that serious critical reflection by Christians grounded in the central values of their tradition may pose basic and profound challenges to established values and institutions, and these ideas, and the people who hold them, may be rejected, persecuted, isolated.

Perhaps this stress on responsibility seems too "activist" a subordination of intellectual and religious values to political ideals and objectives. Yet, it should be clear that such concerns are not new. Monsignor John Tracy Ellis, for example, quite deliberately located his famous 1955 paper, "American Catholics and the Intellectual Life," in the context of the discussion of American values associated with the new conservatism. He agreed with Clinton Rossiter that America was opening in new ways to "religious and moral values," and he welcomed enthusiastically "the radical change from the moribund philosophy of materialism and discredited liberalism which have ruled a good portion of the American mind for better than a century." "The receptive attitude of contemporary thought" was a "unique opportunity that lies before Catholic scholars of the United States, which, if approached and executed with the deep conviction of its vital importance for the future of the American Church may inspire them to do great things." While the terms reflected the polemics of the fifties, the statement was a summons to contribute to a fundamental debate about national values and goals.

Pope Paul VI's Eightieth Anniversary Letter to Cardinal Roy similarly stressed the necessity for "Christian communities to analyze with objectivity the situation which is proper to their own country, to shed on it the light of the gospels." The Pope went on to state very forcefully the imperatives of social and political responsibility, concluding that "Today more than ever the Word of God will be unable to be proclaimed and heard unless it is accompanied by the witness of the power of the Holy Spirit, working within the actions of Christians in the service of their brothers, at the points in which their existence and their future are at stake." The American bishops reiterate the same theme. "Christians are obliged to seek justice and peace in the world," they write. "In today's world this requires that the Christian community be involved in seeking solutions to a host of complex problems, such as war, poverty, racism and environmental pollution, which undermine community within and among Christians."

If, indeed, these matters are intrinsic to the Church's mission and occupy a place of special urgency in our age, then Catholic intellectuals must consider very seriously whether their own efforts might, where appropriate, be directed more specifically to questions of justice and peace. A negative response in effect deprives the Church of the knowledge, creativity, and imagination it so desperately requires while it, in turn, suggests that religious commitment is separate from the scholar's allocation of time, selection of problems, and educational efforts. As Peter Berger has pointed out, Christian thought about the world "must always have the quality of diakonia, of service to the needs of the world," and it is also true that this may mean today "a vigorous reassertion of the necessary unity between reason and moral passion in social thought." Where some would agree with Berger that the reason side of the equation has given way to the passionate in recent years, others quite correctly believe that a lack of passion, commitment, and fidelity to the Christian tradition are far more characteristic of the work of many Christian scholars.

Having opened themselves and their Church to the contingencies and cataclysms of history, and having taken seriously the demands of truth, Catholic intellectuals must now more than ever devote themselves to the service of their people. "We can justly consider that the future of humanity lies in the hands of those who are strong enough to provide coming generations with reasons for living and hoping," the Council Fathers wrote. In our own country, Daniel Berrigan posed the problem for many: "I want to suggest a strong note of reserve, of pessimism, of the ambiguous which it seems are of the very essence of life today, and then to ask: In spite of it all, what are we to do with our lives?" Providing answers to such questions, providing vision and analysis, understanding and resources, those are surely the particular responsibilities of intellectuals, who, if they are Christians, share the specific burdens of that vocation as well. Finally freed from the discipline of institutional authority, they face the challenge in the years ahead of moving beyond an exclusive preoccupation with critical commentary to share in the positive task of realizing the promise of the Gospel precisely within a world that cannot escape its historical character, can no longer share the innocence of those who have not become "aware of their own awareness."

III

My own experience of the fall from grace is not particularly unusual. I lived in a smallish city nestled in the Berkshire Hills of western Massachusetts for eighteen years, went to Catholic schools, and lived all that time in the same parish, whose church my parents had helped to build. In 1956, I went to Notre Dame to prepare myself to join my brother in running the family business. Two years of accounting and marketing proved unsatisfying and I made the fateful decision to switch to history. Two years later, unsure of the future, I won a Woodrow Wilson Fellowship and decided to postpone a career decision by going to graduate school at the University of Rochester for a few years to study American political and diplomatic history. Raised in the Cold War atmosphere of Joe McCarthy, the Boston *Post*, Fulton Lewis Jr., and assorted Maryknoll missioners, I had become, after four years at the center of Catholic America, a liberal, a process assisted by a summer at an international student seminar in Connecticut, where I failed to convince myself or anyone else of the wisdom of Catholic resistance to birth and population control. 1960 was John Kennedy's year; like the president, I and my colleagues were convinced it was time to replace the dull conservatism of Eisenhower Republicans not with the effete liberalism of Adlai Stevenson, but with our own brand of American politics. We believed that we combined the commitment to justice and freedom of the American tradition with a peculiar Catholic sense of the ambiguity of life and the necessity of power: in this

mood John Kennedy was indeed our leader. Despite sixteen
years of Catholic education, I was a relatively unreflective
Catholic, but I thought at the time I was a moderately critical
American. The limits of our criticism were revealed on gradua-
tion day, June 5, 1960. President Dwight Eisenhower gave the
commencement address and Cardinal Montini of Milan, later
Pope Paul VI, celebrated the baccalaureate Mass and personal-
ly handed us our diplomas. The words "God Country and
Notre Dame" enshrined above the doors of Notre Dame's
Sacred Heart Church lived that day; it all hung together.

It doesn't hang together any longer, for me at least. Vatican II, the racial crisis in America, the assassination of our
heroes, the Vietnamese conflict, these provided the context of
my young adulthood and shattered my certainty. As always,
public events were mediated by people, their impact shaped by
accidents. Dorothy Day has remarked that the great actions of
her life almost always happened because someone pestered her
to do something. Like her, I remember people more than
events. When I arrived in Rochester I happened to respond to
an ad for a room with a family who had been involved for a
quarter-century with the local Catholic Worker house. I had
never heard of the *Worker* in my years of Catholic education
and found the paper and the people enormously interesting.
They opened to me dimensions of the Catholic intellectual heritage far more exciting than the sterile theology of Notre
Dame's classrooms. I had chosen the University of Rochester
for a vague reason having to do with its size; I found it popu-
lated by WASP professors and Jewish students from New
York. Bright, articulate, and, in my eyes, enormously well
read, they demonstrated against nuclear testing and the House
Un-American Activities Committee, and participated in inter-
racial political work in the city. The wife of one graduate student had been a pioneer freedom rider in the South; her husband came from a socialist family. Few Catholics had gone to
Rochester as graduate students before, but the times were
good. Pope John and Vatican II stimulated great interest in the
Church, and I found my Catholicism a valuable resource, a
base for participation, rather than a barrier to friendship and
understanding. My four years at Rochester were my real in-

troduction to the intellectual life, facilitated by my fellow graduate students and by a faculty that blended the kindly benevolence of superb older scholars with the excitement of younger
men challenging established dogmas of the profession. Glyndon
VanDeusen initiated me into the tedious work and exciting
rewards of historical research. Willson Coates guided my study
of the philosophy of history, making relativism and historicism
exciting openings to human possibility rather than threats to
cherished traditions. Hayden V. White taught us that history
might be less important than historiography; that the pretensions of historians often provided rationales for the status quo.
History, too, had its history, and like all history, it fell prey to
the tentativeness and reliance on the symbolic that characterizes all efforts to understand man and his world. I can hardly
underestimate the importance of the introduction these men
gave me to historical consciousness; it allowed me, I believe, to
roll with the punches that beset the Church in the sixties, to see
the erosion of certainty as a quite natural fruit of honesty and
commitment to truth, and to regard the new situation, however
ambiguous, as a ground for the renewal of faith and hope.

If great events in people's lives often result from harassment or accident, as Dorothy Day indicated, so the professional involvement of scholars often results from the play of
the academic marketplace filtered through the advice of a faculty director. When it came time to write a doctoral dissertation, Milton Berman encouraged me to explore my own American Catholic heritage, on which so little had been written and
in which American scholars had a dawning interest. The result
was a thesis on Catholic social and political thought in the
1930s, eventually published as *American Catholics and Social
Reform: The New Deal Years*. Previous work on American
Catholic history had featured institutional histories and episcopal biographies, invariably written by men and women
trained in Church history, for whom the American Church was
simply a branch of the Church universal. Only rarely, as in the
case of Notre Dame's Thomas T. McAvoy, was the Church
historian also grounded in American history. Philip Gleason of
Notre Dame and myself were among the first scholars trained
primarily as American historians to study the history of the

Church in this country and to utilize some of the methods of American social science in doing so. As a result we helped to open up the field, which has since attracted a growing number of younger people in immigration and urban studies, as well as in religious history. These new fields in American studies have made Catholic subject matter of interest to a broad secular audience, while changes in theological self-consciousness and new pastoral responsibilities in the American Catholic community have made many Church people anxious to know more about the American context of Catholic life. So the accidents of my biography were particularly fortunate for me personally, giving me an expertise increasingly valued in my community.

The study bore personal fruit in many ways. Knowing fairly well the immediate historical background of Vatican II Catholicism, the changes of the sixties seemed less drastic and the "old Church" seemed far richer than it did to many of my friends. I never experienced any considerable alienation from my family and was thus spared the confusions of personal rebellion and had little personal hostility to pre-conciliar Catholicism. In fact, I developed a considerable respect for its diversity, its realism, and its pastoral effectiveness, while recognizing its cultural sterility and political blindness. One result of all this was that Vatican II and its aftermath were never for me as personally shattering as they were for many of my contemporaries. Unfortunately (perhaps) I was always more interested in the fabric of personalities and symbols that made for Catholic culture than in the deeper spiritual realities that they professed to represent. I was one of those whom Daniel Callahan called "religious slum dwellers," second-class citizens in a Church whose members spoke with increasing frequency of profound personal experiences of faith. This low level of emotional and spiritual expectation was an effective barrier against disappointment. Having had a theological training that was rather shallow, I never thought that the Church had all the answers and thus was not disillusioned when I learned that it admitted some of its limitations. In a recent autobiography, Michael Harrington tells of his years of Jesuit training, when he absorbed, more or less willingly, a Catholic intellectual package that was consistent, complete, and, for a time, satisfying.

For Harrington, Pope John's *aggiornamento*, by opening up questions about parts of the package, called the whole thing into question, leading him to face profound challenges regarding the very meaning and existence of God. In Harrington's case the result was the loss of faith and an existential encounter with a godless universe. In contrast, many religious women tell me that their communities have been able to undertake renewal with more speed and assurance than their male counterparts precisely because the paucity and shallowness of their theological background meant that they have had less cultural baggage to jettison. So, while I often feel deep regret that I lacked the rich classical and theological education received by many of my Jesuit-trained contemporaries, I also wonder whether I might count some advantages to my weakness.

Between 1964, when I left Rochester for my first teaching position at Loyola College in Montreal, and 1974, when I began to write this essay, several personal-social encounters forced me to reconsider the nature of scholarly enterprise and my personal responsibilities as a Christian intellectual. The first of these was simply the five years I spent at Loyola, during the quiet revolution in the Province of Quebec. In 1960, the Liberal party under Jean Lesage unseated the National Union party which for decades had ruled the province by combining demagogic appeals to conservative nationalism and religion with a fine-tuned working relationship with North American capitalism, suppressing dissent and stifling the creative energies of French Canadian intellectuals. Suddenly in 1960 the lid came off, and the province blossomed at every level of society, a boom symbolized by the modernity, the style, and the sheer class of Expo '67.

One major feature of the quiet revolution was the democratization of access to higher education. During and after World War II large numbers of refugees from southern and eastern Europe entered Canada and settled in the French-speaking city of Montreal. There they took advantage of the long tradition of minority rights in education, sending their children to the English-speaking Catholic schools, low in quality, but providing an opportunity for parents to prepare their children for careers in English-speaking North America. When in the sixties the provincial government eased the cost and accessibility of higher education, Loyola was the logical center for the education of these immigrant children. The college had 900 students in 1963; it had 3,400 full-time and 3,000 part-time students when I left in 1969. To the core of Irish-Canadian youngsters who had traditionally comprised the student body were added hundreds of Italian, Polish, Hungarian, Lithuanian, and Ukranian young people, the first generation in college, often trilingual, speaking the ancestral language at home, French in the streets, and English in school. Often poorly educated in secondary school, almost always younger than their American counterparts, they were ambitious, upwardly mobile, tough-minded, and confident of the future. Yet their linguistic facility mirrored deeper identity problems: the *maitre chez nous* character of the Quebec upheaval raised questions about their role in the French province; their own devotion to Canada made little sense in an environment in which Canadian nationalism was the ideology of the economically dominant English minority; their cultural immersion in North American music, film, and media made their sincere devotion to their homeland and their natural anti-Americanism seem ritualistic and superficial. Many seemed to encapsulate within a generation the process of movement from ghetto to suburb to counterculture that took at least three generations in the United States. Living at home with families reared in rural and small-town society in eastern and central Europe, living in the city with French Canadian students attuned to French culture and modern technocracy, themselves attracted to the Anglo-American counterculture, they were frequently torn, always uneasy about who they were, filled with a tension that made for an atmosphere of excitement and enthusiasm, but carried a high cost in nervous and emotional disorder.

In these same years, when American universities were expanding dramatically and Canadian higher education grew even faster, Loyola recruited its faculty where it could: its share of the small but growing crop of Canadian graduate students, refugee intellectuals from one or another section of Europe, and a flood of young American Ph.D.'s attracted by the city and by the tax advantages accruing to American scholars working in Canada. It was a rich collection of people, all highly competent, drawn from a wide variety of backgrounds and experiences, as ready to divide over a question of cold-war policy as over questions of changing curriculum. The Jesuits who owned the school retained top administrative posts but delegated a good deal of academic decision-making to departments and ever-changing faculty government structures.

While simple presence in such an atmosphere was bound to have a profound influence on a young person whose background had been as limited as my own, it was the quality of the history department that made the experience especially profound. Geoffrey Adams, the chairman, was the son of a Toronto Classics professor, a product of Canada's cultural elite whose tolerance, wisdom, and strength of character are enormously impressive. Donald Savage and Terry Copp were Canadian scholars of great quality and both, like Adams, were very active in politics. Robert Ruigh, John McGovern, and Robert Coolidge were, like me, Americans in our first jobs. Adams encouraged us to share responsibility for a growing department and led us in an active effort to shape college policy in a time of rapid change. He provided a unique model of academic leadership, giving all of us a sense of confidence in ourselves and one another, encouraging us to sense our personal responsibility for the college and for that broader world from which our students came and whose future we and they together might help to shape. Working in the Loyola History Department was the best possible experience a young professor could have in the sixties, for it was there that we learned together a sense of the power and responsibility that accrue to those few of us fortunate enough to have the best education society can offer. At a time when my contemporaries in American schools were struggling to survive the tenure race while teaching huge classes, we were rewriting the curriculum, shaping new structures of governance, experimenting with honors and interdisciplinary programs, and sharing in an exciting experience of the kind of community that emerges when very different people are doing work together they think important. I learned many things from my colleagues and students at Loyola, but none was more important than the realization that if people share a broad set of values, however great their disagreement on specific issues, they can be united in creative, challenging, and mutually supportive community; shared purpose, not common belief, is the major source of such community. The ability to shape and share visions of future possibility that at once transcend the existing order and yet are sufficiently grounded in reality to invite the first steps of implementation, seems to me the crucial factor in leadership in the university, the Church and, indeed, in the broader society.

IV

In my early writings I tried to insist that American Catholics were responding to events within their Church out of an American as well as a Catholic tradition. The forces set in motion by the Council were received by Americans within the distinctive contours of their own historical experience. The active leaders of American Catholicism had hoped, as such people had always hoped, to Americanize the Church through a vernacular liturgy, ecumenical understanding, and validation of religious liberty. They had none of the fear of the modern world characteristic of the Vatican, for they had never experienced the perils of modern consciousness that had all but destroyed the European Church in the nineteenth century. The Roman conservative argument that the Church could not change a little, without calling the whole into question, had little meaning for Americans, whose optimism and practicality were sustained less by the sophistication of their faith than by the success of their experience. The liberal Jacques Maritain and the reactionary Cardinal Ottaviani both knew the perils to faith present in adaptation to the modern world, but their warnings fell on deaf ears in the land where pragmatism reigned supreme on the foundations of profound confidence in the beneficence of history. As a result, the crises of faith that occured in the middle and later sixties were, in fact, almost entirely unanticipated in the United States, and for that very reason they were terribly disturbing and far less susceptible to effective pastoral response.

Most Catholics were unaware of the sources of Roman

conservatism, and thus regarded it as obscurantism rather than as a rationale for the survival of the Church. Neither did they understand the American religious experience. Americanization had raised severe problems of unity and discipline for all the Protestant denominations. American pluralism and diversity meant that people could actually choose their religion and thus their identity. Lacking disciplinary sanctions, Churches fell quite naturally into a marketplace mentality, forced to cater to the emotions and prejudices of their actual or potential constituents. The world-shaping power of faith was not lost, but found expression in the Churches of the dispossessed and, even more, in trans-congregational religious movements for missions, education, or for such reforms as abolitionism, prohibition, or peace. In the American context, where Christian faith was removed from the cultural superstructures that had previously supported it, faith itself became problematic. The choice facing Christianity often seemed between a kind of self-righteous sectarian isolation or a reliance upon the cultural context of America itself. Only gradually did the perils of pluralism become at all clear, first finding clear analysis in the writings of H. Richard and Reinhold Niebuhr. Catholics, still battling for their legitimate acceptance into the threefold melting pot of American denominationalism, hardly noticed. They were unprepared to handle the sociological earthquakes unleashed by the social changes following World War II and by the normative shifts of the Council, just as they were unprepared to respond effectively to the intellectual challenges implicit in the call to a new, humble, and mission-oriented understanding of the meaning and purpose of Christian commitment.

As I have tried to indicate, my own training in historiography and philosophy of history, received by a young man not too familiar with or committed to the neo-Scholastic categories of post-Reformation Catholicism, enabled me to welcome, relatively uncritically, the conciliar theology. Emotionally I was an Americanist, enjoying conciliar developments with the same enthusiasm of those young American scholars and journalists who were its major interpreters: Daniel Callahan, Michael Novak, Andrew Greeley, and, from an earlier generation, Xavier Rynne and John Cogley. The years in Canada first began to deepen my awareness of my instinctive Americanism. In the years that followed I urged American Catholics to understand the American sources of their problems and develop pastoral and social responses appropriate to the American environment, and at the same time that they see that environment in a larger, a more critical, context.

In retrospect I think that my secure personal upbringing in the Church, my studies of the American Church in the twentieth century, and some raw sense of humor derived from Irish sources enabled me to survive the perils of Americanization and modernism with faith intact. Throughout the decade, none of its awesome events shook my personal relationship with the Church and the Catholic tradition, despite the considerable personal problems of family life, liturgy, community, and sacraments that my wife and I experienced with others of our generation.

What for me was far more shattering, and exerted far more impact on my personal and professional life, was the American experience of the 1960s, summed up in William L. O'Neill's recent study *Coming Apart*. In retrospect our certainty as Catholics regarding birth control and parochial schools a decade ago is no more striking than the fact that Kennedy-style liberalism marked the limits of our political imaginations. I began to realize while in Canada that our Americanism was as important in shaping our self-understanding as was our faith, and that the collapse of our love for and faith in America would have serious impact on our religious as well as our political beliefs. My Canadian friends taught me a more profound critique of American foreign policy than I had learned from my radical friends at Rochester; the nasty word "imperialism" was a living reality in Canadian life, whatever its sources or intention. Most important was Vietnam. Experiencing that war north of the border, with access to the Canadian and European press, made acceptance of the American line almost impossible from the start. While I offered a moderate, liberal, defense of American policy in the spring of 1965, even then my heart was not in it. Press reports were reinforced by personal contacts with Canadians who had been to Vietnam, and by the summer of 1965 I was convinced that the war was at best a tragic mistake, at worst a revelation of the nation's systematic betrayal of its founding principles. I began to speak and write against the war, not from the point of view of Christian doctrine, but from the perspective of American moral integrity. Believing deeply in the values of self-government and legitimation of authority through consent, I began to understand Vietnam in particular and American foreign policy in general as a history of avoidance of those principles. The manner of the war's conduct added particularly to the outrage, and only at this point did I, personally, draw upon Christian sources. Whatever disagreements might exist about the wisdom of the war, I failed to see how any decent human being, and certainly any Christian, could justify the large-scale slaughter of the innocent which was the war's outstanding characteristic. Like many of my generation, I became almost totally preoccupied with the war. We sponsored fund-raising affairs for the American Deserters' Committee and sheltered a young deserter in our home; we held parties and meetings to encourage resistance and to help Canadians pressure their government to end its complicity.

It was fortunate for me that during this period of my life I lived and worked among Canadian academics of impeccable credentials whose whole lives blended scholarly work with political responsibility and action. Geoffrey Adams and Donald Savage were long-time NDP activists, whose politics enriched their understanding of history and whose historical knowledge gave depth and sophistication to their politics. Terry Copp was a populistic-oriented Conservative, always personally involved in party activity and constantly speaking and writing to help students and the public understand the implications of events. Savage and Adams were devoted internationalists; Copp was passionately dedicated to Canadian independence and integrity. Their example was living proof to me that, far from endangering scholarly work, political involvement was enriching, and that the integrity of scholarly enterprise demanded that the intellectual community bear witness to the Enlightenment values of reason and freedom, which necessarily inform all educational and academic activity.

Vietnam shattered the style of detached objectivity that

had persisted in my teaching despite the impact of Hayden White's historicism. The study of American politics and policy now seemed loaded with moral and political relevance. History-making came to seem to me the goal, not simply of historical study, but of intellectual work generally, a goal long unacknowledged because unchallenged, but now demanding articulation and active reflection. The men and women from the old world who voluntarily faced the perils of migration lived under the power of the dream that they could be responsible for their lives and could share with others the responsibilities of community. This dream united Jefferson and Thoreau, Theodore Parker and William Lloyd Garrison, Eugene Debs and Norman Thomas, Cesar Chavez and Martin Luther King. The war, which first shattered so many of my feelings and thoughts about America, sent me to the American radical tradition and to a reconsideration of the cultural legacy of my own people. It led to a new conviction of the history-making importance of the common experience of Americans: the American experiment, symbolized not only in the Philadelphia convention of 1787 but in the steerage of a thousand immigrant ships, seemed to me to rest on the willingness of people, ordinary people, to risk responsibility for their own lives and risk sharing the life of a national community.

The evil of Vietnam at the end seemed different than it did at the beginning. Then it was a geopolitical mistake, an aberration from a policy of national commitment to self-determination, a mistake costly in its misrepresentation of the intentions and values of the American people. It was an abstract question, thought of primarily in American terms, and evaluated from an American standpoint. At its end it was to be seen as a human tragedy, decent men killing innocent men, women, and children; respectable people at home giving their support to the betrayal of their parents' hopes; murder becoming acceptable as a deepening fatalism gripped the national consciousness. History-making giving way to history-made, confirmed not just by technological slaughter carried on regardless of popular will, but brought home in deteriorating neighborhoods, family breakdown, generational conflict, and almost universal irresponsibility. We faced, it seemed to me, not simply large-scale social change, but a profoundly religious crisis: a people's loss of faith and confidence in themselves and their brothers and sisters. Our religious world had been, I began to understand, not only the world of Catholic tradition and community, but also the world of civil faith. Its collapse was the real religious crisis of the era; it touched us all. Norman Mailer, writing about the Democratic convention of 1972, described it best:

. . . as he stood near McGovern now, there came to him the first strains of that simple epiphany, which had eluded him through all these days, and he realized it, and it was simple, but he thought it true. In America, the country was the religion, and all the religions of the land were fed from that first religion, which was the country itself, and if the other religions were now full of mutation and staggering across deserts of faith, it was because the country had been false and ill and corrupt for years, not in the age old proportions of failure and evil, but corrupt to the point of terminal disease, like a great religion foundering.

However exaggerated the Maileresque language, the point was confirmed in a thousand statements of a hundred anti-war and civil-rights demonstrations.

Daniel Berrigan's play from the Catonsville trial transcript showed each defendant at the bar of American justice testifying not to a renewal of religious conviction resulting in Christian pacifism, but to a personal experience of collapsing confidence in America, its ideals and its people. Each had been active in social ministry at home and abroad, bringing less faith than justice; each experienced America as oppressor rather than liberator and were led by that discovery to the exploration of new vehicles for personal commitment. Christianity provided resources to survive the crisis and to shape new directions, but the crisis was American and precisely for that reason human and secular. The Melville brothers, exiled from their mission work in Guatamala for challenging the CIA and the American corporations; Nicholas Riddell, who had a similar experience in the Philippines; James Groppi, a Catholic Martin King, who placed the American creed against the Milwaukee practice. None were inspired to social ministry by Pope John; rather they were led by what they believed to be both a Christian and an American commitment to justice, freedom, and human dignity. Their radicalism resulted less from their experience of a conflict between American and Christian values than from their shocked realization that America was not, after all, the nation it was supposed to be.

Few of the Catholic radicals seemed to understand this fully. Clearly within the American radical tradition, they failed to claim the American symbols as their own; instead, they often appeared to separate national and religious loyalties. Daniel Berrigan's poetry and Thomas Merton's prose often featured an apocalyptic language that resonated with other-worldly perfectionism. The Catholic radicals often demanded first a personal commitment embodied in distinctive life-style and community, tending toward a sectarianism that would trust to the force of example or nonviolent symbolic protest as vehicles for social change.

For my own part, I hesitated before such personalism and apocalypticism. Instead I found myself increasingly drawn back to the concepts and categories of modern Catholic social and political thought. If Pope John's encyclicals lacked the synthetic structure of older Catholic teachings, they better manifested the never-ending tension between religious authenticity and political realism. A similar tone informed the conciliar documents, which acknowledged the present moment as one marked by both promise and peril. Pope Paul and the Synod of Bishops of 1971 seem to me to carry this spirit forward, incorporating, however imperfectly, the pastoral experience of the Churches of the world as they try to take with full seriousness the contemporary call to mission. Pope John wished to renew the Church to make it a servant to mankind in its struggle for fuller human life in peace, justice, charity, and freedom. This hope is bearing fruit, it seems to me, in hidden ways, in the Church in much of Europe, in the third world, and in many small communities at all levels of the Church in America.

V

It was the war that led me to question my relationship with my country, and it was that experience which caused my most serious break with my Church. Looking back on those years now, I can appreciate the significance of those gradual, hesitant steps by which the Vatican and the Church generally moved to a more powerful emphasis on the Christian vocation of peacemaking and led the American bishops to an ever sharper criticism of the war itself. Yet, the Vatican record on the war was scandalous and, given its position of access to information, far less excusable than the almost equally dismal record of the American hierarchy. I believed then, and I believe now, that the evil of the war's conduct was so great that it could be justified by no conceivable calculus of just war, Catholic or American. I was disillusioned with academic institutions and leaders because of their failures during the war, but my scorn for Church leaders was far greater. Time, and a nose for historical complexity, heals many wounds; so too does the realization of one's own lack of charity and wisdom. Nevertheless, I can testify to the fact that for a moderately conservative person, the experience of active opposition to leaders one has cherished opens tensions in one's life that can never be entirely removed.

It is, of course, natural and good to discover in a small way the burdens of personal responsibility. Yet others, some my friends, bore far greater burdens than I, some the burdens of rejection by family, teachers, counselors, and priests. It is not natural, and not good, that so many, especially among the young, had to bear these burdens alone. The desertion of these people by their Church was a tragedy of considerable magnitude; it angered me then and it continues as a note of bitterness in my relationship to the Church today. Perhaps this is self-righteous; I can only testify to its presence and importance for me. It means that I know something for myself of the goodness and the irresponsibility of the Church, both in the "out there" of ecclesiastical life and in the home territory of my own life.

For me, as for so many others of my generation, the exploration of faith in the light of historical consciousness, and in the equally profound light of experience, has led to considerable doubt, some alienation, and at least a tentative recommitment. We are a generation who actually experienced communities of shared meaning and shared values. In the Church, we once knew that all around us partook of the same sacraments, spoke the same creed, accepted the same authorities. If we differed on such minor issues as parochial schools or the language of the liturgy, we differed within an acknowledged community of faith. Similarly, we knew, or thought we did, that all Americans really did care about liberty and justice and were prepared to sacrifice individual and national well-being for the sake of peace in the world and a better life for all people. Neither of these shared communities any longer exists in quite the same way for us. We have learned too much about our own weakness and self-deception to speak righteously of "them" and "us"; we still cherish the memory and the hope for shared community. But we have come to differ significantly with many of our fellow Americans over the interpretations of those symbols that once united us. For my own part, I feel that the role of the intellectual who is only a critic of those symbols has exhausted itself. Critical scholarship once served human aspirations because it was expressed within a specific historical context of faith in reason and commitment to freedom; the liberal generation was confident that the fruit of critical awareness would be personal and collective self-determination. It is now a fact that such freedom and self-direction has become impossible for large numbers of people, in and out of the Church, and the liberal provides little guidance because he himself has too often lost confidence in reason and in the potential of ordinary people. As a result, his critical stance becomes simply critical; as such it erodes the popular will, contributes to the general cultural disposition to put aside dreams of history-making and accept a world made by forces and powers beyond human control. Only those who are willing to acknowledge quite deliberately a firm commitment to freedom, to evaluate existing structures of society and culture on the basis of that commitment, and attempt to shape personal and collective responses oriented toward maximizing human freedom, deserve consideration and respect. Few are willing to do so; those who are receive too often the ridicule and contempt of their colleagues. Unable any longer to believe that they have indeed mastered the world, our leaders cannot bear to be reminded of their own youthful visions. In academy and Church and community, those who dare to speak and act out the vital symbols of freedom that once nourished us all are driven to the fringes of life, there to try as best they can to find some friendship and some useful work. Meanwhile scholars and priests contribute their share to the mystification of the world, which alone sustains the ever more powerful engines of repression and control.

Given such a view of the contemporary conflict between the values of reason, freedom, and community, and the drift of the world toward a controlled structure of institutionalized injustice and violence, the American and the Christian symbols take on a new appearance. Being American and being Christian become unfinished tasks, unrealized promises, demanding a response of commitment, dedication, and struggle. Throughout the world the Church again stands at the brink, as it did in the nineteenth century; once again it has the opportunity to risk all by joining the forces of peace, justice, and freedom, as Pope John urged it to do. But it also has the choice of setting new limits to the visions its faith inspires, a choice it can make by simply drifting with events, becoming the de facto ally of those who demand subservience to definitions of possibility and practicality set by the powerful and successful. Rather than consistently criticizing, if not condemning, those who are trying to act decisively to counter the drift of events, the Church might take with full seriousness the words of the 1971 Synod of Bishops: "Unless combatted and overcome by social and political action, the influence of the new industrial and technological order favors the concentration of wealth, power, and decision-making in the hands of a small, private controlling group." If this is the case, then the Church must inspire the confidence, trust, and hope that make action possible, and the rest of us must join in the effort to develop, evaluate, and reform new models and programs of action.

To sustain faith, to nourish the spirit, and to plan work we desperately need communities of shared vision, groups of men and women united less by their determination to preserve the old faith than by their common hope to make that faith live in a common life—and by word, witness, and work announce that faith to all who will listen. It is the stance of those who cherish the liberal inheritance of personal and civil liberties, who understand the necessity for democratic procedures, who have few illusions about human perfectibility, but who deny totally that these require an ethical empiricism that holds all values, all creeds, all symbols as equally valuable, and denies that the only test of principles is practice. This stance is conservative in its reverence for the institutions that have been shaped by the long experience of Church and nation. Yet it is a radical stance, because it insists that the purposes of those symbols and those institutions remain unrealized; in fact, they are to be cherished and conserved precisely in order to sustain their promises, evoke new understandings of their meanings, and structure new approaches to living them in life and work. It is activist only in the sense of demanding action; it recognizes that worthwhile action requires personal wholeness and critical reflection. It is utopian only in the sense that it holds a vision of human possibility for freedom, love, and creativity deeply rooted both in the Western tradition and in continuing human experiences today.

VI

The result of all this is far less dramatic than I make it sound. Many ideas that I had taken for granted have come to be questioned, by me and by others; other ideas, long latent, have been forced into consciousness by the events that have touched our lives. The security of our religious and national loyalty has been severely shaken and we can no longer participate in either Church or civic affairs with quite the same assurance and confidence we had before. And yet all of this continues to be mediated by people among whom we live and work. In my own case that means family and friends and colleagues. My wife and I have experienced many of these things together, though we have felt their impact often in different ways. The companionship and care of marriage provide continuity with history as well as personal affirmation and support. The presence of small children contributes a note of ever-present realism, drawing us to the concrete when we are tempted to absorbtion in abstractions. In our experience, wife and husband and children provide one another with many things, not least some constant demand for responsibility; personal demands for integrity and authenticity come within and through our community together. And there is more. In none of these experiences have we been alone; for every disaster and every small problem has brought forth community which, however temporary, has empowered us to some sort of response.

Here in Worcester, Massachusetts, where I live, we have a "floating parish" of Christians who stroke one another when things hurt, support one another in our work and projects, and grope toward some meaningful sharing of our lives. Around that there is a broader community of people concerned with justice and peace who call one another out from time to time and may yet, someday, find the vehicle to overcome the bigger problems that press on us all. We have parties and picnics and celebrations; we are getting to an age when we drink more than we used to and reminisce about the demonstrations and actions of the past. Like our neighbors we worry about medical and dental bills, our children's education, and the cost of heat, gas, and electricity. Like them, too, we appreciate the common goodness of this country, its natural beauty, its fantastic energy, its remarkable ability to preserve hope and confidence in spite of its leaders, the generosity and kindness of its people. We are more patient than we used to be, more aware of the tenaciousness of institutions and customs, less sure that any change will be for the better. We have learned over the years that there are a lot of us in this community, that a great many working people and businessmen, professionals and welfare recipients, students and working mothers share the same concerns about this city and this country. They evaluate their world according to similar moral norms, and they are prepared to sacrifice to make things better, if and when those sacrifices seem credible and authentic. Like the colonial Americans who seemed so passive between the Boston Massacre and the Boston Tea Party, their silence is not satisfied but is in some tough-minded way sullen. Dissatisfaction remains and it will out again. We all pray that when it does come out, there will be responsible and creative leaders and institutions prepared to translate that new energy into work for a more peaceful and just society.

I cannot claim to have found the supportive community for intellectual work which I have claimed is necessary. For many reasons, Catholic colleges and universities have been unable to respond to the call to social and religious responsibility made so clearly by the leaders of the Church and by such men as the Jesuit General, Pedro Arrupe. Like their secular counterparts, Catholic institutions of higher education seem locked into established patterns of specialization and aloofness that inhibit the development of truly critical and creative education and scholarship. While Father Arrupe has called for schools fully committed to analyzing and evaluating the oppressive economic and political structures of the modern world, developing "ideologies and technologies" shaped by the need for the liberation of people, few institutions have been able to respond. Perhaps only in independent research and training centers established for the purpose can we get the kind of committed intellectual work we need.

I have been fortunate enough to experience a taste of a working community in the Catholic Committee on Urban Ministry. Organized by Monsignor John Egan, longtime social activist in Chicago and now on the staff of the Pastoral Studies Department at Notre Dame, the committee is a network of social-action people around the country who offer one another personal support and shared resources in the overall effort to move the Church toward the implementation of recent social teachings. As a member of its board and as a staff member of its summer program in pastoral and social ministry at Notre Dame, I have had the privilege of working closely with people in social ministry, whose interest in my work has been particularly supportive and whose lives have been an inspiration to me. CCUM has attempted to encourage people active in ministry to understand that their experience of faith is the ground for a theology of social ministry, and that such a theology must emerge from their reflection, rather than from the academy alone. It has also attempted, with less success, to encourage scholars to become involved with people in ministry, not simply as resource people but as colleagues sharing their experience and participating in common work.

The universal Church in my lifetime has moved gradually, but certainly, toward a more integral vision of social responsibility. It continues to encourage and sustain a wide variety of types and styles of Christian life. In the past the Church has had both very diverse congregations and a sense of common belief and purpose. There are today many examples of new congregations operating in varying degrees of affiliation with the institutional Church. The multiplication of such alternatives, and the diversification of opportunities for service and ministry, remain matters high on the Catholic agenda. In the lives of priests, sisters, and lay people around the country, I personally have found signs of hopes and witnesses of new possibilities, just as I have long found support and strength among Catholics of more traditional orientation. In a stance of invitation rather than regulation, the Church might be able to tap more fully her always incredible resources of talent and good will. Whether she will do so or not, whether the promise of the past will find fulfillment in the future, is far from clear to me. To those who always tell me that my hopes have no possibility of fulfillment, I can argue with Max Weber that without reaching out for the impossible, even the possible would not be achieved. In fact, the limits of the possible are always greater than they seem; definitions of human possibility always presume present inertia and pessimism. Throughout my life, people in and out of the Catholic community have constantly helped me to discover unknown parts of myself. I continue to believe that we in the Catholic community could do great work in the world if we could constantly offer one another a challenge and an invitation. The challenge—to change our lives to become more fully a people living for others—and the invitation—to be part of a community of people trying to do the same—both derive from continued faith in Jesus Christ, whose promises remain ever before us, calling us to be better than we thought we could be, together, all of us, with him. I, for one, have nowhere else to turn than to the tradition that inspired and empowered my parents and shaped and formed me. I cherish that tradition and retain a confidence in the final fidelity of God, because I have experienced in my own life and in the lives of those who have touched me the mysterious but wonderful benevolence of Providence. It is perhaps all best summed up by Thomas Merton in words I have often found personally consoling and profoundly Catholic:

My Lord God, I have no idea where I am going. I do not see the road ahead of me. I cannot know for certain where it will end. Nor do I really know myself, and the fact that I think I am following your will does not mean that I am actually doing so. But I believe that the desire to please you does in fact please you. And I hope that I will never do anything apart from that desire. And I know that if I do this you will lead me by the right road though I may know nothing about it. Therefore will I trust you always though I may seem to be lost and in the shadow of death. I will not fear, for you are ever with me, and you will never leave me to face my perils alone.

Growth (Hopefully) in Wisdom, Age and Grace

CHARLES E. CURRAN

This essay intends to look in a reflective way on how events, ideas, and personal experience have influenced my theological development. Both personal and intellectual experiences have helped to shape the thinking of every scholar. The theologian is also influenced by experiences within Christianity and within the Church. This article will reflect on the personal, intellectual, and ecclesial influences that have shaped my own theological reflection in the area of moral theology or Christian ethics.

Reflection shows that my personal experience has been influential in shaping my approach to moral theology even on the most abstract and fundamental questions. One of the basic questions in any ethical theory is the ultimate ethical model. In theory, I have been influenced on this question by the thought of H. Richard Niebuhr and his disciples. Traditionally, ethics has been divided into either teleological or deontological types, although lately a third type of a relationality-responsibility model has been introduced. The teleological model understands ethics in terms of the goal or end and the means to obtain it. One first determines what is the ultimate end and then coordinates and subordinates more proximate ends and means as the way of achieving the ultimate end. Thomistic ethics generally follows such an approach as is evident from the fact that Thomas Aquinas begins his discussion of ethics by considering the ultimate end of man. Deontology sees the ethical life primarily in terms of duties, laws, and obligations and is well illustrated in the philosophical approach of Immanuel Kant. In practice the ethics proposed for daily living in the Catholic Church with its heavy emphasis on law and the Commandments followed the deontological model which was probably common for most Christian Churches.

Theoretical reason argues that the teleological model is too purposive and ordered. Likewise, in the midst of both enormous complexity and great historical change the older understanding of eternal laws based either on the scriptural revelation or on the essential nature of human beings does not seem adequate as the primary ethical model. These and other reasons only exclude the deontological or the teleological as the ultimate ethical models even though there must always be some place for norms and for goals and ends in moral theology.

My own life and development as a theologian and as a person did not follow the teleological or the deontological model. I did not sit down and figure out what my goal was and decide on the best means to achieve it. My personal and professional development as a theologian has been something that I did not and could not see in advance. My theological growth depended very much on my response to the new and changing situations with which I came into contact and was not the unfolding of a well-conceived plan. There were too many aspects in my own development over which I had no control. I never experienced the luxury of feeling that everything was under my influence and I could plan my own future development in a very detailed way for a long period of time. Obviously some such plan is always necessary for organization and results, but reflection made me realize how often I was called upon to respond to other events that entered my life.

I never planned to write an essay on this subject, but after some hesitation I responded positively to the editor's invitation. The conscious awareness of the influence of experience on my theological development as mentioned above led me to accept this invitation for further reflection. Perhaps a chronological arrangement will be the most logical way to proceed, although at times other considerations will be introduced.

Theological Studies

My theological studies were done in the context of preparation for priestly ministry at the North American College in
Rome. I was studying for the Catholic priesthood for the diocese of Rochester, New York, and had received my B.A. from
St. Bernard's Seminary in Rochester having followed the usual
college-seminary course. I began my theological studies at the
Gregorian University in Rome in September of 1955 without
any intention or goal of ultimately becoming a teacher or
scholar in the area of theology. In fact, I had purposely not
chosen a religious community because I had no overwhelming
drive at that time to devote my life to either teaching or scholarship.

Theology in Rome in the 1950s was still generally unaffected by the winds of change that would come with the advent
of the Second Vatican Council. The teaching methods were of
the old school—the professor read his lectures, which would
often be available in mimeographed form, to an audience of
students which regularly numbered well into the hundreds.
(There were many more students on the first day and on the
last day of class!) No papers were required, and there was just
one final examination (oral in the major subjects) at the end of
the year. Lectures and the examinations were all in Latin,
which was not too great a problem for me. Despite all these
very negative aspects of the education itself, I am glad I was
exposed to it. It put me into contact with working theologians
and even at a distance I was able to appreciate some aspects of
what they were trying to do. Later I would change many of the
ideas I learned in those years, but I remain grateful for the experience.

I was in no sense a rebel student, but would have accurate-
ly been described as a docile student who did his work and was
faithful in class attendance—doing also a moderate amount of
outside reading. Now I can recall only two or three issues on
which I seriously disagreed with a professor—the question of
religious liberty and the fate of unbaptized infants. I did not
see how the mercy of God could not find some way to bring
these "souls" to the fullness of life. I was ordained in 1958 at

the end of my third year of theology and shortly thereafter the bishop of Rochester told me that I would be staying on for graduate studies in moral theology because I was going to teach moral theology at St. Bernard's Seminary. I had no burning desire to teach; but after more than three years of theology the prospect of teaching seemed acceptable, although naturally I had no say whatsoever in the matter. At the time I thought it might be more interesting to study and to teach canon law because the practical application and concrete working out of ideas have always been appealing to me.

My two years of graduate study proved most formative. I was told to obtain my doctorate at the Gregorian University. With the exception of a newer vision and approach to moral theology that Father Joseph Fuchs was trying to impart, my earlier theological formation at the Gregorian University had been in terms of very traditional moral theology. However, I was very much attracted to my professors such as the German Franz Hürth, who was known as a most influential member of the Holy Office, with whom I occasionally chatted for lengthy periods in Latin about different kinds of moral problems. Since I was familiar with the approach to moral theology of the professors at the Gregorian, I tried to broaden my horizons. I enrolled in courses at the Academia Alfonsiana, which under the direction of the Redemptorists at that time was in the process of initiating a program of studies leading to a doctorate in moral theology. In the end I obtained a doctorate from both institutions.

My experience at the Alfonsiana brought me into contact with a much broader view of moral theology. This institution demanded much more course work on the doctoral level than the Gregorian and opened up vistas in the area of biblical and patristic morality, the historical development of moral theology, and different philosophical approaches. These newer approaches and vistas were epitomized in Father Bernard Häring, who almost singlehandedly pointed Catholic moral theology in new directions in the pre-Vatican II Church. Häring's insistence on overcoming the dichotomy between moral theology and spiritual theology not only countered the legalism and minimalism of the manuals of theology but also gave moral theology a scriptural and liturgical dimension that it had previously lacked. Häring's insistence on the biblical call to perfection also brought with it an emphasis on growth, change, and development in the Christian life that paved the way for my own future appreciation of historicity. Likewise, his dependence on Max Scheler's philosophy also opened up new philosophical horizons for me. In the light of Häring's insistence on the primacy of the Spirit and the virtue of *epikeia* (equity), positive laws and exceptions to such laws were more properly understood. Häring in those days created quite a stir by maintaining that the obligation to pray the breviary was such that at times one should not use Latin if the language became an obstacle to the primary purpose of prayer.

A practical and compassionate side of Häring's moral theology was also underscored in the law of growth that would not insist on imposing more than an individual was able to do at a given time. What appealed so profoundly to me was the wholeness of his approach which was mirrored in his own life and personality. There was an authenticity about his teaching and his life that spoke volumes. Ours was not a particularly close relationship at the time, but my enthusiasm for his moral theology was demonstrated by the number of fellow graduate students from the North American College whom I invited to attend some of his lectures.

Our personal relationship grew with the years. I was instrumental in setting up Häring's first theology week in this country in Buffalo in 1962, although the primary invitation had already been extended to him by the Benedictine Fathers at Conception Abbey for a six-week summer course. Very significant for me personally was the backing Häring gave me in the midst of two public struggles I later had. In 1972 I was happy to be able to express publicly my gratitude to Bernard Häring by dedicating my new book to him on the occasion of his sixtieth birthday.

As the 1960s moved on and post-conciliar period of the Church opened, I was somewhat disappointed to realize that Häring's publications were no longer breaking new ground in a systematic way. We had a discussion about this while he was a visiting professor at Yale Divinity School in the

1966-67 school year. Häring pointed out that the was devoting much of his time and energy to bringing the idea of renewal in the Church to an ever-wider public, for he felt this was the most important need for the Church at the present time. I respected that decision and could understand it very well. One can say without fear of contradiction that no one has spoken to more people in more countries about contemporary Christian moral life than Bernard Häring. In the process it has been impossible for him to publish on a high, scholarly level, and thus he has not been able to continue charting the future course of moral theology. However, even now his insights are often valuable and fruitful for the discipline of moral theology. The moral theologian who is a committed Christian and Churchman will always experience the tension between the scholarly understanding of Christian ethics and the practical proclamation of the Gospel as it affects the lives of people.

Graduate study in moral theology thus gave me a new vision of the subject and made me very discontent with the older approaches. Here the seeds were already sown for many of my own future developments, but my doctoral research did not wholly mirror these new attitudes. My doctoral dissertation at the Gregorian University under the direction of Father Francis Furlong was of a very traditional variety—*The Prevention of Conception After Rape*. At the Alfonsiana I wrote a dissertation of a more historical nature on *Invincible Ignorance of the Natural Law in Saint Alphonsus*. My director, Father Domenico Capone, also helped me by insisting on the need for a systematic approach to put together all the other aspects of moral theology.

One incident that occurred just before I returned from Rome in the summer of 1961 stands out in memory. Francis X. Murphy taught patristic theology at the Alfonsiana, and we had lunch together just before my departure. (Some of our conversation that day, plus the fact I knew his mother's maiden name was Rynne, helped me partially solve the riddle of the author of what later appeared as the famous letters from Rome about the Vatican Council in the *New Yorker* magazine.) We discussed what would happen upon my return to the States to teach moral theology. Murphy encouraged me to write and continue my scholarly pursuits, but also cautioned me to go slow and not make too many waves, because he was aware of my dissatisfaction with the older approach to moral theology. He suggested that I begin by teaching my classes in Latin (this had been somewhat of a tradition in the past at St. Bernard's Seminary in Rochester) so that first attention would not focus on the newer approaches I was teaching. The strategy worked quite well—for a while. I was known as the one who taught in Latin for the first three weeks before going into English at the request of the students.

The First Years

Teaching a new approach to moral theology in a pre-Vatican II seminary environment was an exhilarating experience —especially since my approach was different from that of all the other theological professors. Newer approaches to theology challenged many students and created a real interest in theological study. The faculty was expected to follow a textbook, but my "introductions" became notorious. One year the introduction finished in March, and only then did I bring the textbook into class. A number of faculty colleagues were also quite supportive in many different ways even though they might not have fully appreciated what I was trying to do.

My first venture in writing was in response to a request for a pamphlet on Christian morality for a Doctrinal Pamphlet Series to be published by Paulist Press. This pamphlet was written in the spring of 1962 and published early that summer. (Two years ago my final take-home examination for students in the introductory course in moral theology was to criticize this particular pamphlet. They were quite negative—and rightly so!) Also, there were a few other comparatively small and insignificant articles. Probably because there was no other Catholic theologian who had shown in print any sympathy for the newer developments in moral theology, I was invited to give a paper on conscience at the Roman Catholic-Protestant Colloquium sponsored by Harvard University in March of 1963. I was fearful about accepting, but finally agreed and enjoyed the entire experience. After that time I tried to deepen my contact with Protestant ethical thought and often taught seminars on the subject at the Catholic University of America, which gave me the opportunity to read and discuss with my graduate students the outstanding figures in the Protestant ethical tradition. Previously, as was typical of most pre-Vatican II Roman Catholic theologians, I had little or no contact with Protestant ethical thought.

During the early 1960s I began to give talks not only in the Rochester area but also in various places around the country on topics of renewal in Catholic moral theology including an address to the convention of the Canon Law Society of America in 1964, arguing against the continued need for the promises to be taken by both parties to a mixed marriage to raise all the children in the Catholic faith. I was also warned on a number of occasions by officials of the Diocese of Rochester that my teaching was at times too progressive and I should be more careful.

The major issue at the time was artificial contraception. Only at the end of 1963 did some Catholic theologians begin openly to question the teaching of the Church on artificial contraception. I followed the debates and reported on them sympathetically in an article published in the summer of 1964 in *Jubilee*. Shortly thereafter I became convinced of the need to change the teaching of the Roman Catholic Church on birth control and before the year was out wrote an article to explain my views and gave addresses on this topic.

As a moral theologian teaching in a diocesan seminary and as a priest helping out weekends in a parish, I came into contact with a large number of young married couples. Often I was asked in those years to give talks to parish groups on questions of marriage. Likewise, many couples were sent to me by others to talk about their problems. I was jarred by the discrepancy between theory and practice. Those couples who were practicing artificial contraception did not seem to be sinning. At first I had justified their position by saying that objectively what they did was sinful, but subjectively there was no sin. They were showing all the signs of a good Christian life. What was wrong with what they were doing? I was also troubled by the fact that many other couples who were trying to follow the teaching of the Church seemed to be under such difficult pressures and tensions in their lives.

This somewhat jarring personal experience caused me to reconsider the reasons that had been proposed in favor of the teaching against artificial contraception. Looking back at that article which was written in 1964, I see that it really set the parameters for much of my work in the next few years—although I obviously did not recognize it or understand it at the time. Any thoughtful discussion of the question of artificial contraception must face the question of natural law and the teaching authority of the Church. These were the two areas I discussed in that article. The teaching against artificial contraception seemed to be based on only one aspect of the human —the biological; but the moral judgment can never be absolutely identified with the biological. Research for my thesis helped me to show that the Catholic teaching was proposed at a time when all thought the seed was the only active element of human reproduction, so that every single act of sexual intercourse was open to procreation. Today we know that this is not true. In the section on the teaching authority of the Church I pointed out the possibility of change in the light of the change in other Church teachings and also based on the changing understanding of human sexuality and reproduction.

In retrospect, so much of my scholarly interests for the last decade were set by that discussion. In September of 1973 I published an article in *Theological Studies* on the present state of Roman Catholic moral theology arguing for a pluralism in moral methodology and a pluralism with respect to specific moral teachings in the Catholic Church. This article had originally been given as the presidential address to the American Society of Christian Ethics. Two of the three major divisions of that article were natural law and authoritarianism in Church teaching. In the ensuing years I had investigated in greater detail the question of natural law, since it was generally accepted that Roman Catholic moral teaching was based on natural law. An interest in history and an appreciation of historical mindedness (which I learned explicitly from my former professor, Bernard Lonergan) helped me to show that for the most part Roman Catholic moral teachings were not based on *the* natural law understood as a monolithic, philosophical system with an agreed upon body of ethical content in existence throughout the centuries. Although many thinkers had employed the term "natural law" in the course of history, they did not mean the same thing by it. In addition, it seemed that the individual teachings came into existence first, and only later was the theory introduced as a way to explain the already existing teachings. However, in the nineteenth century the authoritative, hierarchical teaching office of the Church imposed Thomistic philosophy and theology as *the* Roman Catholic approach. In ethics, emphasis was placed on the natural law as the Catholic approach. Most contemporaries grew up in the context created by the nineteenth century and thus did not realize that Catholic moral teaching for the most part had not been based on *the* natural law.

The very ambiguities in the concept of natural law occasioned problems. Ulpian, a Roman lawyer in the third century, had defined the natural law as that which is common to man and to all the animals, such as the procreation and education of offspring. He distinguished natural law from the *ius gentium* which was proper to man because of human reason. Thomas Aquinas later defined the natural law as right reason, but at times he did accept Ulpian's understanding of natural law as that which is common to man and all the animals. Consequently, the natural easily becomes identified with the physical and the biological, and human reason cannot interfere in these natural processes. This seemed to me what happened in the Church teaching on contraception and in the famous teaching on the primary end of marriage. But it also explained other problems in moral theology. In fact the debate about situation ethics in the late 1960s, in my judgment, ultimately centered on those areas where the human was identified with the physical and the biological—questions of medical ethics such as contraception and sterilization; the question of when human life begins; the solution of conflict situations by the principle of double effect that defined the direct effect in terms of the physical structure of the act; sexuality in which the sexual act as described in physical terms is always wrong outside marriage;

and there are also traces of this problem in the treatment of the problem of divorce. I do not at times deny that the moral and the physical can be identified, but this insight helped to explain and situate much of the debate about situation ethics.

The early treatment of the teaching office of the Church in moral matters, as found in that article written in 1964, centered on the possibility of change in such teaching. Later reading and investigations showed other instances of such changes, and again the recognition of the importance of historical consciousness gave a theoretical basis for such change. Even before the encyclical *Humanae Vitae* in 1968, I insisted on the accepted Catholic teaching about the right to dissent from authoritative, noninfallible Church teaching. This aspect has developed at much greater length in the controversy following the organized theological dissent against the papal condemnation of artificial contraception in 1968. Naturally, too, the possibility of dissent was seen as extending to all other specific moral questions, because in the midst of such complexities one cannot achieve a level of certitude on specific moral questions that can exclude the possibility of error. Thus, my first articles set the tone and the parameters of much of my theological writing for the next ten years. But we are getting too far ahead of the chronology.

Back in 1964 and early 1965 a call for change in the teaching of the Catholic Church on contraception was bound to cause some ripples. There were pressures put upon officials in the diocese of Rochester from outside the diocese, but there was also discontent within the diocese itself—although there existed for some time a reluctance to touch me. There were some warnings, and I knew the situation was tense. I tried to strengthen my own position by sending to the diocesan officials various offers I had to teach at Catholic universities in the United States, but in all cases they told me that I could not be spared from St. Bernard's. In late July of 1965, the ax fell. I was called in and told that I would no longer be teaching at St. Bernard's, but I was free to accept the offer from Catholic University or any other offer I had received. My reaction was not very strong, for I was realistic enough to know that sooner or later this was bound to happen. I can truthfully say that neither then nor since have I really experienced any great bitterness over it, but I have always been grateful for those who supported me and spoke up in my defense at that time.

Catholic University and Controversies

After a few weeks of negotiations, mostly by telephone, I accepted the invitation of Dean Walter Schmitz and the faculty of the School of Theology of Catholic University of America to join them. I had previously taught in the summer sessions of the Department of Religious Education of that university under the chairpersonship of Gerard Sloyan who had also wanted me to join his faculty full time, but Father Schmitz had originally been in touch with me more than three years previously. Early in September after I had just arrived at the university, I was called in by the vice-rector on the basis of a letter that had been sent to all clerical members of the faculty questioning my orthodoxy because of the various positions I had taken.

I enjoyed the new surroundings and was made to feel at home by my colleagues, some of whom had been in graduate studies with me. I continued my work which in the light of the circumstances included continued writing and speaking on the question of artificial contraception. In the fall of 1965 I arranged with Fides Publishers of Notre Dame to publish a collection of essays under the title *Christian Morality Today*. The book was published in September of 1966 and contained essays on many facets of the Christian moral life emphasizing newer developments in terms of scripture, the liturgy, and the Gospel call to perfection as well as discussions of natural law, authentic Church teaching, contraception, servile work, and the promises in mixed marriages. There were further meetings in which university authorities expressed misgivings about my teachings. In October of 1966, my faculty unanimously expressed confidence in my teaching and orthodoxy and objected to the harassment of me and the unspecified charges made against me.

In June of 1966, I was scheduled to give a paper on masturbation at the annual meeting of the Catholic Theological Society of America and spent the second semester working on the subject. Again, the approach followed the same format as in the case of contraception. Catholic teaching maintained that in the objective order masturbation was always a grave sin, although in the subjective order grave fault might not always be present. The actual practice and experience of people seemed to contradict that statement. In the light of a better understanding of the meaning of sin, in the light of a more personal and less biological view of masturbatory activity, I argued that even in the objective order masturbation should not always be considered grave matter. Historical investigation pointed up the poor biological understanding that may have influenced the teaching attaching such great importance to human semen. To my knowledge, this was the first article by a Catholic theologian attacking the accepted position that masturbation always involves grave matter.

It seemed expedient at that time to show that the call for new methodological approaches in Catholic moral theology and for a change in some of the past teachings on specific questions was coming from more than just a few theologians on the fringe. I conceived the idea of a book on the question of absolute norms in moral theology concerning many of the disputed topics, with articles written by various professors teaching in Catholic universities and seminaries. In February of 1967 a contract was signed with Corpus Books, and I contacted seven other Catholic theologians, working out specific articles with them. With the help of my colleague and friend, Daniel Maguire, the edited book finally was published in the spring of 1968. But the spring of 1967 was to bring its own surprises.

On April 17th I was called by the rector (the president) and finally asked to come to his room. He was flanked by all the executive officers of the university and informed me in the presence of Dean Schmitz that at the spring meeting the board of trustees voted not to renew my contract. The rector insisted that he was not speaking in his own name but as an agent for the board of trustees. The board of trustees had met in Chicago on April 10th. Later newspaper reports indicated that about twenty cardinals, archbishops, and bishops participated in the voting while the six laymen on the board of trustees abstained. (At that time the Board of Trustees of Catholic University consisted of every archbishop in the United States as an *ex officio* member plus some other members including laymen.) These same later reports indicated that a committee composed of Cardinal Krol, Archbishop Hannan, and Rector McDonald had been constituted to undertake a study of my writings and make a report. It seems they looked at the book from Fides (which incidentally was published with the *imprimatur* of the Bishop of Fort Wayne, Indiana) and also at the paper on masturbation published in the *Proceedings* of the Catholic Theological Society of America. Newspaper reports at the time also indicated the hand of the Apostolic Delegate, Archbishop Vagnozzi, in the matter. A few years later Roy Meachem, a journalist who covered the whole affair, wrote in the *Washingtonian* that Archbishop Vagnozzi, the apostolic delegate to the United States, told Meachem in an interview that he was responsible for my firing because Rome wanted to make an example out of a liberal American priest, and I was chosen.

Since there had been previous meetings with officials of the university, I was quite suspicious when I was called to the rector's rooms. My reaction to the rector's news was to protest that I had been given no hearing. I pointed out that the action was all the more incongruous because earlier in the academic year the faculty of the school of theology and the academic senate of the university voted unanimously that I be given a new contract in September and promoted to the rank of associate professor. After realizing the decision was final, I mentioned that the only recourse available to me was to bring the whole affair to public attention, but I agreed to keep it quiet for twenty-four hours. I left the rector's rooms and went to teach my 11:00 A.M. class as if nothing had happened.

That afternoon (Monday, April 17th) I told a few friends and colleagues. From there things quickly spread. The theology faculty met on Tuesday at noon. A public rally was scheduled for Tuesday night, and the crowd overflowed the 400-seat meeting hall. The rally had all been arranged by a very efficient and hastily put together faculty-student group covering all the various schools of the university. Here for the first time the facts were made public. The steering committee of students had sent out flyers advertising the meeting, and my faculty colleagues, Robert Hunt, Daniel Maguire, and Sean Quinlan, spoke eloquently and moved the crowd. Petitions were signed demanding the trustees rescind their action. The momentum was obviously building. The Wednesday morning *Washington Post* headlined the story on the front page, and at ten o'clock that morning a rally of over 2,000 persons was held in front of the rector's quarters. At Wednesday noon the theology faculty voted unanimously that, "We cannot and will not function unless and until Father Curran is reinstated. We invite our colleagues in other schools of the university to join with us in our protest."

As the front pages of Thursday's newspapers continued to tell about the story, students quickly joined in the cessation of classroom activities. Faculties of other schools met and with one exception joined in the strike. On Thursday afternoon the entire faculty assembled and voted to endorse the strike, but even on Thursday morning classrooms were empty. The strike was on. Demonstrations and rallies continued. My room was turned into "strike headquarters," but the whole operation was truly collegial with many people working together who had never even known one another before. The media continued to give immense coverage to the strike both in daily papers and on evening television news programs.

The pressure was building. There were some cracks among the hierarchy as Cardinals Cushing and Sheehan as well as some other bishops spoke out against either the firing itself or the way in which it was done. Negotiations began, with Dean Schmitz courageously standing up for his faculty's decision. Finally after a long Monday afternoon meeting between the Chancellor of the University, Archbishop O'Boyle, the rector and the theology faculty, it was announced publicly at 6:00 P.M. that evening (April 24th) by Archbishop O'Boyle and the rector to a crowd assembled in front of the library that the action of the trustees was rescinded and I would be given a new contract with a promotion to associate professor as of September 1, 1967.

Throughout the strike we purposely made every effort to keep the basic issue as narrow as possible—proper academic procedure was violated because the trustees fired me without giving reasons or a hearing despite the unanimous decision of my peers that I be promoted. This was the formal reason, but everyone knew the real reason was my teaching, especially in the areas of artificial contraception and also masturbation. In the final victory our tone was also purposely restrained—we had now been given not an ultimate victory but an opportunity and a mandate to continue our efforts on behalf of Catholic University, scholarship, and Catholic theological investigation.

This successful strike of an entire university community in 1967 was unique. One campus historian claimed that it had not occurred since the Middle Ages! But I am also sure that it could never happen again. The fortuitous confluence of many circumstances allowed it to happen. I was a comparatively unknown figure on the campus outside my faculty, having been there for only two years. I taught no undergraduate students. However, there had been a long-smoldering resentment against the administration of Rector McDonald. Academic freedom and theology had been involved in many earlier issues, especially the banning of four prominent liberal theologians from speaking on campus and the "firing" of a Scripture scholar, Father Siegmann. There were also many other dissatisfactions about arbitrary decisions and the bypassing of the academic senate. The time was ripe. My incident just ignited the immense mound of tinder that had been accumulating over the years. The timing was fortunate—who wants to picket in the middle of winter? Or who wants to go on strike the week before final examinations are to begin? In my judgment, all those facts would never again come together to make possible a strike by the entire university community. For one thing, after ten years on the same campus and having been scarred in many battles, I am sure that I could never get the type of unanimous support which I obtained at that time. Such are the contingencies of history.

Little did I realize that this event set the stage for a future development. The 1967-68 school year proceeded with the usual ups and downs. I prepared another collection of essays for publication that touched on a wide range of subjects beginning with a discussion of the radical ethical teaching of Jesus and including a long chapter on conversion as the fundamental moral message for the Christian. There was no explicit chapter on contraception, but the essay on masturbation was included. I obviously did not want to see my function only in terms of speaking out on the one issue of artificial contraception. But that question did not die.

I had hoped that ultimately the problem of birth control would be handled in such a way that artificial contraception in practice would not constitute a moral question or problem for Roman Catholics. As 1968 dawned there were signs that perhaps Pope Paul would not take the recommendations of the majority of his special commission studying the question of birth control who called for a change in the teaching of the Church. That summer I had agreed to give six lectures at St. Bonaventure University in Olean, New York, and would spend the rest of my summer there reading and writing. In July rumors began to fly that an encyclical condemning artificial contraception was imminent. I was in frequent contact with colleagues at Catholic University and throughout the country. The strike at Catholic University the year before had the effect of catapulting me into a very prominent leadership role on this question of artificial contraception and the Roman Catholic Church.

We tried in vain to raise enough publicity to prevent the issuence of any encyclical. It was my judgment that an encyclical at that time reaffirming the older teaching would be catastrophic. Many people would think that they could no longer be loyal Roman Catholics because of their decision to practice artificial contraception. Priests would be searching for guidance and would also be thrown into great crises of conscience. I was convinced that most Catholics and priests did not even know about the right to dissent from authoritative, noninfallible, hierarchical teaching. Plans then began to take shape to formulate a response to the encyclical that was rumored to be imminent.

On Sunday evening, July 28th, it was reliably reported on radio and television that an encyclical would be issued on Monday, July 29th. The encyclical was released in Rome on that Monday morning (at 4:30 A.M. New York time). I already had contingency reservations to fly back to Washington about noon on Monday. After numerous phone calls Sunday evening and Monday morning, a meeting was set for Caldwell Hall (my residence) at Catholic University that afternoon for a group of theologians to assemble and discuss a response to the encyclical. Copies of the encyclical were promised to us at that time. Other calls were made to theologians around the country telling them that a statement would be forthcoming and asking them to be prepared for a phone call later that evening asking them to sign the statement.

A group of about ten theologians met in Caldwell Hall, read the encyclical, and discussed a response. I insisted that the statement could not hedge, but would have to meet head on the question of dissent. After a fruitful discussion I typed out the final draft on my typewriter with help from Dan Maguire, but the whole enterprise had been the fruit of the contributions of those present at the meeting. It was agreed to hold a press conference Tuesday morning to announce the statement, and in the meantime we telephoned the other theologians around the country to get their names for the statement. At the press conference I was the spokesman for the group and issued the statement in the name of eighty-seven American theologians. The number later swelled to over 600 signatures of people qualified in the sacred sciences as a result of a mailing to members of various professional organizations. Naturally this response became headline news throughout the United States and in all the television media. In fact we were able to hold subsequent press conferences in the next few days in an attempt to obtain as much coverage as possible.

Our quick, forceful response supported by so many theologians accomplished its purpose. The day after the encyclical was promulgated American Catholics could read in their morning papers about their right to dissent and the fact that Catholics could in theory and practice disagree with the papal teaching and still be loyal Roman Catholics. Other theologians around the world joined in and also even individual bishops and later some conferences of bishops. But our response as a quick, well-organized, collegial effort was unique. This, I hope, solved some problems for many Catholics, although I am sure that it also created problems for many other Catholics, who could not understand this type of dissent.

The statement that a small group put together within hours after the encyclical was published has in my prejudiced judgment stood the test of time remarkably well. It was short, respectful, pointing out the good aspects of the encyclical, but also clearly showing its flaws both from the viewpoint of moral theology and ecclesiology. It ended with a short reminder about the existence of the right to dissent in the Roman Catholic Church from such authoritative, noninfallible, papal teaching, and clearly applied that right to dissent both in theory and in practice to the use of artificial contraception. In the ensuing furor, two false charges tended to ruffle me more than usual. Some claimed that we never read the encyclical. (It is true that our response was published before even many bishops had received the encyclical.) Such a charge is not only false, but anyone who read our short critique had to be convinced that it was a direct response to the reasoning of the encyclical itself. Others claim that our action was precipitous. My answer to that is: What is the virtue in delay? Our statement has stood the test of time much better than many that were written weeks or even months later. No, it was imperative to act both with speed and theological accuracy to accomplish our purpose. There was absolutely no virtue in delay.

As was to be expected, this organized dissent caused quite a stir in the Roman Catholic Church in the United States. Catholic University was the center of focus in the academic discussion because the core group had many members associated with the university, and I was recognized as the principal animator of the group. There were a number of meetings and discussions that have been described elsewhere between dissenting theologians and bishops. A special meeting of the Board of Trustees at Catholic University was called to discuss the matter. Cardinal McIntyre of Los Angeles introduced a long resolution stating that the utterances of Father Curran, his followers, and associates with regard to the encyclical *Humanae Vitae* constitute a breach of contract that admits of no other consideration than termination. Such an approach did not prevail, perhaps because of the experience occasioned by the strike the year before. The board of trustees finally called for an inquiry in accord with academic norms and due process to determine if the theologians had violated their manifold responsibilities.

The academic process was a full-scale hearing before a faculty committee at which we were given (wrongly) the burden of defending our actions. Thanks to the inestimable generosity of the law firm of Cravath, Swaine, and Moore of New York City and to the professional skill and extraordinary personal concern of Mr. John F. Hunt, a member of the firm, and his associate Terrence R. Connelly, our case was presented in a most cogent and professional manner, both in terms of written submissions and of oral argument. The hearing dragged on for almost the entire academic year, and it was only at the beginning of April that the unanimous decision of the faculty hearing committee acknowledged that we had in no way violated our responsibilities. All "the subject professors" worked together on our defense; but my friend and colleague, Bob Hunt, and I organized and directed the effort. The written submissions were modified somewhat and published as two books—one written primarily by the theologians considering the theological aspect of the question and the other written primarily by the lawyers discussing the academic freedom aspects of the case.

The longer, more detailed study of dissent on this occasion opened up the further door in my thinking that such dissent was going to be more and more frequent on specific moral issues in the Roman Catholic Church because on such issues one could never attain the type of certitude that excludes the possibility of error. Thus, in the future the dispute over contraception would be paradigmatic of a growing pluralism in the Roman Catholic Church on such issues as abortion, divorce, medical ethics, and some questions of sexuality. In all probability as discussion on these issues becomes more public there will be further tensions within the Roman Catholic Church. The Church must learn that its unity is not to be found in terms of absolute agreement on such specific moral teachings.

The reaction to the papal encyclical was obviously a very significant event in terms of the life of the Church, of Catholic theology, and of my own development. My participation in it also increased my own desire to continue my theological investigations as best I could in the field of Roman Catholic theology. Over the years despite the problems involved in this and other disputes I had also experienced support and encouragement from many different people. In my view this only made it more incumbent upon me to continue my theological research.

Other Influences

One of the fortuitous and influential developments affecting my thinking was contact with the ethical thought of other Christian communities. This gave me another vantage point in the attempts to criticize my own tradition. But my critique of the Catholic tradition was also heavily based on a critique from within, considering especially scriptural, historical, and contemporary insights. Despite these criticisms by myself and others that have called for significant changes both in methodology and in the teaching on specific questions, I believe my own theological ethic stands firmly within the tradition of Roman Catholic theology. I wholeheartedly accept the fundamental premise of that theology which insists that God often and usually acts mediately with human beings—through the medium of creation and not just through Jesus Christ, through the medium of the ongoing tradition and not just through the revelation in Scripture, through the "koinonia" of the Christian Church with its hierarchical teaching office and not just through an immediate I-Thou relationship between God and the individual.

My more concentrated study of Protestant ethicians has reminded me that my theological approach is basically within the Roman Catholic tradition. I spent a sabbatical year in 1972 at the Kennedy Center for Bioethics at Georgetown doing research on the Christian ethics of Paul Ramsey. Ramsey often comes to conclusions quite congenial with more traditional Roman Catholic conclusions and is thought by many to be a crypto-Catholic in his ethics. On the other hand, some in the Catholic Church claim that I follow a Protestant ethic. Late one night in one of my many discussions with Ramsey, I told him that I could correctly summarize my research by saying that the differences between us are that Ramsey is more Protestant than most people think and I am more Catholic than most people think!

In theological ethics the Roman Catholic approach asserts the ability of human beings through reason to arrive at ethical wisdom and truth. The Catholic moral methodology based on natural law tries to incarnate this basic reality, but in my judgment certain aspects of this approach have to be changed. Protestant and some contemporary Catholic approaches have helped me in developing a criticism of what I believe is a fundamentally sound assumption. First, the natural is not an order in itself, totally cut off from the "supernatural." There is only one historical existence for all of us. By concentrating only on the natural and human reason, Roman Catholic moral theology tended either to forget and ignore all that belongs to the "supernatural" order or at most saw the "supernatural" as something added on to the "natural."

Many recent emphases in Catholic moral theology have followed from a better understanding of the question of the natural and the supernatural—the call of all Christians to perfection; the need for continuing change of heart; the fact that the Kingdom of God calls us now to cooperate in trying to build a new heaven and a new earth; a call to strive constantly to change the structures of society in the light of the fullness of the Kingdom; an emphasis on the Spirit and a corresponding growth in the moral life; the role of the Scriptures in moral theology; the importance of the liturgy in the Christian moral life; an attempt in theory and in practice to overcome the dichotomy between faith and the daily life of Christians; a corresponding realization that one could no longer accept such a dichotomy between Church and world.

The recognition that we live in only one historical order also influenced my understanding of the relationship between Christian and non-Christian morality. The question of the self-identity of Roman Catholic ethical teaching first came to the light in terms of its relationship to Protestant ethics and prompted my investigations into pluralism in Catholic moral theology, including a pluralism on specific moral teachings. In

the light of personal experience and historical evidence, but-
tressed especially by the realization that all human beings live
in one and the same order, I have come to the conclusion that
non-Christians can and at times do arrive at the same attitudes,
goals, dispositions, and concrete acts as Christians. Thus,
Christians cannot claim self-sacrificing love as belonging only
to Christians. The level of difference is on the transcendental
level and not the categorical. Our Christian understanding affects the motives and the reasoning processes employed in ethical thinking. The methodologies on a more reflexive level will
be different, but Christians cannot claim for themselves a monopoly on such attitudes as love, care for others, or willingness
to give oneself for others.

Also the Roman Catholic insistence on reason and the
goodness of the natural tended to forget about the effect of sin.
Protestant thought exemplified in Reinhold Niebuhr and also
in contemporary writings by Paul Ramsey reminded me of this
important aspect missing in Roman Catholic thought, although
I would insist that many Protestants of the classic Lutheran
tradition as well as Niebuhr and Ramsey have overemphasized
the notion of sin. The presence of sin in the world influenced
my thinking on a number of significant questions—opposition
to utopian views of man's possibility for human progress; acceptance of the probability of conflict in human affairs, at
times even the use of violence in the service of justice; a willingness to accept a more negative judgment about human social and political structures at any given time in history, and
the need for change with the realization that all human structures will always be imperfect; a theory of compromise applied,
for example, in the question of homosexuality in which the
presence of sin in the world (not personal sin) sometimes forces
people to be content with less than what would be required if
sin were not present and in this sense justifies homosexuality
for the individual.

With this background, I was also prepared to realize a
danger that emerged in theology in general, and in Catholic
theology in particular in the 1960s. In rightfully realizing the
importance of overcoming the dichotomy between the natural
and the supernatural, some theologians tended to forget the

limitations and sinfulness of the present and especially the fact that the fullness of the *eschaton* is not yet here. Too often, a naively optimistic theology arose from a too easy identification of the future of the Kingdom with the here and now. The fullness of the Kingdom lies beyond history, and we will always live with the tensions of eschatology, which is part of our theology.

These various considerations led me to develop what I call a stance, perspective, or horizon of moral theology, which is logically the first step in any systematic development. This perspective is formed by the fivefold Christian mysteries of creation, sin, incarnation, redemption, and resurrection destiny. Any approach to Christian ethics that forgets one of these elements or overemphasizes one element is in my judgment inadequate. What traditional Catholic moral theology said about the ability of human reason is basically correct, but it must be integrated into a more complete picture or perspective.

This perspective also reinforced a fundamental attitude that I came to verbalize and explicitly recognize as governing much of my thought in the last few years. Reality in moral matters is more complex than most people realize. Error more often than not comes not from positive error, but rather from failure to give importance to all the elements that must be considered. This emphasis on complexity and the need for a wholistic approach is appealing to me because I tend to be realistic and practical in my personality rather than idealistic and utopian. In theory it has been developed especially by H. Richard Niebuhr and is often at work in the contemporary writings of James Gustafson. I find particularly impressive how Gustafson in his writings, as well as in his own person, shows a balanced and sensitive approach—a basic Christian and scriptural vision of reality with a critical openness to philosophical and empirical understandings of the human.

The same insistence on the need for a more wholistic approach that would see all the aspects of the question and not absolutize any one element was behind my critique of the traditional Catholic understanding of the human as incorporated in the Catholic philosophy of natural law. Roman Catholic theology in a few cases absolutized the physical and made the moral and human identical with only the physical aspect, although others have failed to give enough importance to the physical element as exemplified by our contemporary problems of ecology and pollution. Catholic natural law theory overstressed the objective aspect of reality at the expense of more subjective considerations. The emphasis on continuity and the unchanging tended to obscure discontinuity and change. More relational and personalistic emphases will also change some of the older emphases in the Catholic understanding of the human.

There is no doubt that such an insistence on complexity and on a more wholistic approach with the corresponding danger of polemical exclusion has exerted a great influence on me. I cannot reduce all morality to any one content virtue, even love, nor can I see moral norms based only on consequences unless these are interpreted in the broadest possible sense. My Christian perspective recognizes that the cultural, political, social, and economic structures of society will contain both positive and negative elements. Christian life in the paschal mystery will experience both the suffering of the cross and the joy of the resurrection. Social reform requires both a change of heart on the part of individuals and a change of the cultural and economic structures of society. I am also cognizant of the danger that such an approach, striving to hold in tension all the aspects of our human existence, will at times fail to speak the prophetic voice and be tempted merely to adopt a middle position; but I hope that by constantly asking this question I can avoid some of the pitfalls connected with it.

Critical Retrospection

In retrospect one should also be critical of the development in one's own thinking. In the light of my basic insistence on complexity and the danger of forgetting or slighting certain aspects of the question, such a critical appraisal of my own development is especially necessary. I think there have been underemphases in two very important areas of concern for the moral theologian that have been somewhat influenced by the biographical aspects considered in this essay. The Catholic moral theologian is both an academic and a committed Christian member of the Church, and these two aspects will always exist in the person of the theologian and create some tensions. There are the academic concerns for the discipline in attempting more satisfying explanations and synthesis. But there is also the fact that the Catholic moral theologian is intensely interested in the way in which Christians should live out the Gospel in daily life and influence the world in which we live.

In terms of the more theoretical aspects of the discipline, the events of the last few years have concentrated attention on some specific teachings accepted in Catholic life and have also witnessed the breakdown of the monolithic Catholic natural law methodology so that today on all levels there is a growing pluralism within the Church.

The next step must be to attempt a more positive synthesis of moral theology—a step which is just beginning. Here I feel the need for deeper philosophical and empirical understandings that will be necessary to develop more systematic approaches for bringing together all the different aspects contributing to moral meaning in the midst of our complex time and culture. My own philosophical approach up to now has tended to be eclectic, bringing in elements from personalistic, phenomenological, transcendental, and value philosophies. Despite the gigantic task involved, moral theologians like myself must strive for a more synthetic approach bringing together all the scriptural, theological, philosophical, and empirical data. In the future, in the light of my past interests, I will most emphasize the philosophical and empirical considerations of the human.

The moral theologian is also intimately involved with the life of the Church and the living out of the Gospel message in the world. The developments of the last few years have focused attention on calling for a change in some of the areas that might be called personal morality. However, I have also tried to stress the call of the Christian to perfection and the need for a more faithful response to the Gospel in social life. Social morality and its problems have been discussed, but not enough, because so much attention has been given to particular questions of personal morality. There is need now and in the future to develop at greater depth the Christian recognition of the responsibilities to change society. In my writings on social morality I have attempted to apply the general fivefold stance so that one can avoid both the danger of utopianism, with the resulting danger that after a few years of small or meager success people will just give up the struggle for social change, and the opposite danger of merely accepting the status quo. With this and other friendly amendments I accept the basic thrust of contemporary liberation theology, but must also point out that liberation theology has tended to be more theological than ethical—in other words, it has not really analyzed with systematic ethical reflection the concrete problems of social and economic structures.

It seems that the most pressing problem facing the Church and the members of the Church concerns the fundamental problem of a better and more equitable distribution of the goods of this world. The Church must raise its own consciousness and the consciousness of its members to this particular problem, which is especially apparent in our consumer-oriented American society. The Catholic Church in the United States to its great credit has an historical tradition of social liberalism and social justice gained from its attempts to prevent laissez-faire capitalism from overriding the just claims of workers to a share of the goods of this earth. But in the past this social teaching very often was not present at the level of the pulpit and the daily lives of Christians.

Today the problems are more complex and difficult, but there is even greater need for raising consciousness and attempting some solutions. The problem was somewhat easier when the victims of injustice were "our own"—that is, Catholic workers. Today the problem is more complex because we realize it is worldwide in scope. It is not just a question of a more equal distribution of the goods of creation or of justice for workers in the United States; our horizons now must also be worldwide, with all the resulting complexities and difficulties of finding solutions. In addition, even here in the United States, the question is of more equitable distribution of the goods of creation for those people who have been outside the establishment to which Roman Catholics now belong. This is a gigantic task facing the Church, and I believe that moral theologians like myself must strive to make our contribution to it. I am also aware that our efforts in this area will not be as dramatic and as attention-catching as our criticisms of particular past teachings of the Church, but they are even more important than those earlier efforts.

Personal Influences

Up to this point my theological development has been considered in terms of events and the thoughts of others that have influenced me. Before closing a few things should be said about me—my personality and how I see this affecting my theology. Obviously, in this area, the possibilities of self-deception are even greater!

I am a committed Christian believer belonging to the Roman Catholic Church. Like many, I have had my ups and downs, but Christianity and Roman Catholicism are very significant and important to me. The recognition of complexity and tension together with the understanding of sin and its effects, even within the Church (in my first years teaching moral theology in Rochester I caused some consternation by insisting that there were five marks of the true Church of Jesus Christ— one, holy, catholic, apostolic—sinful!), have helped me to cope with some of the problems of life in the Church. Although I am constantly impatient with the rate of change in the Church, the recognition of my own sinfulness and of how slow I am to change has made me more patient (perhaps too patient at times) with regard to progress and change in the Church.

Such a view of the Church has helped me to cope with the inevitable tensions and oppositions that I have experienced in the Church. Because of the stands I have taken on a number of issues, and the wide publicity given to them, as well as the fact of my professorship at the Catholic University of America, which is supported by the American Catholic bishops and people, I am a *persona non grata* for many people in the Church, especially some bishops and priests. There is still a long list of dioceses in which I am even now forbidden to speak. I have been looked upon with suspicion and never been appointed to any official Church committees for my own Roman Catholic Church. In 1972 the Catholic Theological Society of America bestowed on me its annual award for outstanding contribution to Roman Catholic theology, but the prelate who sponsored the award did not agree with that judgment. I am grateful to the courage of my colleagues who changed the name of the award and named me the first recipient of the John Courtney Murray Award! (I shall always treasure the citation for that award which was written by Richard McCormick, a most perceptive critic of all moral theologians but also a source of personal support and encouragement to me.) However, there have also been other bishops who both publicly and privately have supported me.

There have been many people whom I have never really met or known who have in one way or another encouraged my continued efforts, in addition to the encouragement I have received from a large number of friends and acquaintances. I realistically expect controversy and do not mind it (maybe the predominantly Irish genes in my genetic make-up dispose me to like a fight!). The somewhat vitriolic attacks in the conservative Catholic press and hate mail are things I can readily shrug off. By temperament I am not a brooder, so none of these things really ever gets me down. I can relate them with very little emotional response on my own part. Most of these problems never cause me any pain or anger, but rather I just keep on doing what I feel is right.

The public stands against some Church teachings have attracted attention, and in the eyes of some I am a rebel and a radical. I do not think that I am, and at times I really wish I were more of a rebel and more of a radical—something that might be hard for some people to believe! Although I have critically called for a change in some teachings of the Church, I am deeply committed to the Church on a very profound level. There is no doubt that I am inclined to speak out and call a spade a spade. Perhaps again this is a part of my character that wants to see things work out in practice and is unable to easily accept discrepancies between the theoretical order and the practical living out of reality. I cannot deny, however, that there is a stubborness in me that also contributes to my willingness to take such stands. Nonetheless, I think that I am today in some way the same type of person who obeyed the seminary rule because I was convinced that was the right thing to do in practice.

In reviewing one of my books in late 1974, a Catholic moral theologian identified somewhat with an older approach described my moral theology as radical even though his tone was sympathetic and open. As for being a radical, no one who stresses complexity can really be a radical. In life and in theory I am not a radical, but there are times when the simplicity of the radical does appeal to me. This is probably why I say that at times I wish I were more radical, but "common sense," or is it "common nonsense," and a sense of practical reality usually win out. My fear is that an acceptance of sin and complexity will at times make my theology too middle of the road.

I am sure that there are many other factors contributing to my own theological development of which I am not even conscious, but I believe that the characteristics and traits mentioned in the last few paragraphs have had some bearing and influence on my own theological development. In fact, my own experience in writing this essay has made me even more conscious of the influence that personality, events, personal history, and the thoughts of others have had on my theological development.

The Mandalas Do Not Break:
A Theological Autobiographical Essay

MONIKA KONRAD HELLWIG

"Theology is the critique of praxis." When I first read those words in an essay by Gustavo Gutierrez, I recognized them immediately as a description of my own experience. Christian theology is the critique of the praxis of trying to live by the Gospel of Jesus Christ within a constantly changing world. Catholic theology is the critique of the praxis of doing it within the framework of the Catholic community and its traditions. Following through this line of thought, one also comes to the realization that there is indeed a characteristically lay theology, a characteristically feminine theology, and a characteristic theology of the uprooted, just as there is a characteristic and uniquely powerful theology that springs again and again from the bitterly oppressed and overwhelms us all from time to time in our comfortable entrenchments.

I was born in Breslau in Silesia in December 1929. I was born into a city, a culture, a civilization, and an extended family that, despite all their graciousness and self-confidence and sophistication, were cracking at the foundations and were soon to fall apart completely. Before I was old enough to go to school, Hitler was in full sway, freedom and privacy were disappearing, Jews were being persecuted viciously, and all the adults I knew looked apprehensive, spoke in tense whispers, and hurried along the streets minding their own business as unobtrusively as possible.

Both sets of grandparents lived in Breslau during my earliest years. My father's parents lived close to us in the suburbs, but in any sense other than the geographical there was little proximity between us, though we children enjoyed these grandparents well enough and liked the attention from my father's two sisters, then still unmarried. I learned later from other relatives that grandmother Hellwig had bitterly resented her son's marrying a Jewish girl, and one who was a sculptress and wore slacks and smoked besides. My mother was, in fact, Jewish by the Nazi though not by the Halakic definition, having a Jewish father but a gentile mother. My father was killed in a motor accident when I was six years old, and we soon lost touch almost completely with his side of the family, as Jews active in the arts and professions were forced to flee Germany. I discovered later, from family documents, that my father had been born in Riga, Latvia, though the name is German, and that he had been stateless when he died. The family on that side was Catholic and steeped in the folkways of Eastern European Catholicism. Of their doings beyond that we learned little other than that grandfather Hellwig in his old age sold an early variety of washing-machine, which an aunt on the other side of the family assures me entailed much more work than simply washing the clothes by hand.

The grandparents Blaauw, on the other hand, became a constant and intimate part of our family life, and after my father's early death grandfather Blaauw remained for the rest of his life the chief father-figure in my life. The father-image applied to God has for me the primary analogue of grandfather Blaauw, and it is a wholly fortunate one, for he was the gentlest of men whose power was his wisdom, his sensitive perception, his love of music and of art in any form, and his very extraordinary compassion. He did not rule our family but he inspired it and permeated it with his presence. I never had the privilege of meeting Abraham Joshua Heschel, but photographs of him bear a very striking resemblance to grandfather Blaauw, and his writings have the same feeling-tone as my grandfather's conversation.

Grandfather Blaauw was a Sephardic Jew whose family had fled Spain at the end of the fifteenth century and settled in Amsterdam where they founded an early printing and mapmaking business. As a young man he had gone to Germany, qualified in medicine, and lived for a while in Bonn, where he met and married my Lutheran grandmother, Marianne Lotze, granddaughter of the philosopher Hermann Lotze. Later they had moved to Breslau, where there was a considerable Jewish settlement at that time. If my grandfather followed any Jewish observances we certainly did not know it, but then the Nazi era was a time for Marranos like none other in history. He did not pass on in our family any explicitly Jewish teaching, though when I began to read extensively in the Jewish tradition as an adult, I realized how much of the distilled wisdom of it had gone into our upbringing.

Unlike my mother and my aunts, my grandmother was completely absorbed in her family and found it totally satisfying. She had six children, the youngest of whom died in infancy. Caring for the remaining five kept her busy enough. Though my grandfather was a medical man, they were not at all wealthy as doctors are in the U.S. today. My mother and her two older sisters and two younger brothers told stories of living a quite Spartan but extremely hospitable family regime. They felt very welcome to bring extra mouths to the family table, but it was a scrubbed wooden table across which my grandmother would deftly roll potatoes boiled in their jackets towards each hungry diner, to be eaten with salt and rather small quantities of ham or cottage cheese or other poor man's fare.

As a very small child I was frequently taken to see these grandparents, who then lived in a high apartment in a very gracious old quarter of the city. My strongest memories are the musty smell, the elaborately carved and ornamented stones on the face of the building, the dark solemnity of the approach to the apartment, and the lush vines gracing the balcony on which my cousin, Miriam Meier, and I constantly played when I stayed there for an extended period. As I remember my grandmother at that time, she was always in the kitchen cooking, and there was usually someone there talking to her—sometimes my father who was permitted liberties, like sitting on the kitchen table, which were forbidden to everyone else.

My grandmother had become a Catholic when her daughters were in their late teens and her sons much younger. The whole family had been in close contact with a Benedictine monastery over a lengthy period of time, and had been charmed and deeply impressed by the vision and way of life of the monks. The girls and the older boy eventually decided to become Catholics by their own conviction, but the younger boy was pulled into it by his mother who tricked and deceived her husband in the process. This left its own scars in the family.

My mother was unconventional even in that family. She was a cultivated and widely knowledgeable person as well as an artist, and it came as a great surprise to me when I discovered as a teen-ager that she had demanded to leave school at the age of thirteen. My wise grandfather allowed it and she never went back, having been thoroughly disillusioned by what went on in school under the name of education. She went to art school soon after and became totally absorbed first in drawing and then in sculpture. But she read voraciously and for those days daringly, and she was constantly in dialog with her father. As an adult, I was fascinated to learn that Edith Stein, also growing up in Breslau in a Jewish family, had similarly demanded to leave school at the age of thirteen and been permitted to do so, going on to become a gifted philosopher.

Relatives have told me since my mother's death that she suffered from terrible depressions and was difficult to get along with, and that she probably would have preferred to express the total reality of her being in her art rather than have children. As a child I never had that impression, though I knew she suffered from migraine headaches, was extremely sensitive to noise while she had them, and was often caught into an ecstasy of artistic creativity when she came out of them. When I was still very young, my mother told me that her migraine headaches were always accompanied by very severe visual disturbances, but that when she came out of them she would see lines, shapes, colors, and light qualities as though for the very first time in her life—as though the world were being created in front of her anew. This has remained for me the paradigm of redemptive suffering. There is no value in pain and confusion; the value lies in the rearrangement of the elements of experience which leads to clearer vision, more immediate access to the real, and greater transcendence of the givenness of one's life. My mother never drew any connection between this experience and that of childbirth. Having my own children by adoption, I am not personally able to do this either. But I have heard hints of it in the conversation of other women, and was delighted to meet it in the writings of Margery Kempe, who sees the passion and death of Jesus in terms of childbirth.

My strongest early memory of my mother is that of slipping unobtrusively into her studio and sitting there absolutely still, looking and looking at the sculptures and watching her work until she was ready to take a break. She would put her tools down, wipe the clay or stone dust from her hands, come over to where I was and, with her eyes and attention never straying from what she was working on, she would size up lines, proportions, angles, her arm all the while around my shoulders as I leaned against her and she called me very softly and caressingly by my family pet names. After a while she would resume her work. I might stay a little longer, but soon I would slip away again. That was all the communication there was on these occasions and I was super-satisfied by it. Her studio was like a temple where I went to pray. Whether she was priestess or goddess I do not know, but it was enough to know myself called by name and loved.

My mother did not raise us. She was a life-giving and affirming presence in our lives, but schedule, discipline, baths, clothes, and meals were presided over by a succession of nannies. My sister, Marianne, and I were close enough in age to do everything together almost like twins. She is eleven months younger than I, and our other sister, Angelika, four and a half years younger than I, seemed to us as we were growing up to be another generation entirely. The nannies, who were with us constantly until we were of school age, were usually young women getting experience because they were about to get married. Their values were tradition and common sense; their methods orderly and disciplinarian. In their world there was no such thing as permissiveness, and impropriety was the ultimate sin. My sister constantly rebelled. I took their world as inevitable. I do not believe that either of us ever took their world as the real world. The real world was where our parents were, and we were aware that judgments and decisions in that real world were made on a very different basis from that provided in the world of the nannies.

My father was different in almost every way from my mother. He was one of those lighthearted people who always sit loose in the saddle and seem to be able to give their attention to a half dozen things at once without any strain. I was told he was a very talented mathematician who could do extremely complicated calculations in his head, apparently without having to concentrate too much effort on the task. By profession he was an economist, taught part time, consulted part time and did a great deal of traveling. Whenever he was at home it was his pleasure to play with us and take us out. He had a dog with which he went rabbit hunting, he was an adept and well-practiced clown, and he used to do crazy dare-devil stunts that totally delighted my sister Marianne and terrified my mother and me. Some of these had to do with driving the family car with or without the family inside it. The one I remember with most terrifying clarity is that he went diving under passing steamboats in the river Oder while we watched. Until his cheerful grin greeted us from the other bank, I fully expected to see the river turn to blood and chopped-up pieces of my father come floating up from under the propeller.

There was a serious and deeply religious side to my father too, but he wore it rather lightly. It was he rather than my convert mother who provided me with basic paradigms for apprehending our Catholic heritage. He was a superb storyteller, knew a wealth of religious and secular songs, accompanying his singing on any of several instruments, and was an enthusiast for liturgical and paraliturgical celebration. I do not mean that he took us to church. In fact I do not remember that he ever did that. I mean that he had a flair for the family celebration of the Christian calendar, was keenly aware of the liturgical cycle, and passed this consciousness on to us. If I had to sum up in one word his impact on our lives, that word would be "celebration."

Shortly before I was six years old, we moved to the suburbs of Berlin, rather far away from most of our relatives. That winter, three days before Christmas, my father was killed driving back to Berlin from a consulting job on roads that were heavily iced over. He was found with a carload of toys he had bought us for Christmas. With the help of relatives, my mother made that Christmas a normal and a very happy one for us, which may have been partly responsible for my strong sense that my father had passed through a veil but that we were still in communion with him. We did not see him laid out and we were not taken to the funeral.

However, my father's death changed the family situation radically. That Christmas was the last thing to be normal for a very long time. The Nazi persecution of Jews was well under way. My psychiatrist aunt and my uncle who was then training in surgery were both unable to practice, and both had been at our house in Berlin. Now my mother could no longer exhibit or sell sculpture. She had been successful as an artist and could have supported us, but that was closed to her now when she really needed to do so. Besides, rumors and threats were mounting all the time. So, soon after the move to Berlin and the death of my father, we had to move again in search of a livelihood. As her father had come from the Netherlands, my mother scouted around for opportunities there and was offered a contract by the coal-mining interests in Limburg to set up simple ceramic studios to train local boys and absorb some of the increasing unemployment in the area.

We moved to Limburg and changed to a much simpler standard of living—a change we children scarcely noticed, though for my mother it meant very long hours of work and very little help in the house. Again many relatives visited and helped. All branches of the family were looking for ways to get established outside Germany in those days, and some did not realize how little time they had. Newspapers were kept away from us children very carefully, but we heard much of what was going on in Germany since we had left, and there were constant rumors of war and of the Netherlands being easily overrun.

Meanwhile, we went to school in the villages and towns in Limburg in which my mother set up a series of studios. Shortly before I had gone to school in Germany, my cousin Miriam had taught me to read. From the day that I made the breakthrough to assimilating meaning from the page, books became a very important part of my life and I was reading fluently in German before we went to the Netherlands. But books belonged to my home rather than my school life. They extended my experience of what I took to be the real world of my parents, while school extended that other world of the nannies. From kindergarten to defending my Ph.D. thesis, I found school interesting but always very much secondary to what I received and assimilated at home. The same applied to Church and catechism classes. It is with a certain sense of puzzlement that I have begun to realize quite recently that for most of my American friends being Catholic is primarily a relation to clergy and schools and a way of life taught in catechism classes by priests and sisters. For me being Catholic has been constituted primarily by a way of life that is very free because it has very deep roots. It is a way of life rooted at home, not in school or the parish church. It consists of the stories that shaped our thinking from earliest childhood, the feasts that measured and shaped time for us, the visual symbols that were the backdrop to all we did, and a very secure sense of belonging to a community and having a task in the world. Prayer has always seemed to me the most natural and spontaneous human activity, because my parents prayed and allowed us to enter into their prayer, and because my relationship with both of them and with grandfather Blaauw provided an obvious, almost an inescapable, analogy for prayer.

But school took its toll and left its scars. I made my First Communion in Limburg tormented by all kinds of anxieties carefully fostered by the official training—anxiety whether I would be able to swallow the host properly, whether I would forget part of the planned ceremony and commit some sort of sacrilege, and so forth. As a matter of fact, this particular village school prided itself on its very high catechetical standards. Whereas in other schools the catechism question would be proposed and the candidates for First Communion were supposed to give the answer, in this school the number of the question in the catechism would be called out, and the pupil was expected to recall the question and the answer! Another school that we attended later prided itself on cultivating a refined conscience. We sat in the pews on Sunday terrified lest our attention stray for a second during the "essential parts" of the Eucharist, and we hurtle headlong into mortal sin. Questions were not allowed in catechism classes, even requests for clarifications.

During these years I knew well that my mother and my Catholic relatives took a very different attitude to prayer, Church, and Sunday. I did not think they were un-Catholic or out of communication with God. Yet the indoctrination I received at school was like water dripping on a stone, and it succeeded in building up personal anxieties that were not shed in a day. Sometimes I would come home and report to my mother things I had been taught at school which I knew well to be factually false, concerning Protestants and Jews, or concerning life in Germany or certain persons of whom I knew something from reading or from home. My mother would say, "Sweetheart, they are simple village women who entered the convent as young girls with very little schooling. They are doing their best and you must be respectful and kind to them. It is too hard to be a teacher if the children are not kind and respectful." That was my only pathway to reconciling home and school.

In those days there were no children's lending libraries where we lived. I could never get enough books. A couple of weeks after each birthday I would have exhausted all the new literature that had arrived in our house by way of birthday presents, and similarly after Christmas. Nowadays when there is always much more being published in my field than I can possibly keep up with, and when I can buy almost everything in paperback, I feel a great nostalgia for that era when my hunger and zest for more books never abated. The only book I recall that gave me indigestion was my father's doctoral dissertation of which we had hundreds of copies in the attic and which had to do with the growth of the American banking system. My mother had many avant-garde German novels on her shelves that I appreciated but which were always being removed from my reach. When I was eight I recall being caught in the secret study of midwifery, which I must have taken up in desperation. My surgeon uncle or psychiatrist aunt must have unloaded some textbooks from an earlier stage of training in our house. I was discovered with the diagrams folded out from the book, and I was stretched out on the living room rug, practicing how to slip my hands in to turn the baby in a breech presentation. Another set of books disappeared from my reach.

I need not have worried. We were soon to begin studying English. Outside the ambit of our rather stable and secure life at home, things were worsening steadily. After weeks of great tension and anxiety, the grandparents Blaauw were spirited out of Germany and came very quietly and without advance notice to stay with us in Limburg. They had no change of clothes and barely any personal effects. A friendly Limburg burgomaster had brought them across the border one day "for a picnic." Aunt Ruth, the psychiatrist, already widowed some years, had left for Scotland without her daughter Miriam because of visa and livelihood complications. It was hoped Miriam, staying with another aunt and uncle, would join her soon. Uncle Konrad, the surgeon, had tried to settle in Vienna and had had to flee to Amsterdam, only to find that that would not be safe either. He was leaving for Scotland too with no idea whether he could get accreditation from the British Medical Association. His wife was then pregnant with their first child.

Clearly, the Netherlands would be overrun very soon. A special refugee visa to the United Kingdom was available for children who were Jewish by Nazi definition and we qualified, but adults had to wait for quota assignments. My mother could not get out for some time, and even then she would have been unwilling to abandon her elderly parents to try to escape the Nazi horror on their own. She made the difficult decision to get us out in any case, and sent us off to boarding school in Scotland when Konrad left, hoping she and her parents could join us there but suspecting she would never see us again. It was a leave-taking much harder and much sadder than my father's death. My mother came alone to the ship at Hoek van Holland to say good-bye. "You will have to be a mother to the others now," she said to me, and both my sisters have assured me many times since then that I took that admonition far too seriously and proceeded from the age of nine to exercise tyrannical control over them.

From that day we knew we had to begin a radically new

life, and that we might lose touch completely with what we had thought to be the real world. In fact, we did see our mother again after the war for three months before she died of a combination of lung disease and malnutrition. Grandfather Blaauw died peacefully in my mother's house in Limburg, undiscovered in the hunt for Jews. Grandmother survived the war by some years. Miriam was not able to get out of Germany and grew up practically a stranger to her mother before they could be reunited. Konrad and Ilse had to go to Borneo to make a living. All three of their children were born there, two in a Japanese concentration camp in very great hardship. Ruth had a checkered and tragic career and died about the age of fifty, a woman totally broken by suffering. The others remained in Germany and survived but with very great suffering, and with the threat of much worse hanging constantly over them.

What does it mean to come into adolescence emerging from a context like that? I have often reflected upon that with reference to my subsequent theological career and my ultimate convictions about reality and about the meaning of my life and that of other persons. My experience seems to me to have had the following outcomes. First, paradoxically, I have a far greater sense of stability in my life, my values, and in my association with institutional structures, including those of the Church, than most of my American friends appear to have. I am quite sure that the cumulative wisdom of the ages in my own tradition is an adequate base for creative solutions to our problems today. I am equally convinced that without recourse to the cumulative wisdom of one's own tradition, one can not be creative. I also believe one must be very much steeped in tradition to be at all innovative.

Secondly, I am deeply convinced that the traditional wisdom is not passed on primarily by purely intellectual connections. When I reflect on my own experience I am aware that although I am in many respects a "head person" with aptitude and inclination for abstraction, logic, and rational discourse in general, I was born from the womb of sculpture and music and fairy tale, and my head has always had much deeper levels of tradition to draw upon than the purely intellectual. This seems to me a very solid asset; my thoughts are deeply rooted in my being and my being is constituted by a long history so much greater than I am, which I have been able in large measure to appropriate. Convictions formed like that are not easily swayed by fad or fashion nor are they overturned by slick argumentation.

Thirdly, it seems to me that one comes out of such a childhood with a certain sense of universality rather than allegiance to any particular group. I have always felt a strong affinity to the uprooted and the deprived, probably because I have never been able to see the status quo of any society as normative. Stability for me is not in attempts to preserve any status quo but in the dynamic of history appropriated through the vision of a creatively projected goal. One works with history as a resource, never with history as a prison. But one works *with* history, not against it or without it.

Moreover, one comes into adolescence with a very strong will to survive and to do so with style and zest, coming out of a childhood such as I had. My adolescence began early, with the parting from my mother on the boat at Hoek van Holland when I was nine and a half years old. It was then that I realized that my own experience was valid knowledge and that I would now have to live by it. New voices would only be normative for me in a very secondary and relative way. I arrived in Scotland knowing that my childhood had stayed behind on the other side of the English Channel. Within a few months war was declared and all ties with my mother cut off. Soon after that the bombing began and our school was evacuated from Edinburgh to the far north of Scotland.

My adolescence had two phases and the first was almost entirely transitional. My sisters and I were almost always together, but everything else changed constantly—the relative who officially had charge of us, the series of boarding schools and private families in which we were placed, the geographical locations in Scotland and England in city and country, the religious context varying from convent boarding schools to the home of a Scots Presbyterian minister and that of an atheist or agnostic doctor. In the early part of the war, conditions were very hard physically. We suffered from malnutrition and sheer deep hunger and roamed neighboring woods stripping bark off trees to eat. The debilitating effect of that constant hunger is unforgettable but would be hard to describe. In addition, we were very inadequately protected against the cold of the winter in northern Scotland. We slept in unheated attics and the bowls of water in which we were supposed to wash in the morning often contained only ice. I think mentally and psychically we simply hibernated most of that time.

The later years of the war held much of challenge and excitement for me intellectually. For the most part we were in rather small schools and worked almost individually. We had come to Scotland bilingual because of the stay in the Netherlands and were then, of course, forced to learn English rapidly. But we were also introduced to French immediately, and when I was ten I began Latin on an individual tutorial basis and was young enough to enjoy the grammar as though it were a series of puzzles. When I was thirteen a Sister at one of the convent schools offered to teach me Greek and I accepted with alacrity. Both the classical world and the origins of Christianity had sparked my enthusiasm. As to the latter I had become an avid private reader of the New Testament. As to the former, we were taught classical languages out of books that introduced history and mythology and a whole way of life. Besides, I had heard an adult friend make a remark that seemed to me to be so much wiser than she was. I asked how she came by the idea and she said she had read it in Plato as an undergraduate. Having no access to a library containing anything of Plato I saved up enough pocket money to buy one volume of the *Dialogues* and was immediately enthralled.

In the schools I attended until I was fifteen, science was barely taught, perhaps because the size of the schools did not warrant the equipment, but mathematics was rather well taught. I always enjoyed it and was usually able to work at my own speed even if that was far ahead of the class at a particular school. English composition, English literature, English history, and world geography were the core of the curriculum. In literature we always worked with primary sources, with at least one Shakespearean play each year along with a selection of novels, essays, and a great deal of poetry. I wrote poetry myself and was constantly encouraged in this by my teachers at the various schools. Dancing, graphic art, music, and exploratory trips into the countryside were also part of the curriculum that was simply taken for granted. It was an enjoyable education, maximally stimulating, minimally competitive. Toward the end of the war we were again under rather heavy bombardment in the south of England, where we then were. I was so caught up in the intellectual and cultural realms opening up to me at the time that I barely noticed the fear and disturbance of the "doodlebugs," the unpiloted missiles that constantly interrupted our routine.

In our religious education, at least in the various schools run by the Benedictines and by the Sisters of Notre Dame of Namur, I believed we fared far better than most of our contemporaries in the U.S. The New Testament was at least as important as the catechism, though the Hebrew Scriptures were known to us only through Bible stories. We were given a good and relatively unbowdlerized introduction to Church history. Under the title of "apologetics" we received a fairly sober justification for taking a Catholic stance. We were also introduced to the papal encyclicals on social justice and the understanding of society and morality underlying them. Besides this we were given very good experiences of the liturgy as it then was, and were taught the correct and beautiful rendering of the Gregorian chant which became for me a very important form of prayer and a very revelatory medium of our Catholic tradition.

The second phase of my adolescence began, when the war ended, with the news, after years of silence from across the Channel, that my mother had survived the war but was now dying. My psychiatrist aunt, with whom we were living at that time, made great efforts and was finally successful in getting us a special visa to visit my mother in the Netherlands for three months. At that time we had no legal right to return to the Netherlands and quite apart from her health she had no legal possibility of getting out. It was a frightening trip, not only because of the devastation of the war and the sheer physical complexity of getting through the Netherlands to Limburg, but also because we well knew she might be dead when we arrived, and that if she were still alive we might have grown so far apart in those years that it would be worse than finding her dead.

For me those were three extraordinary months of rediscovery and of getting in touch with the sources again. We did not go to school during those months, but lived almost timelessly in between the times. It was like living in a myth or fairy tale where the ordinary laws and measures do not hold. People were still in a daze in the immediate aftermath of the bitterest time of the war. They had lived very close to starvation for some time. There was a great deal of damage to roads and canals. The suspension of ordinary business reminded me forcefully of Holy Week as celebrated in my childhood years in Limburg. But the atmosphere in the little town, as in our family, was one of quiet faith and confidence and gratitude. The trial was over and we had survived. People were grateful and encouraged by such very small things—that there was bread for sale in the bakery, that the potatoes in the back yard had grown to a good crop, that it was possible to plant tulips again, that letters were now coming through from relatives abroad. Life was very simple but it was on the upswing.

My mother was very ill with silicosis aggravated by the years of malnutrition and anxiety. I took over much of the task of nursing her and slept on a couch in her room so as to be close at night. To my immense relief I remembered German well enough to converse colloquially and easily. She was exhausted. Speaking cost her a great effort and she knew she was dying. When she spoke it was seldom of practical matters for which she could signal; she did speak of what life had meant to her, what we had meant to her, of her most cherished convictions. She quoted poetry a good deal, most frequently Goethe and Rilke. I had never been with someone consciously approaching death like this. Instinctively I knew that the most important thing I could do was simply to be fully present and to try to understand. I was profoundly influenced by the realization that she had so totally lived her life. There was no anger or self-pity or regret in her reflection on it, only a total appropriation of its reality and its truth. She also fully and consciously and personally died her death. It did not just happen to her. We were not there at the very end. We stayed to the last day of the emergency visa. When we left, her doctor had her admitted to the hospital for lung surgery. He had always been more sanguine about her condition than she had, and thought he could collapse one lung to heal it. She died in the course of the surgery and the autopsy showed that both lungs were so far gone that nothing could have been done.

While my sisters remained with our aunt to go to school, I returned to Limburg almost immediately to settle the estate, try to make proper provision for my grandmother, and see to the storing of the sculptures that remained until they could be exhibited for sale. The biggest job was to clear the house and to sort through great accumulations of family records, correspondence, and miscellaneous papers. I was then barely sixteen. Our lives had been such that I simply took it for granted that I would handle these responsibilities. In that context there was no room for an adolescence that rebels against adult controls, against traditions and established patterns.

When I returned to England, my two younger sisters were living in furnished rooms in a friend's house, cooking for themselves and somehow getting themselves to school. There had been a terrible crisis in my aunt's tragic life. She was then hospitalized and unable to care for them in any way. With advice and financial help from friends, I took my youngest sister back to a boarding school in the south of Scotland where we had been very happy and where a German Jewish doctor's family had always taken a great interest in her and had frequently had her to stay for holidays. When I returned to Liverpool, my sister Marianne and I planned what we should do because we had no financial resources. She was in her last year before the School Leaving Certificate examination and wanted to take this and then go to an art school. Clearly she had to finish. I was enrolled in a sixth-form science program, preparatory to going to medical school, but I had already discovered that because I had top grades in a wide range of subjects in the School Leaving Certificate, I was eligible for the matriculation certificate without further sixth-form work. I did not return to school but found a job, on the proceeds of which my sister and I could barely live.

Meanwhile, many people were concerned about us. The

London refugee committee that had originally procured British visas for us before the war was informed that we were managing like this on our own, and summoned me to London to inform me that there were funds available to supplement what I was earning. A colleague of my aunt, a Sister of Notre Dame of Namur, happened to work both in practical clinical psychology and in a teacher-training college where she taught some courses. We were on her mind, and over a cup of tea in the faculty room she turned to a colleague and said, "Mrs. Whale, do you know of anyone who could offer a home to two teen-age girls who just lost their mother?" The person addressed, who had never heard of us before, said without a moment's hesitation, "I don't see why I shouldn't," and added a little later, "but perhaps I should consult with my husband." Over that cup of tea we were conceived into a new family. The Sister had spoken of two girls, but in due time my sister, Angelika, was also rescued from her boarding school and joined us.

If a council of wise and compassionate men and women had searched all over England and Scotland they could not have found a better set of second parents for us than Barrett and Winefride Whale. At their request we always called them by their Christian names because they did not want to do anything to dim or diminish the memory of our first parents. They were then middle-aged and had not been able to have children of their own. As we grew to know and love them intimately I came to realize that what may seem to have been improvident and precipitate haste in Winefride's response to our plight, was in fact a totally deliberate act springing from long-cultivated attitudes and convictions based on her personal understanding of divine Providence and the way God acts in history—something which she, though herself Catholic, claims to have derived from her own mother's Anglican background.

Winefride was then, and continued for some time to be, the professor of geography at the Mount Pleasant Training College. Before her marriage she had taught at the London School of Economics, where she met Barrett. Subsequently she had taught for many years at Strawberry Hill Training College in London. Barrett was an economist, had taught at the London School of Economics, at Cambridge during the war and at

Birmingham, and was the chairman of the Economics Department at the University of Liverpool at the time that they virtually (though not legally) adopted us. Barrett was an agnostic, although he had been raised as a Methodist and then an Anglican. Because of his great moral and personal integrity, his extraordinary compassion and concern for all those unjustly treated, and his intellectual honesty and humility, his agnosticism made a profound impression on me, reversing many of the assumptions that my convent education would have disposed me to make. This was accentuated and underscored when, a few years later, he died a truly extraordinary and serene death, making appointments to see the young lecturers who had worked with him at the university, thanking them for their cooperation and taking leave of them, and likewise quietly saying good-bye to all of us.

In the years before that, Winefride and Barrett lived very graciously and introduced us to a wide circle of cultivated and humane friends. They always had more leisure than I have ever had in my academic life in America, and they used that leisure well to enhance the society, the city, the country. During this time I enrolled at the University of Liverpool and read law. It never occurred to me to return to the sixth-form program and try for a scholarship to Oxford or Cambridge—I valued the life we had at home with Winefride and Barrett too much to want to live away from it. When I graduated from the law school, I continued in an interdisciplinary social science program, for which the University of Liverpool was famous, and went from there into family casework with an independent and non-denominational social service agency. I was living at home with Winefride and my sister Angelika. Barrett had already died and my sister Marianne was in London staying with friends and studying at an art school.

Had I remained there I would probably have returned to the University to teach political philosophy, for I was subsequently invited several times to do so, but the family casework was absorbing and dealt with such obvious need that I found it very satisfying. I used to go to and from work some miles away by bicycle and would also make my home visits that way. This brought me into very immediate relation to the dock hinterland and all the suffering and degradation it contained. There had been a lot of suffering in my life and that of my family, but not the kind of degradation and dehumanization that I saw and experienced in Bootle. At that time of my life, I began to feel an urgent need to set aside substantial periods of time to pray. It was like coming out of a place with a stifling odor and needing to breathe.

Meanwhile, I did not stay in Liverpool. For some years I had been in touch with the Society of Catholic Medical Missionaries. I had heard them speak of the situation in which they were working in India, of the difficulty of getting trained people to go where the need was greatest, and of the responsibility of the British as a colonizing people to go back and deal with the havoc that had been created by the impact of the West. I had thought of religious life before. Indeed many Sisters in the convent schools I attended had approached me with the suggestion, but I could not see myself in the school situations where I saw them. I had also thought of joining a contemplative community earlier in my teens, but had been wisely dissuaded from this goal by a Benedictine priest who was a good friend to us through all the strange adventures of our adolescent years. But the Medical Mission Sisters were different. Their life was built around a definite need that I could appreciate, and it seemed to me with my social service training and experience that it was a life and a task for which I was fitted. I joined the community in England when I was twenty-two years old, and remained in it for fourteen years, but my experience was very different from what I had anticipated.

I had assumed that I would be doing some type of social-service work in India in connection with the Society's hospitals or its public health and clinic projects. From the beginning, however, the Society had me earmarked to teach in one of its novitiates. My own novitiate experience was profoundly revelatory. One important matter that became clear to me was the brutalizing and destroying power of certain types of physical work. I had certainly not realized how destroyed people are when they have to do work that involves constant stooping. At the University I had been in frequent dialog with Marxists, but the notion of work as alienating, and the difference between work that fulfills and work that oppresses, is something that I learned in my religious novitiate. That is the only time in my life that I had the experience of being literally destroyed by exhaustion and physical strain, doing things in totally inefficient ways because the person in charge was too unintelligent to organize it better and too insecure to accept suggestions.

At this time I also learned the possibilities of a truly communistic society. The communes that are religious communities sometimes work supremely well, and in the most tangible way provide eschatological witness. They demonstrate that neither possessions nor expertise, nor yet family connections, need be the basis for personal dignity or identity or relationship with others. Community is constituted by the simple will to accept others and to subordinate personal goals to the common goals. Because of my experiences of religious community life, the vision of the reign of God among men seems to me quite realistic and functional.

During the time of the novitiate I had opportunities for very slow, unpressured, meditative reading that I appreciated, for I have never had such opportunities in the rest of my adult life and had not sought them when I was younger and always read with the speed of one who was starved. In these novitiate years there were times when I had no access to anything that interested me except the Bible, but I was given and was permitted to keep a Jerusalem Bible, then only available in French. On Sundays, in the long silences of the evenings, and at retreat times I read and reread, following the marginal cross-references given in the Jerusalem Bible and learning to hear the echoes of one passage within the other. We did not have access to library shelves as novices, but read the books that were given to us individually. Someone must have had the idea that I would be reading too intellectually and not "spiritually" enough, so I was given the same book over and over and over again. It was one of the books of Dom Columba Marmion. I cannot remember which one. It made a deep impression on me, because it affirmed my trust in the cumulative wisdom of the generations past in my tradition. Besides, Marmion had also heard the echoes of one biblical passage in the other, and he heard them as rendered in the liturgy.

The community at that time had built its whole prayer life and spirituality around the liturgy. The cycle of the liturgical year became even more tangibly the shape of all time for me than it had been in my childhood. We learned and chanted a great deal of the Gregorian music in the liturgy, and there of course the echoes and resonances of biblical and traditional themes emerge in a new dimension, as meditated and reflected through the ages. The Gregorian chant in the liturgy remains for me to this day the most central vehicle of tradition in Western Christianity. I have no doubt that he who sings prays twice and that he who sings Gregorian chant prays triply. It is a matter of deep regret to me that the chant was passed on in forms too complex for congregational use in parishes and that we have therefore temporarily lost it. Having experienced first hand the wealth of prayerful reflection on the praxis of the Christian life that is in it, I cannot believe that we have lost it forever. Moreover, having participated in Anglican liturgies in England, I am convinced that the chant need not be linked to the Latin language, though I myself dearly loved it and enjoyed it that way.

Whenever I reflect now on our Society's living of the liturgy in those days, I am struck with the thought that we were so little dependent on the clergy. Of course, we had priests preside at our Eucharists, but even there the spirit and shape of the experience came almost exclusively from community planning, preparation, and participation. We were still dealing with the one compulsory Tridentine Canon with the old single cycle of readings, and dialog homilies would have been thought an international scandal. Yet the fact that we always prepared and discussed the readings beforehand with the help of a liturgical cycle of commentaries on the readings and the feasts, the fact that we ourselves prepared the chapel and the decorations, the fact that we sang so much of the propers and that we carried the singing and therefore the themes over into the divine office, made the liturgy very much an experience that we shaped and for which we took the responsibility. If there was a good homily or a truly liturgical participation by the main celebrant, that was an unexpected bonus with which we were delighted, but it was by no means necessary in order to make a high celebration out of it. The experience of liturgy among the Medical Mission Sisters before Vatican II will forever inform my understanding of the possibilities of lay initiative even in the "churchy" activities of the Church.

The novitiate also provided me in many ways with a desert wrestling place. The isolation, the long and deep silences, the extremely monotonous routine, the absence of responsibilities and distractions, the disappearance of historical time into a bland sort of aeviternity brought me to terms with my own possibilities and limitations with a rather terrible simplicity. One could not go through that desert and come out the same.

To my bitter disappointment, when I completed the novitiate, I traveled west to the U.S. instead of east to India, and was channeled into further studies and an academic career rather than going back into direct involvement with elemental human needs as I had anticipated. That year I studied theology at the Catholic University of America, minored in anthropology, and completed the master's degree, thesis and all, in two semesters—not an impressively thorough theological foundation on which to presume to teach for the next seven or eight years. However, I was assigned to the U.S. novitiate to teach and we had an excellent library, and after the years of fasting from intellectual reading I had acquired an insatiable appetite for it. Moreover, my reading and reflection was guided by some excellent summer sessions at C.U.A. and at the University of Notre Dame's summer school of liturgy.

As I reflect on this earlier stage of my theological training, I realize that my entrance to it was quite unconventional. I did not come into it by the usual Catholic philosophical route, though philosophy had earlier been a passionate interest. Having been enamoured of Plato at thirteen, I thoroughly enjoyed the more theoretical debates of jurisprudence in my first year in law school when I was sixteen, and felt I was really at home with Aristotle when I discovered him in a political philosophy course I took at age nineteen. Although there was a good deal of philosophical content in the program in which I was then studying, the focus was always on the historical emergence of the social sciences out of their philosophical matrix. We studied psychology, political theory, sociology, and economics this way. During those same years, I had attended lecture series arranged by the Catholic chaplaincy at the university in Thomistic philosophy and theology which I found fascinating. When they ended, I arranged with a group of friends to invite a Dominican priest, Rupert Grove, over from Manchester on a regular basis to work through the *Summa Theologiae* on a seminar basis. The university setting was predominantly logical positivist, and in that context our pursuit of Thomist thought was a radical protest that was met with good-humored and puzzled tolerance on the part of our professors when it came out in our essays and examinations. At that time I felt that a highly sophisticated tradition of thought had been undeservedly and all too lightly ignored.

To anyone not acquainted with the British university scene it may seem strange that at the same time in which I was engaging in this study of Thomist thought as a radical protest, I was passionately caught up in the study of Marxism under the aegis of the university's (duly registered and authorized) Communist Society. I never had any intention of becoming a Communist, but I was convinced that Marxism contained much serious and sophisticated thought about the human situation, the meaning of being human, the possibility of understanding and appropriating history, and the possibilities and limitations for the construction of a social order. I simply wanted to make sure I understood what Marxists were saying, and that I was not getting a garbled version at second hand.

During the time in which I was doing social casework and no longer studying full time, I had continued to extend my reading, especially in the areas of psychology and cultural anthropology. During my religious postulate and novitiate years my reading was confined practically to Scripture and liturgical commentary. When, therefore, I began the M.A. program at Catholic University, I approached it with a pleasant curiosity as to what might be the distinguishing characteristics of a Catholic University in general and its handling of theology in particular. I was amazed to find it so provincial. The general assumption seemed to be that a liberal education could be very specifically defined in a more or less standard curriculum, and that theology was something that came after philosophy, which was also defined by a specific sequence of courses that totally excluded most of the great thinkers in the world's history.

In terms of my background, everything that I learned could only appear as one strand of thought or experience among many others, each justified only in terms of its own frame of reference. The year at Catholic University was salvaged for me by three professors. The first was Father Gerard Sloyan, who later became the chairman of the department and transformed it, and who always combined respect for tradition with a genuinely scholarly and critical approach. The second was Godfrey Diekmann, O.S.B., who gave me a very penetrating introduction to the Fathers of the Church, thereby introducing a dimension into my perception of the Christian heritage that was revolutionary, because it put me in possession, for the first time, at least in principle, of the missing element I needed in order to resolve doctrinal questions creatively myself. I do not mean, of course, that I felt equipped after a few courses to theologize competently on my own. I only mean that I knew I now had the keys to all the doors, and that if I never returned to formal study, I should nevertheless be able to acquire all that I needed by reading. The third professor was Friedl Lang of the anthropology department, who had done all his research and thinking in ethnology fully conscious of his own religious assumptions as a Catholic, and always reflected on Catholic questions fully conscious of what he had observed in crosscultural studies. I had many very insightful discussions with him, and with Regina Herzfeld, then chairwoman of the Anthropology Department, although I had no classes with her.

In the summers at the University of Notre Dame, I had inspirational and visionary accounts of many aspects of Christian tradition from Jean Daniélou (not then conservative in relation to his contemporaries at all), from Louis Bouyer, Bonifaas Luykx, Ermin Vitry, Cornelius Bouman, and Josef Goldbrunner. What characterized the Summer School of Liturgy in those days was a very solidly founded optimism about the possibility of reintegrating Catholicism for our times.

After some years of teaching in the novitiate, during which I managed to get not one inch nearer to India, I was sent to the University of Oklahoma for linguistics training with the Wycliff Bible translators, some of the most interesting, heroic, and singleminded Christians I have ever known. After that, while still teaching in the novitiate and also putting in time as spare cook, bottle washer, chauffeuse and switchboard operator, I embarked on a doctoral program in South Asian Studies "full time" at the University of Pennsylvania. The Department of South Asian Studies was a very well organized and perceptively planned interdisciplinary program. Participation in it was a good experience, apart from the sheer fatigue of doing it alongside other "full-time" occupations. One experience within it which was explosively illuminating was a course in Indian iconography given by Stella Kramrisch, then already an older woman, who had spent many years in India as a museum curator in Benares. In showing the symbolism of the Indian traditions, she opened my eyes (or so it seemed) for the first time to the symbolism of my own tradition. My own mandala began to become visible to me in those classes, and ever since then I have seen mandalas emerging, diverging, converging, in people's lives and in various traditions. People's life experiences change, drastic things happen, disasters threaten or strike, but the mandalas do not break. They transcend all this because they are made of the cumulative vision and wisdom of many generations.

My mandala does not break either. In the midst of this frantically strenuous program, I suddenly got word to drop everything and prepare to proceed to England—no explanation forthcoming. It was a grim experience. One's nervous system does not so easily unwind from doing three jobs at once to doing none at all, nor from fierce concentration in planning and keeping track of many things at once to the condition of suddenly having no knowable future to plan. There followed six months in the small English novitiate in which no one else seemed to know why I was there either, and I spent most of my working hours punching out on an addressograph machine plates for all the priests in England which were probably never going to be used. The desert Fathers with tasks of watering dry sticks and unweaving baskets really had very little edge on the Medical Mission Sisters in England in the heyday of that regime. In my free time I concentrated on remaining sane in case the Lord might have something else in mind after the file was finished. I borrowed translations of the Fathers of the Church, volume by volume, on interlibrary loan through the local public library and proceeded to make myself a file of quotations on topics I was particularly interested in pursuing.

The addressograph file was well advanced but my project on the Fathers really just begun when, at the end of six months, with equal suddenness I was summoned to Rome. I left with barely a change of clothes, expecting to be back within the week, but stayed three years first ghost-writing a book for a Vatican official, then beginning a file of materials from Vatican II, which I was able to follow day by day from the reports of speeches in *Osservatore Romano*, then out "on loan" for two years to the Better World Movement at the Centro Pio XII in the castelli, and finally back to complete the Vatican II file for the society's forthcoming general chapter.

At the Centro Pio XII, I participated in a different kind of Christian commune, cutting across ages, languages, and nationalities, states of life, educational levels, the sexes. Tempestuous and difficult as it was, it was in its own way a very extraordinary eschatological witness, and I had the opportunity to meet and to observe some very extraordinary Christians, as well as some of the great European scholars far beyond the small circle I had earlier met at the Notre Dame Summer School of Liturgy.

Among the scholars whom I had the opportunity to hear at this time were Yves Congar, Edward Schillebeeckx, Barnabas Ahern, Salvatore Marsili, Bernard Häring, and others whose influence was less sustained. Many of these men made a profound impression on my thought. What impressed me most in those I have mentioned by name was their collossal patience in mediating between the pastoral and the scholarly exigences of any question under discussion. Having the opportunity to discuss theological questions with a great number of bishops, frequently those from so-called missionary countries, and following the Council speeches daily as they were reported verbatim by *Osservatore Romano*, I myself could not think of theology as an elitist university game. At that time I came to reflect very explicitly on the nature of theology as a practical art. I

came to see it as resting on a great many levels of scientific inquiry, which must be competently and fully pursued, but as not
actually consisting of scientific inquiry. I understand theology
to be essentially not a science at all but an art—the art of interpreting the symbols inherited within a tradition, in such a
way that they are recognized and accepted by those who live
within the tradition as offering continuity, inner coherence, and
an adequate and appropriate response to contemporary questions about human life. This is why I believe that the books one
has read, the ideas one has exchanged, the great minds one has
met, all represent a very small constitutive factor in one's approach to theology, when placed beside basic personal life experiences.

When I was alone in the strangely mixed community at
Centro Pio XII, I began to realize with an entirely new depth
what is the characteristic vocation of the vowed religious. Ironically, almost as soon as I had this realization I became involved at the Centro in a counseling clientele I could scarcely
have refused to serve, but which was to lead me in short order
to ask and obtain a dispensation from my religious vows in
order to complete the task I had undertaken. My juridical exit
from the society was peaceful and friendly and I have been able
to maintain strong bonds with the people who had become my
family. But it was not an easy decision, in spite of the fact that
I had excellent advice both within and outside the Society. In
retrospect, I am more sure that I "followed my vocation" in
leaving than in joining the Society of Medical Missionaries, but
at that time in spite of the background from which I had come,
the institutional pressures were so strongly internalized in me
that it was very difficult for me to conceive of fidelity in other
than rather simplistic institutional terms. It was not as common then as it has become since to leave a religious institute.
Most who had done it to my knowledge had left bitter and
disillusioned or had left to get married.

Clearly, I could not live by the sort of counseling I had
been doing. Of the various options for earning a living that
opened before me, I chose, after prayer and reflection and advice, to do the two things that I would initially never have
chosen on my own. I returned to the U.S. and to the academic

life. Helped and encouraged by Gerard S. Sloyan, I completed the Ph.D. at Catholic University of America, settled down to college teaching in the Theology Department at Georgetown University, and tried to tune in to the Spirit to hear what else there might be to do in my spare time. I may or may not have heard correctly what the Spirit whispered. The messages I picked up led me to lecture rather widely to adult audiences in institutes, workshops, and summer sessions, and to write in short popular books such material as seemed most urgently and obviously to meet the needs of today's adult Catholics in the U.S. I also adopted two children, but it would take a whole book to explore the change in perspective from theologizing as a celibate to theologizing as a parent. The experience of being a parent is revelatory in many dimensions, and that of being a single parent has a distinctive slant to it. (One of my friends among the Medical Mission Sisters commented, "Good old Cuthbert does everything upside down. Other people leave to get married and then maybe they have children. Cuthbert leaves and has children and then maybe she doesn't get married.")

My return to Catholic University, after years of reading and teaching, study at the University of Pennsylvania and the University of Oklahoma, more extensive reading in Patristics, the experience of the Council years in Rome and the experience of the team reflection at Mondo Migliore, really began a third phase in my experience of theology. This time I came with a much clearer vision of what I needed to learn, and this time I found a very well-organized program that offered me all possible opportunities of doing it. The emphasis in the doctoral program was on a very thorough coverage of systematic theology and on adequate preparation in all the fields necessary to make the systematic theology an intellectually honest enterprise. It was a far cry from the provincialism I had met ten years earlier and it was the type of program I realized I needed at that point. I knew enough already to realize that no one can be competent today to do all the necessary research on a contemporary theological question from the beginning and from primary sources. I knew it was above all important to know how to articulate into the available resources for teamwork, and that for this purpose one needs to have an overview of what is happening in each field and some understanding of the basic craftsmanship and tools of each field, to be able to assess what kind of information is retrievable, what kinds of questions make sense, what kinds of hypotheses have any probability.

Again, I was profoundly influenced by the teaching of Gerard Sloyan and in particular at this time by the method implicit in everything he did. As far as I was able to decipher the method it was the following—a meticulously careful description of the phenomenon of the historical unfolding of a question, or the historical development of a statement, so as to allow the intrinsic configurations to appear, all leading up to conclusions stated as questions or stated very tentatively as to contemporary interpretations. Thinking of systematic theology as essentially an art, I was impressed by the power of Sloyan's approach, combining the thoroughness of historical investigation and exposition with the classic understatement of the conclusions. He was still conducting the seminar in doctrinal theology for the doctoral candidates at that time.

My doctoral studies also took me for the first time deep into the literature of post-biblical Judaism, in itself a thrilling and deeply satisfying experience, and beyond this powerfully suggestive of ways to practice theology as an art. This journey into Jewish religious literature was in some ways a continuation of what I had learned years before from Stella Kramrisch in the Hindu iconography course—an induction into the appreciation of the religious use of symbols. I do not believe my thought has taken any major turn or leap since then. As far as I can know it, I am still in that third phase of my experience of theology.

When I reflect on what theology is for me now, I realize that first of all it is not a career I have chosen but a task that somehow landed in front of me to be done. Secondly, it is a task that is done primarily from the resources of my own life experience within a great tradition that I am very happy to have internalized, for which I have the deepest affection and respect, and for which I consider myself co-responsible. Beyond that it is a task in which intellectual endeavors are only the tip of the iceberg that shows. The reason I engage in it is mainly that it gives me great satisfaction and that it seems to meet a need as basic as those I set out to meet in Liverpool and had hoped to meet in India. In particular, it seems to me that there is great confusion, uncertainty, and a crisis not only of understanding but also of confidence among Catholics today. I do not think Catholicism is the only way to live. I believe I would have found the same kind of deep-rootedness had I been raised Jewish or Hindu, but of my own tradition I know unfailingly from the inside that it makes total sense. I want to draw on my experience to assure my fellow Catholics that the mandalas do not break.

Theology as the Search for Self

EUALIO BALTAZAR

I would like to recount here how my personal life and experiences have affected and influenced my mode of theological reflection and the kind of theology I espouse.

In my personal life, I should note at the outset that there is nothing of divine illumination or mystical experience, which some privileged souls have been granted, to influence my theologizing. When I speak then of the influences of my personal life on my theology, I mean the influences of culture and heredity.

My cultural background is threefold. Being a nativeborn Filipino, I have the indigenous Malayan culture. But I also have the old-world and new-world Western culture, since Spain colonized the Philippines from the middle of the sixteenth to the end of the nineteenth century after which the United States took over. The Malayan culture influences me, I believe, at the deepest level of the unconscious; the Spanish culture, at the subconscious level; and the American culture, at the conscious level, since all my formal schooling has been under American or American-trained teachers.

Hereditarily, I am one-third Chinese. I do not know how much this fact has influenced my temperament. It is true, however, that my present philosophy and theology, which are a mysticism of the earth and a oneness with nature, conform and harmonize with basic Oriental mysticism. Paradoxically, however, it was not through a formal study of Oriental philosophy or parental teachings that I arrived at my present theology-of-the-earth, but through Western science. If one's theology is an expression of self, then my theology has been the expression of

147

my search for cultural identity. My selfhood, at the deepest level of the unconscious as conditioned by my Oriental culture, is mystical. But to reach it, I had to get away from it dialectically. I had to go from East to West culturally in order to come back and possess myself. Thus, my theology has had three phases: first Thomistic, then Teilhardian, and finally, Third World.

Before I joined the Jesuit order I had gotten a bachelor of science in agriculture degree from the University of the Philippines. I mention this fact because my scientific background with a specialization in genetics and evolution would later on in my life help my conversion from Thomism to the Teilhardian world view. But more on this later. Reflecting on my college days, I was not really interested in becoming an agriculturist. Going to college was the thing to do and since at the time I did not exactly know what I wanted to be, I enrolled at the college that was most convenient and accessible for me, namely, the college of agriculture in Los Banos, Laguna, where my father was a professor in agronomy.

In college, my scientific interest was not so much in the mathematically oriented sciences like agricultural chemistry, engineering, physics, or economics, but in the biological sciences: botany, zoology, and special biological fields like genetics and plant breeding. I do not know if this choice was influenced by my basic temperament which was poetic and imaginative rather than empirical and logical. But while managing to get a B plus average in college, my mind was not totally absorbed in my studies. I had other intellectual interests. Half my time was spent in the college library where I read the works of Locke and Hume and other philosophic thinkers.

In joining the Jesuit order I hoped to find intellectual and spiritual fulfillment. Of course, this was not my main reason for joining the order. It was to become another Christ by helping others through one's service, preaching, and fellowship. But to accomplish all this, I first had to find myself. The Jesuit spiritual and intellectual life helped me to find part of myself. If I had not studied philosophy and theology, I would have been an unhappy man. I found joy in the study of philosophy in the seminary. A vast region of the intellectual world was suddenly opened to me and I felt an expansiveness of spirit, the more so when I was introduced to the Thomistic metaphysics of being. I marveled at the great philosophical minds of Plato, Aristotle, Augustine, Thomas Aquinas. I became deeply involved in philosophy and distinguished myself in it.

Besides the study of philosophy I also had learned Jesuit spirituality. Whatever be the distinctiveness of Jesuit spirituality from that of other religious orders' spirituality, they are all one of a piece with the medieval metaphysical approach to spirituality. What I am saying is that as the metaphysics so the spirituality. The Scholastic metaphysics of being emphasized the categories of transcendence over that of immanence, of being over becoming, of substance over process, of the supernatural over the natural, of the other-worldly over the this-worldly, of the metaphysical over the physical, of the metempirical over the empirical, of immutability over change, of the eternal over the temporal and historical. Church spirituality following from this metaphysics of being created a dualism between the religious and the laity. In accordance with the categories of transcendence, seminaries were withdrawn from towns and cities and situated far out in the country; the religious garb also symbolized the separation of the religious from the laity, while the religious life itself was far removed from lay life, being centered on heaven and things eternal rather than on the mundane plight of poor people and the injustice and oppression that were visited upon them.

Somehow living the dualistic kind of spirituality based on the Scholastic metaphysics of being left me uneasy and unfulfilled. It did not agree with me. But I did not question the spirituality; I questioned myself. It was only later on after I had left the seminary that I read in the writings of Teilhard de Chardin that he too had the same problem. In his first writings, Teilhard expressed passionately his excruciating spiritual experience of being torn apart by two allegiances, his love for the world, on the one hand, and the demand of his metaphysically expressed Christian faith that required withdrawal from the world, on the other:

For after all must one renounce being human in the broad and deep sense of the word, bitterly and passionately human, in order to be a Christian? Must we, in order to follow Jesus and to participate in his celestial body, renounce the hope that we are getting the feel of and preparing a little bit of the Absolute each time when, under the blows of our labor, a little more of determinism is mastered, a little more truth is achieved, a little more progress realized? Must one, in order to be united to Christ, keep himself disinterested concerning the progress peculiar to this cosmos?

At once so intoxicating and cruel, this progress carries us along with it and comes to light in the consciousness of each one of us. Does not such a process risk making mutilated, tepid, and weak personalities of those who apply it on themselves? This is the existential problem in the heart of a Christian where the divine faith which supports all human effort, and the terrestrial passion, which is its sap, inevitably collide.[1]

Judged by the metaphysical ideal of withdrawal from the natural order into the supernatural, I was a "bad" religious. I was still a layman at heart, in the sense that my heart was still with the world. Like most lay people, I had a schizoid spirituality. Teilhard noted in the following passage:

I do not think I am exaggerating when I say that nine out of ten practicing Christians feel that man's work is always at the level of a "spiritual encumbrance." In spite of the practice of right intentions, and the day offered every morning to God, the general run of the faithful dimly feel that time spent at the office or the studio, in the fields or in the factory, is time diverted from prayer and adoration. It is impossible, too, to aim at the deep religious life reserved for those who have the leisure to pray or preach all day long. A few moments of the day can be salvaged for God, yes, but the best hours are absorbed, or at any rate cheapened, by material cares. Under the sway of this feeling, large numbers of Catholics lead a double or crippled life in practice: they have to step out of their human dress so as to have faith in themselves as Christians—and inferior Christians at that.[2]

The tension in my soul came to a head in my study of Scholastic theology, which covered the last four years of a Jesuit's training. In theology I understood how the relationship with the natural order and the supernatural order was formulated in terms of Scholastic philosophy. The key Scholastic concept was that of "nature." It was to this concept that the notion of the "supernatural" was related or grafted. According to the Scholastic concept, nature has an exigency or claim to those things necessary for its perfection. God who created nature cannot frustrate it, cannot create a nature in vain *(Deus non creavit frustra: natura non potest esse inane)*. It follows from this that what is due the given nature cannot also be gratuitous. Now the supernatural is a gratuitous gift of God to man. The Scholastic question then becomes that of relating the gratuity of the supernatural to a frame of reference consisting of the twin categories of *nature* and *exigency* or *being* and *justice*. Because of the a priori frame of reference, the supernatural cannot be constitutive of nature, cannot be part of *substance*; it can only be accidentally related to nature, otherwise it would lose its transcendence and gratuity. But if the supernatural is accidental to nature, then it is really *extrinsic*. Nature can be conceived apart from it; nature has its own natural end; the supernatural end is something superimposed.[3]

Many theologians who may be called intrinsicalists found the extrinsic formulation of the supernatural inadequate. For how can we in our theological formulations say that natural man can be understood apart from Christ and the supernatural when the whole tenor and basic message of the New Testament is to affirm that in Christ we move and have our being; in him all has been created; and not only man but the whole universe is "ontologically suspended from Christ and completely unintelligible apart from him"?[4]

Christ is our meaning. To know him is to know ourselves and to know ourselves is the basic meaning of redemption. Now, original sin is precisely the loss of the image of what we are. Thus, Christ came to earth to restore that image in us which is none other than himself. But the Scholastic formulation based on the Greek concept of nature borrowed from Plato and Aristotle claims that man can understand himself apart from Christ and the supernatural. If so, what need redemption? If Christ is just a superimposed meaning, an added meaning, that is not really constitutive of our natures, then he is not all that necessary to human history and fate. But this runs counter to the constant teaching of the Scriptures that Christ is the focal point and supreme center of the universe. In fact, so necessary is it to man that he know Christ that the punishment for this lack of knowledge and loss of Christ is hell fire that touches the very marrow of our beings. Now this would seem to be a cruel and unjust punishment if we follow the Scholastic formulation that portrays the loss of Christ and the supernatural as merely a loss of a superimposed or superadded meaning which are not necessary to the integrity and intelligibility of human nature.

Unless the supernatural is constitutive of human nature, constitutive of temporality and history, nay, the *essence* and *substance* of human nature and the material universe, it cannot be the principal redeeming force and energy in the universe and is of little significance to human activity and human goals.

The Scholastic formulation, it seemed to me, was valid for the medieval age—the age of *religiosity*—and by this term, I mean, a metaphysical world view, in which man's orientation was toward the other-worldly rather than to this world. But our modern age has become historically conscious. Time is no longer peripheral to man's thinking. Time is constitutive of man's reality. As Robert Johann has expressed it, "time is the creative process itself, in which the real is coming to birth."[5] He has developed this point more fully thus:

This awakening of man to the creative possibilities of this life and to his here-and-now responsibility for achieving an ever more human world has occasioned a new wave of religious skepticism. For there is the widespread feeling that traditional religions, with their emphasis on extratemporal salvation and the rules for reaching it, have served to distract the mass of men from wholehearted commitment to enhancing the present scene and really meeting its needs.[6]

And Walter Ong has confirmed this widespread modern outlook:

We are living in an age in which man is identifying himself more and more with the material universe by pinpointing the network of connection between himself and the rest of God's material creation. Darwin's discoveries mark a state in this movement whereby man finds himself more and more truly by finding the cosmos in which he lives. This movement is the contrary of that of Platonism and other ancient philosophies which drift away from a consideration of this world to a world of separated and supposedly "pure" ideas.[7]

I shared the views of these two perceptive thinkers. My scientific education, in which the study of biological evolution was a central part, proved to be a major influence in my questioning of Scholastic theology in particular and of Scholastic philosophy in general. I saw that all of Scholastic theology was formulated from a metaphysical and other-worldly point of view. I saw that this other-worldly and transcendent attitude prompted the Church to be aloof from the world, to emphasize her spotlessness and immutability and consequently to refuse to admit that she is a pilgrim people in need of redemption. In line with this other-worldly view, grace or the supernatural had to be separated from the impurities of the temporal. Its transcendence was emphasized, not its immanence.

The clash between my scientific orientation with its evolutionary outlook, on the one hand, and Scholastic philosophy and theology with its nonevolutionary perspective, on the other, produced a tension in me. The latter forced me to withdraw from the modern world into the medieval, but in so doing a part of me rebelled. I was driven back into the modern world, but I did not as yet have the proper intellectual and philosophic categories to relate my Christian faith to it. Before abandoning Scholastic philosophy and theology, I examined the efforts of Henri de Lubac and Karl Rahner, to see whether their reconciliation of the supernatural with the natural was adequate. In his book, *Surnaturel*, de Lubac made an effort to make the supernatural intrinsic to human nature. But the encyclical *Humani Generis* put a stop to this noble attempt. However, even de Lubac's hopes were false, for I believe that as long as one persists in trying to see the relation of grace to the world in terms of the Scholastic categories of nature and supernature, as de Lubac did, there is no way grace can be made constitutive of and essential to human nature. Even to attempt to do so is to verge on heresy, as *Humani Generis* warned, for what is constitutive of and essential to nature is also *exacted* by that nature, thus destroying or nullifying the gratuity and transcendence of the supernatural which is a truth of faith.

Karl Rahner, using Heideggerian existential philosophy in support of his basic Scholastic philosophic orientation, developed the novel category of the *supernatural existential*. Prescinding from my general criticism of existential philosophy as an adequate frame of reference for theological formulation,[8] my specific criticism of Rahner's efforts is that in the end, after claiming that his supernatural existential is the "central and abiding existential of man as he really is,"[9] and that to this extent this potency is "what is inmost and most authentic in him, the centre and root of what he is absolutely,"[10] he nevertheless admits that the orientation of man to God is not so basic that human nature cannot be conceived apart from grace. Now here precisely is the apparent contradiction, for if the supernatural is not constitutive of human nature, if human nature can be conceived apart from the supernatural, as Rahner ultimately admits, then he does not really mean what he says when he asserts that the supernatural is the center and root of what man really is. The supernatural existential may be an abiding and original equipment of human nature, but all that this means is that one cannot conceive *temporally* of one without the other. It is still possible *logically* to conceive of one without the other, and this is the crux of the matter.

Besides the reasons I have just described, there were others that slowly eroded my faith in Scholastic philosophy and theology. One of these was the dry and highly abstract theological discussions characteristic of the Scholastic method in which theological categories so far removed from the concrete and living categories of the Scriptures were employed. I went into the study of theology expecting an expansion and deepening of my personality and being as they came in contact with the word of the living God, but I found only aridity. Scholastic philosophy and theology became a barrier to my religious enlightenment.

Another shortcoming of Aristotelian-Thomistic philosophy and theology is that its metaphysical structure and orientation cannot present the historical and sequential character of revelation as presented in the Scriptures. Revelation is there presented as the successive saving events of Yahweh visited upon his chosen people. How is it then possible for a metaphysical theology that looks at truths in an immutable and nonhistorical way to present unique and temporal events without distorting their historicity, temporality, and uniqueness?[11]

My dissatisfaction with Scholastic theology and philosophy convinced me of the need for a new philosophy that had to be historical and evolutionary. However, during my years of theology (1955-59), the development of a new philosophy or the search for one was deferred for the sake of a more pressing and personal concern, namely, the solution of the problem of the supernatural. My efforts were directed at finding out a way to make the supernatural constitutive of man. My goal centered on the search for new categories that enabled the supernatural to be constitutive of human reality while at the same time safeguarding its transcendence and gratuity. My method was to approach the problem of the supernatural from the side of grace rather than from the side of nature. From the side of grace I hit on the category of love, for grace is love. It was the divine call to man to enter into a *koinonia* with Yahweh. The category of love in turn led me to the category of *person*. In my exploration of the category of personality, the little book of Martin Buber, *I and Thou*, exercised tremendous influence. It furnished the categories of I and Thou with which I began to relate grace as love. I assured myself that this line of reasoning was the right one, for if grace is a divine call of love, then it is to the *person* not to *nature* that the call is addressed, for nature is impersonal and universal and therefore unable to respond to a call of love. Love is between persons.

Another observation that convinced me that I was on the right track was the fact that love and gratuity go together. Grace as gratuitous could not be properly related to the category of nature for nature is in the context of justice, exigency, and necessity, not gratuity. But the context of love is the context of gratuity. In other words, love is not something forced or coerced. It is a free, gratuitous gift of oneself to the other.

With the above considerations, it is now possible to show the intrinsic ordination of the I to the Thou not only temporally but logically, not only existentially but constitutively. For love to be possible between the I and the Thou there has to be a structuring of one to the other. Love means union. Union requires affinity, proportionality—hence, a structuring of one to the other. And if one is talking of the highest type of love, namely, supernatural love or grace, then the structuring of man for it must be total, for the higher or the deeper the love so too the degree of structuring.

The paradox of love and the I-Thou context is that it is possible to affirm both the gratuity of grace and the intrinsic ordination of man to it. It is possible to say that grace is constitutive of man, that man is unthinkable temporally and logically apart from grace while at the same time safeguarding the gratuity of grace; for now we are not relating grace to the framework of nature and exigency but to the framework of love and I-Thou.[12]

I wanted to share this solution to the problem of the supernatural with others by having it published in the *Theologian*, a publication of the Woodstock College seminarians. But it never saw the light of day. The editorial reader and reviewer of the article, a fellow seminarian, told me personally that he could not understand it. And he added that one of the professors who also read the article made the remark that seminarians should not be writing articles like this.

After I left the Jesuit order, my interest in theology did not wane. But I knew that if I was to do any theological writing I had to develop or find a philosophy that proved an adequate framework for theological reflection and reconstruction of the metaphysical theology that so dissatisfied me. Consequently I concentrated on a study of philosophy, taking a doctoral degree in it. During this time, my philosophic stance was that of interpersonalism. I was a devotee of the I-Thou philosophy, and because the *person* was the central category of existentialism, I was attracted to this latter philosophy. I explored the possibility of the reformulation of theology within the context of an I-Thou perspective. I had already worked out to my own satisfaction the relation of grace to man within this frame of reference. I was aware too of the works done by Protestant theologians using the existential frame of reference, for example, Rudolf Bultmann, and among Catholic theologians, Karl Rahner. But I felt that the existential frame of reference was too narrow, being restricted to human temporality alone. The total compass and scope of redemption, however, includes not only human temporality and existence, but also material creation. As St. Paul tells us, creation itself is groaning until now to be redeemed.[13] Thus, existentialism brackets the material universe, refusing to see that the roots of human temporality extend all the way back to the evolution of the material universe. Existentialism has no commerce with technology, seeing it merely as an impersonal reality, an impersonal *It* that depersonalizes man, submerging his identity as an *I* or *Thou*.

In my view, another shortcoming of existentialism is the restricted scope of the phenomenological method. Thus, the phenomenological method is a valid and effective method for the study and exploration of human temporality, that is, of human existence here and now, but is unable to cope with the dimension of the future, and by future here I mean the category that the Scriptures call *eschatological*. Much of theology, if not its basic orientation, has to do with the eschatological future. In sum, existentialism not only does not go far enough into the past—but also does not go far enough into the future —to that future which transcends historical time. But the Scriptures speak of the absolute beginning of the universe—its creation; of its middle—the redemptive process; and of its end or consummation—the eschaton or Parousia. To express these data theologically, we need a frame of reference that is coextensive with the material.

After having considered existentialism, I next examined empiricism. I asked whether it was adequate to present the data of Scriptures purely empirically, that is, as a historical theology. It would seem that the empirical framework was effective and valid for the presentation of the data of Revelation, which as presented in the Scriptures take a linear rather than a cyclic pattern of temporality. But it did not take long for me to conclude that an empirico-historical method can handle only part of the data of Revelation. In other words, not all of the data are historical. As we mentioned earlier, the eschatological dimension, which is central to the message of the Scriptures, transcends the historical dimension. The transition from the first creation to the New Creation, the old Adam to the New, the Old Jerusalem to the New, the Old Earth and Heaven to the New Earth and the New Heaven is a radical change, a change from the historical-empirical dimension to the eschatological dimension which latter is transhistorical, transphenomenal, and transempirical. The empirico-historical method is thus unable to comprehend the extraordinary, the miraculous, the transcendental.

Like the phenomenological method, the empirico-historical method is unable to deal with the prehistorical past and with the eschatological future. The historical method valid for the realm of human history may indeed be applicable in the study and formulation of the historical accounts of the dealings of Yahweh with his chosen people. But the Scriptures, as we mentioned earlier, start with a prehistorical event—the first creation, and end with a transhistorical event—the new creation. I felt therefore that the historical method was limited in its scope. What was needed was a method and a frame of reference that could handle and properly formulate eschatological realities. The historical method, valid for explaining the temporal dimensions of the historical past and the historical present, is unable to deal with the category of the eschatological future.

Reviewing the various theological methods used by theologians, I noted that they could be categorized into two divisions: the metaphysical and the empirical. The strength of the metaphysical method (usually Platonic or Aristotelian) was its ability to portray transcendence. But it attained this, it seemed, at the expense of immanence. It took us to the region of the eternal or timeless but at the cost of abandoning the world, the temporal and the historical. By way of contrast, theologians who tried to emphasize the value of the temporal and historical understandably used empirical philosophies as frames of reference. But these philosophies too proved unsatisfactory, for historical and empirical theologies, while able to emphasize the immanence of God and of grace, were unable to preserve the transcendent value of these same realities. What was needed was a dynamic philosophy that preserved both immanence and transendence.

I next examined the dialectical philosophy of Hegel. It appealed to me as a dynamic philosophy that presented reality as an evolution or process according to the dialectic of thesis-antithesis-synthesis. But it was idealistic, that is, its dialectical starting point was bare timelessness, which then evolved into its opposite, the temporal, which in turn would evolve into the fullness of timelessness. This final result seemed to me not the fulfillment of time but the destruction of it.

Karl Marx's reformulation of Hegel's dialectic started with concrete temporal man, who then created his antithesis in religious and metaphysical man, who in turn had to be transcended to attain the full concreteness of man. In my view, the Marxist dialectic, which presented humanization as the creation of a new man on earth, was closer to the scriptural view of a New Heaven and a New Earth in which God will dwell with man forever, than was the traditional metaphysical view or Hegelian view in which we leave time and temporality to dwell with God in timeless eternity. I realized that Marxist philosophy was atheistic and for this reason unchristian, but there was no reason why the end of the dialectic had to be an atheistic state of man. It could just as well have been a theistic man as long as religion was presented as this-worldly rather than other-worldly. Compared to empirical philosophies, Marxist philosophy had the advantage of being able to provide the dimension of transcendence here on earth in the form of the promise for a better society and of a new man who is fully humanized. Thus, the dimension of the future was prominent in Marxism. It had an eschatology.

But a basic reason for my rejection of the Marxist frame of reference for theologizing was the inadequacy of the dialectical method itself. For me, the dialectical method was too rhythmic, too pendulum-like and mechanical to have properly served as a mold for the interpretation of the dealings of Yahweh with man and man's response to Yahweh. In the Scriptures, man's response to the divine call was a free response. Thus, free responses are not predictable nor so automatic and mechanical as to be properly comprehended by a dialectical frame of reference. To attempt to interpret sacred history and the salvific events within it in terms of the dialectical method would have been to distort the very character of unpredictability and miraculousness of the facts.

The philosophy I finally chose as the least objectionable and as being able to portray both immanence and transcendence was process philosophy. It was not however the process philosophy of Alfred North Whitehead but that of Teilhard de Chardin which I preferred, although the former was better known in philosophy for his express and formal treatment of process than Teilhard's. But more on Teilhard's philosophy of process later.

Let me deal briefly with my objections to Whitehead's process philosophy, which has become very popular today among many American Protestant theologians and some Catholics.[14] Whitehead has said that philosophy (Western) was nothing but a series of footnotes to Plato. As a matter of fact, Whitehead's philosophy was basically Platonic. What he owed to Plato, among other things, was his concept of God's primordial nature as eternal timelessness. And what he owed to Heraclitus was the concept of God's consequent nature as a perpetual becoming. Now this dualistic concept of God was difficult for me to accept. I just could not see how the timeless and the temporal could coexist in one and the same reality, God. Timelessness to me was a relic of a metaphysical outlook, hence an abstraction and a figment of the imagination. It could be an acceptable philosophical postulate and category but improper and unsatisfactory for the purposes of understanding the God of the Scriptures—the God of Abraham and Moses. For the eternity of God in the Scriptures was conceived in terms of time, not timelessness. Yahweh who was spoken of as "he who is and who was and who is to come" (Rev. 1:4; 4:8), as Oscar Cullmann aptly noted, implied time, not timelessness.[15]

Now with respect to Whitehead's concept of God's consequent nature as a perpetual becoming that never terminates in being, I accepted the Eastern or Oriental philosophic critique of it, namely, that this was *karma* or illusion. Liberation in the Eastern sense meant to have done with "becoming," with "doing," and with "having," so that one may simply *be*. A never-ending round of impermanent existence did not appeal to me. From the philosophic point of view, a becoming that never terminates in being appeared to me to be unintelligible. For the intelligibility of a given process is based on the *fruit* of that process. A given tree is named after its fruit. Thus, a tree is called an *apple* tree because its fruit is an apple. From the evolutionary point of view, there is no empirical basis for a never-ending process. All the evolutionary processsess we are aware of, cosmic evolution, cellular evolution, etc., have had a goal or terminus. And, finally, from a theological point of view, the Whiteheadian philosophy of a never-ending process ill-suited the scriptural view that the first creation is the first stage of a salvific process that will terminate in the fullness of the New Creation or that the old man will be transformed into the New Man in Christ, the old Jerusalem into the New Jeru-salem, and the old earth into the New Earth.

I now turn to Teilhard de Chardin's process thought. First of all, let me observe that during the time I was studying philo-sophy (1959-1962), I came across Teilhard de Chardin by ac-cident. True, in my theology days, I was aware of Teilhard de Chardin. But he was not popular among the intellectual pace-setters at the seminary. Besides, his writings were not available then. In 1959, the magnum opus of Teilhard, originally pub-lished in French as *Le Phénomène humain*, appeared in English translation as *The Phenomenon of Man*. A friend of mine gave the book to me as a gift. It proved to be the kind of world view I was looking for for years. It provided a magnificent and original synthesis of science and theology. Within Teilhard's evolutionary world view, Christ had a central place. He was the supreme center, the fulfillment, the Omega of the whole macrocosmic process. He was no longer peripheral to the world process as in the Scholastic formulation,[16] but its very essence and substance. It was to be expected that so original a work would be misunderstood, not only by the highest Church authorities in Rome, but by many well-known theologians at the time. To make Christ the Omega point of the evolutionary process was to destroy the gratuity of the Incarnation, it was asserted. Others, more sympathetic, forgave Teilhard de Chardin his view of Christ-Omega by saying that Teilhard was not a trained theologian, that his work was not a treatise in theology but mere poetry. If Teilhard's writings tended to be poetic, I did not consider it a shortcoming but rather a sign of profundity, just as the poetic form of the Scriptures attest to its profundity.

Indeed, Teilhard was not a trained theologian nor a trained philosopher. He did not speak the language of the disciplines. But I considered his great work to contain more authentic theology and philosophy than many of his theological and philosophic critics had ever done.

Because of the many and deep misunderstandings attendant on Teilhard's writings, I endeavored to be one of his many apologists. The first task I set myself was to develop the philosophy implicit in his world view. This task provided me with the subject matter for my doctoral dissertation which was entitled, *A Critical Examination of the Methodology of The Phenomenon of Man* (Georgetown, 1962). The result of this study plus the article I had done on the problem of the supernatural were later incorporated in book form under the title, *Teilhard and the Supernatural*.

By using the process framework of Teilhard, the data of the Scriptures can now be translated into modern categories and be shown to speak about this world in process. God's creative action, which formerly was thought to be timeless, is now shown to be expressed in time under the form of evolution. God is the ground of this world process. God is also the Omega of this process.[17] God's own eternity is not a timelessness but the Fullness of Time in accordance with the scriptural view that God's eternity is endless time.

In Teilhard's process thought, one does not need to go outside time to attain transcendence. Transcendence is resituated in the eschatological future. The eschatological future is not a historical future, that is, some historical date in the future, say A.D. 2000. The historical future is the region of transcendence of biological realities and of cultural ones such as nations and civilizations, but not the region of spiritual transcendence. To use Teilhard's terminology, the historical future is the omega of biogenesis and noogenesis. But noogenesis in its turn has its own omega—the level of Christogenesis. This latter is a new time dimension. Evolution may be seen as a process of transcendence, but transcendence in this case is a transition from one time level or dimension to another, never from time to timelessness. Thus cosmic time evolves into biological time, biological time into historical time, and historical time into Christ time, and Christ time into the Fullness of Time which is eternity.

If I reflect on the influences that helped me to prefer process philosophy and an evolutionary world view over other philosophies and world views, certainly one of them would be my scientific background in biology. Teilhard de Chardin's world view thus appealed to me. But whatever be one's background, I think it is wrong for any theological systematization and formulation that approaches a global or universal perspective to ignore the world of science. The metaphysical world view of two orders, the natural and the supernatural, separated the world of science and the world of religion, the former speaking of this world, the latter of the other world. The result was that theology and the Churches were left in splendid isolation, forgotten and ignored by the ongoing world process. The Scriptures do not speak of two orders. Rather there is only one order, this world itself, and it is a supernatural process of redemption. Teilhard's world view has come to terms with the world presented by science. He may not have been able to show precisely how the supernatural fits into it, that is, he did not give us a formal and explicit explanation how, if Christ is the Omega point of evolution, the gratuity of the Incarnation is safeguarded. But his insight was valid. What I have tried to do is to show, by using the philosophy of process implicit in his world view, how the gratuity of the supernatural is safeguarded.

While having been influenced greatly by Teilhard, I refuse to be classified as a follower of Teilhard. I am not a slavish follower of Teilhard nor of any thinker, for that matter. Likewise, I refuse to be pinned down to process thought and be classified as a process thinker. My philosophic interest basically is to arrive at a more or less common universal philosophy. This may be wishful thinking to some, but I believe that there are basic commonalities in Platonic dialectic, Hegelian-Marxist dialectic, and process thought. If the Platonic world of pure forms is resituated in the eschatological future, then Platonism ceases to be an escape from this world. It becomes immanentist; its idealism, instead of being metaphysical and other-worldly, becomes futuristic. It is possible that future studies on Plato will confirm that this was his original and authentic view. But it was not how Western philosophic thought understood Plato.

My present state of philosophic and theological reflection is one of transition from process thought to poetic and mystical thinking. There is profound truth in the saying that a philosopher is a frustrated poet. Having been educated in the West, my thinking has been for the most part scientific, logical, and rational as opposed to the imaginative and poetic ways of Eastern thought. Process thought and philosophy are the product of conceptual, rational, and logical thinking. But reality is deeper than what can be grasped by rational, conceptual, and philosophic thinking. The Scriptures were not written from a scientific, rational, or conceptual point of view, but rather from a poetic and imaginative point of view. The sacred writers were not writing history in the sense that we understand the term today. They were communicating transcendent realities. And as great mystics tell us, the most effective way to communicate these realities is by the use of concrete poetic images, symbols. Of course, to have insisted on communicating the message of the Scriptures couched in the language of the agricultural societies of the past to conceptually and rationally oriented minds of the West would have been futile. There was need of reformulation into a scientific and rational theology. But today, with the increasing interest in the occult, the mysterious, in the religions of the East, perhaps a theology based on the imagination and expressed in poetic form would be a more effective means of leading the modern mind to a communication with the Transcendent. We must insist here however that Transcendence is not found by an escape from the world, but through the world; and the world where the Transcendent is found is in the suffering, the sick, the oppressed, the exploited, the poor. If Christian theology is to be authentic, then it must conform to the mission of Christ, namely:

The spirit of the Lord has been given to me,
for he has anointed me.
He has sent me to bring the good news to the poor,
to proclaim liberty to captives
and to the blind new sight,
to set the downtrodden free,
to proclaim the Lord's year of favour.

Luke 4:18-19 (Jerusalem Bible)

Unfortunately, very little of Western theology is devoted to the problems of Third-World peoples. In theological conventions held around the world, the topics discussed hardly include the problems Jesus was concerned with. And Third-World theologians are scarcely represented. But I believe that any valid theology done today must be Third-World rather than the onesidedly bourgeois theology of the recent past. Consequently my present interests are centered on Third-World theology of which black theology is part.[19]

NOTES

[1]See "La view cosmique," 1916. (Quoted from Claude Tresmontant's *Pierre Teilhard de Chardin* (Helicon, 1959), p. 79.

[2]See his *The Divine Milieu* (Harper & Row, 1960), p. 34.

[3]For a discussion of the problem of the natural and the supernatural, see my book, *Teilhard and the Supernatural* (Helicon Press, 1966).

[4]Joseph Huby's commentary on Colossians. See *Teilhard and the Supernatural*, p. 69, where this is quoted.

[5]See *Teilhard and the Supernatural* where this is quoted, p. 69.

[6]*Loc. cit.*

[7]*Loc. cit.*

[8]See my article, "Process Thinking in Theology," in *Transcendence and Immanence*, ed. Joseph Armenti (The Abbey Press, 1972), pp. 23-30.

[9]See *Teilhard and the Supernatural*, Chs. I & II, where Rahner's theology is discussed.

[10]*Loc. cit.*

[11]See "Process Thinking in Theology," *op. cit.*, p. 24.

[12]For a full-length discussion of this problem, see *Teilhard and the Supernatural*, especially Ch. VIII.

[13]Incidentally, Eric Mascall makes a similar criticism: "It is significant

that for existentialist theology there are no problems about the relation between science and religion, for it ignores those facts about man from which the problems arise. . . . There is little sense of the Pauline assertion that the whole of creation groaneth and travaileth awaiting redemption; rather it is man who groans and travails awaiting redemption." (See his review of W. Richard's book, *Secularization Theology*, in *The Thomist*, 32 (1968), pp. 106-115.

[14]My comments here could very well be open to misunderstanding for their very brief nature. Perhaps, at another time, a fuller critique of Whitehead's process philosophy as applied to theology will be forthcoming.

[15]Please see my discussion of this point at length in my book, *God Within Process* (Newman Press, 1970), Ch. IV.

[16]As Berdyaev comments, "the natural order according to the Aristotelian and Thomist conception is not penetrated by divine forces; it lives according to its own laws, and is only subject to the organized action of external grace." (See his *Freedom and Spirit*, Charles Scribner's Sons, 1935), p.352.

[17]A reformulation of the notion of God in terms of process is attempted in my book, *God Within Process*.

[18]See *God Within Process*, Ch. IV.

[19]My latest work, *The Dark Center* (Paulist/Newman Press, 1973) is the attempt to develop a black theology.

"Nothing but a
Loud-mouthed Irish Priest"

ANDREW M. GREELEY

Four points by way of introduction:

1. I write this autobiographical sketch against my better judgment, but one of the things I learned growing up on the west side of Chicago is that when your friends ask you to do something, you do it. The editor of this series asked me to write this essay, and since he is a good friend, here it is.

2. I propose to sketch out as best I can some of the environments, people, and ideas that have influenced my thinking ("intellectual development" strikes me as too pompous a label). Hence this essay is not "the story of a soul," or an intimate memoir, or anything of the sort. Some day I may try such an exercise, but too many people are still alive for me to attempt it now.

3. I am not a sociologist, a writer, or even a theologian despite the editor's gracious bestowal of those titles upon me. I am a parish priest who, by a series of chances more than choices, ended up doing sociology, writing, and now a bit of theology. I may not be able to practice the parish ministry just now, and I may never do so again. Still, it is a parish priest I set out to be; it is the work of the parish ministry that brings me the greatest happiness. That is the core identity that I claim.

4. Let me endeavor to answer at the beginning three hostile questions that are addressed to me quite frequently, so that those readers who begin to read here seeking answers to these questions will not have to go any further. (a) How do I

write so much? I work hard. (b) Why do I write so much? I like to write. (c) Why do I wander all over the intellectual outfield instead of settling down and doing one thing? Why shouldn't I?

Twin Lakes

The first memories are of grassy terraces, a great old castle-like building, wooden outbuildings, a shimmering silver lake, the bell calling us to delicious meals in the dining hall, another faint, tinkling bell at Mass on the great, sweeping lawns, thick old trees, boats on the lake, the rough concrete of the "pergola," running madly down the hill and scraping my knees on the rough gravel path.

Commodore Barry Country Club, Twin Lakes, Wisconsin, the early 1930s. "Country club" indeed; it was really only a rough-hewn summer camp approached by a slow, laborious milk train and then a bumpy truck ride from Chicago. But for the lower middle-class and a handful of upper middle-class Irish-Catholics from the west side of Chicago, it was the greatest place to go for a summer vacation. My father and mother met there, and for many years our family was at Twin Lakes from July 4 to Labor Day. The "club" is gone now, weakened by the Great Depression, rendered obsolete by the surge of prosperity that swept up the Irish after the Second World War, and finally replaced by a subdivision of "second" homes. Still, for a decade or so, it represented the zenith of immigrant Catholicism, a warm, friendly cocoon that provided the social support, the recreational opportunities, the organizational experience, and the religious convictions to sustain the children of the immigrants as they pushed their way into the white-collar world of the 1920s, hung on desperately to their respectability through the Great Depression, and then finally "made it" after World War II.

Immigrant Catholicism, in my experience of it, was benign. It may have been narrow (you didn't encounter very many non-Catholics at Twin Lakes) but it was not oppressive and, as I remember it, not very rigid. It was ground on which to stand, a place of your own. If you were still excluded from the more posh watering places in society, that didn't make much difference. With a spot like Twin Lakes, no one cared what anyone else had.

The Catholicism of my parents was not ostentatiously pious or rigid, neither hangdog nor defensive. It was a matter of course, something as natural as breathing the air. You were loyal to the Church, but you hardly even thought of it as loyalty. It was simply an important part of your life. We were always on the fringes of the parish, and although my father was deeply committed to the Knights of Columbus he rarely went to Holy Communion. My mother used to joke that she hated to think what would happen if my father were forced to choose between Bary Council and his family.

My father was a man of extraordinary integrity. Indeed, he once refused an opportunity to make several million dollars in a tax warrant transaction because Anton Cermak, then mayor of Chicago, demanded a half-million dollar cut of the profits. In my early years of parish work an occasional old-timer would come up to me and ask if I was "Andy's son" and then invariably say something about his integrity and "fairness." He was a political liberal and a New Deal Democrat, and despite Cermak, he was a loyal member of the Cook County organization. He worked terribly hard (indeed worked himself into an early grave) and was a conscientious and effective organizer and administrator. He wrote quite a bit for the Knights of Columbus journals. He drank not a bit and smoked far too much.

The Great Depression broke my father's spirit, and the somber, serious side of his nature was what we saw most of the time. There was a strong strain of the leprechaun in him, though, a wild west-of-Ireland wit that erupted on occasions. He had an incorrigible sense of flair that got him into trouble occasionally with humorless friends (as it would later for two of his children). He was an avid reader, a skillful writer, and I think had an absolutely first-class mind. He did not get beyond high school (my mother went to work at Sears when she was fifteen), but he had the erudition and the intellectual style of a college graduate.

Contributions to the Church were always anonymous or given to the parish priest with my father's insistence that they not be published in the monthly "scandal sheet" (which listed the contributions of the parishioners). I cannot recall priests ever coming to our house for dinner, yet my father had many close friends in the priesthood and at a time when it was absolutely unthinkable, he was on a first-name basis with several of them. Indeed, they often came to him for advice, which in retrospect was an extraordinary thing in the 1930s.

There was sorrow and suffering in our family, mostly caused by the Great Depression, but that is beyond the scope of this sketch. From my family environment I drew my ease with the Catholic Church, my intellectual curiosity, my political convictions and commitments, my obsession with work, a leprechaun strain, ambition, and a tendency to dig in my heels when I am pushed too far. The older I get the more I see in myself the "old fellow" when he told off Anton Cermak.

I also, heaven forgive me for it, inherited, as did my sister Mary Jule, my father's incorrigible flair. When presented with alternative courses of action—one quiet and inconspicuous and the other spectacular—my sister and I aren't even really free to make a choice. It is not merely enough that you wrestle a doctorate from a grudging University of Chicago; you do it spectacularly, one of you in twenty months while you're a full-time parish priest, and the other at one class a quarter for nine years while you're a full-time mother of six, and then seven, children.

That will show the so-and-sos!

Still, it's fun, and when you know what the ground is on which you stand, you can afford to gamble for high stakes.

My sister insists that Grand Beach is Twin Lakes reincarnate, a place by a lake where the memories of childhood stability, security, and happiness are reawakened. I'm sure she's right. Twin Lakes was a good place to begin; Grand Beach is a good place to be today.

The Neighborhood

Lines of single-family brick bungalows, 1936 Fords puffing down the street, red streetcars on Division Street and North Avenue, a wooden church and an auditorium, then a great white stone Gothic, walking lazily to school and even more lazily home, touch ball games in the street, the Austin bus and the Lake Street El downtown, trouble with the nuns over handwriting, sitting on the front porch talking on hot summer evenings, Motto's drug store, the Rose Bowl ice-cream parlor, shopping for my mother in the pre-supermarket Jewel, making a mess out of model airplanes, hearing of the Pearl Harbor attack as the great 1941 Chicago Bears played the then Chicago Cardinals.

My memories of the neighborhood and of the parish are benign. I am always astonished when other Catholic writers describe their own parishes as dreary, oppressive, benighted places that stifled their spirits and from which they had to revolt in order to be free and to be themselves. By contemporary standards, I guess, the St. Angela's of the 1930s and the 1940s was not overwhelmingly enlightened, but neither was it punitive or hostile to the rest of the world. We had dialogue Mass in the late 1930s, there were Catholic Action groups in our parish almost before the name was invented. One of our priests, John Hayes, was among the early "labor priests." So the parish was, I suppose, more aware of the social action dimension of Catholicism than were most. We were part of immigrant Catholicism, surely, but we were not belligerent or militant. We were mostly Irish—with some Italians and Germans—but our Irishness, like our Catholicism, was unselfconscious. (One of my friends insists that I only became Irish in 1965 when I discovered that you had to be something at the University of Chicago.) We knew nothing of Irish history or Irish culture, and we were quite unaware that our grandparents must have spoken Irish as their first language. To be Irish was like being Catholic. What else was there to be?

We had our policemen and our firemen, our precinct captains and our undertakers, our clerks and our small businessmen, our handful of managers (like my father), and professionals. You didn't automatically go to college when you graduated from high school, especially if you were a girl. Perhaps half the boys in my class and only three or four of the girls went on to college. (A decade later, of course, this would be completely changed, at least for the Irish.) The Great Depression ground to a halt, World War II ended in victory, but still we were cautiously conservative about our personal lives. We were used to hard times and used to a timeless Church. The changes in our economic and social environment that were to begin in 1947 (the year I went to the major seminary) and in the Church a decade later with the Vatican Council were beyond our wildest imaginings.

For most of us there was no need to imagine those things. Despite the hard times the environment of the neighborhood was pleasant enough. Everyone knew everyone else, we all understood the tremendous importance of loyalty to one's friends, standing by your "own kind." There were a few well to do among us, and they were respected but not envied, I think. Whatever had been our heady ambitions during the 1920s, they were gone by 1945. Enough that we had made it into the middle class. No one expected much else, and what in the world was a Ph.D. anyway?

The neighborhood was the decisive experience for American Catholicism, I believe, and perhaps it was the most unique creation of the American Church. Since we all grew up in neighborhoods we take them for granted. Some of us, like me, remember them benignly; others are still angry at their oppressiveness; and still others are profoundly ambivalent. In fact, though, the neighborhood was and is something unique and special, an experiment in community in the midst of modern urban society which when properly reflected upon and understood may be able to make a considerable contribution to the humanizing of city life. My neighborhood was not nearly so intense as the one in which I first worked, but it had everything from the haunted house, the cranks, the crabs, the characters, the baffling (and ofttimes baffled) Protestant ministers, the hangers-out at the drugstore corners, the school yards, the precinct captain, to the all-powerful parish priests.[1]

In retrospect, I was surely on the margins of the neighborhood. My decision to go to the seminary, my intellectual interests, my parents' reluctance to get involved in neighborhood social life, my tendency even then to imitate my father's leprechaun flair set me apart somewhat from my peers. (It is a bad thing to know more than your teachers; it is a worse thing to let them and your fellow students know it.) But the point about the neighborhood was that it had great broad margins. There was room in it for lots of different kinds of people, including future clerics who knew too much for their own good. I miss the old neighborhood, I miss St. Angela's. I have been back to Twin Lakes only once since 1945; I do not think I could bear to go back again. But I occasionally drive through St. Angela parish, always with a lump in my throat and a tear in my eye. It was a good place to grow up, and I miss it. The people who built it and the people who were part of it responded to the challenge of their times with ingenuity and courage and faith. I cannot abide those who write them off as benighted relics of the past. We should do as well with our challenges as they did with theirs.

One cannot go home again, perhaps, though in a way I feel that I have never left St. Angela's because I have brought so much of it with me. But while one cannot recreate the past and should not try to, one can be open to the possibility that our predecessors were not howling savages. They knew some things about what Christianity could mean in the modern world that we may have missed. I am and always will be a neighborhood person even if I never live in a neighborhood again. I am not alienated from my St. Angela's of the 1930s. I am not ashamed of it; it was a good place.[2]

Seminary

Basketball on Thursdays by the garage behind my house, long winter rides on the Chicago Avenue streetcar (the red rocket), the smelly cracker-box gym, the great gray Gothic chapel with the stained-glass windows, Cicero, Xenophon, fights with civilian-defense fire extinguishers in the corridor, Tom Grady trying unsuccessfully to be a stern disciplinarian and succeeding at being a great English teacher; Georgian buildings spread across a northern Illinois countryside, red brick, greenery, blue lake and sky; writing letters and darning socks in Scripture class, two precious hours of visiting on Sunday, making cocoa in the room between classes, walking around the lake discussing philosophy; John Courtnay Murray telling us the World Series score in the middle of a retreat;

Time magazine smuggled up and down the corridors, the imaginary click of high heels on the concrete walks, incessant sermons about obedience, the fierce clang of the bell at 5:25 in the morning. And finally, ordination day, the coldest May 5 in history. (Ed Roche: "Did anyone say it would be cold day in hell when you guys would be ordained?")

In retrospect it was a hell of a way to train young men to be priests in the city of Chicago. The trouble was no one knew what lay ahead. The seminary was rigid and timeless. It did not change; it did not have to because the Church would not change. The rules were strict; life was regimented. There was a time for everything and everything had its time and place. You memorized answers and turned in essays, listened to the lectures in Latin, got two weeks at home in the middle of the year, plus the summertime, and did not have to make many decisions (once you made the one to be a priest), and the seminary life had to be endured—seemingly forever—as a necessary precondition.

There was little intellectual stimulation or challenge. Indeed, one was warned of the dangers of pride and exhorted to practice conformity and obedience. Maturity, as we would define it today, was thought to be counterproductive. One learned to do what one was told. The spiritual life was geared to produce men who would be docile assistant pastors for most of their lives. It might have worked reasonably well were it not for the Vatican Council. For so many priests who went through that seminary system the answers they had memorized were no longer adequate, the rules they had kept no longer meant anything, the conformity that had been imposed on them was collapsing all around. The external structures of the Church as an organization and the intellectual structures of apologetic Catholicism collapsed almost overnight, and we had the choice of either growing up or of getting out. A lot got out. A few lucky ones like me were prepared and found the transition to be relatively easy and even enjoyable, but we were, I think, the minority.

But when all this is said, I must still insist that I was happy in the seminary years. I did not find it difficult to make my peace with the system. If you did what you were told, it left

you alone. Nobody really bothered much about what you
thought or what you read. There were good friends and good
times and one did not have to make the kind of decisions about
education, career, marriage, military service that one's contemporaries were making. It was an ivory tower but one with a
magnificent gymnasium, swimming pool, private bath in each
room, and a vast library full of books. It was no place for
growing up, and you were turned into the world still very much
an adolescent, but then that is apparently what most of the pastors in the archdiocese wanted in those days.

There seemed to be no particular point in fighting it, and
as long as you left it alone, you had all the time you needed to
read and write and think. It was in Quigley, the minor seminary, that I first discovered the world of ideas. Theodore
Maynard's *The Story of American Catholicism*, given to me as
a prize at the end of my freshman year, opened up to me the
world of history and of the incredible heritage of American Catholicism. Conrad, Dickens, Thackeray, Scott, Wilkie Collins,
Willa Cather, Churchill, Hawthorne, Melville, Sinclair Lewis,
Chesterton (still my favorite), Newman, Belloc, Dawson—
these occupied most of my time when I was not at school, or
not sleeping, or not playing basketball (badly, alas).

During the years in the preparatory seminary I became interested in politics and social problems. My political orienta-
tions were liberal Democratic by inheritance, and there was
nothing in my adolescent reflection on the subject to cause me
to change my convictions. A reading of the social encyclicals
when I was about fourteen persuaded me that the social reforms of the New Deal were in harmony with the Catholic
social tradition. At the same time the columns of the young
George Higgins began to appear in the Catholic press. These
articles had a great impact on me because Higgins' pragmatic
liberalism seemed to resonate with so much of my own. His
columns helped me to articulate my developing social convictions. George would later become a good friend and start me
on my own column-writing career. He did so with the full
awareness, I am sure, that I could easily emerge as a rival for
the limited space in the Catholic press. I have often wondered
whether if the positions had been reversed, I would have been

equally generous. (Of course, some Catholic papers have the good taste to publish both of us.)

At St. Mary of the Lake, the major seminary at Mundelein, Illinois, I escaped from the dullness and monotony of the philosophy and theology classes[3] by reading social and labor history and economics. I discovered more or less by chance the theological ferment in Europe after the Second World War. I could read French moderately well and plowed through Congar, de Lubac, the younger Daniélou, and then I turned back to their predecessors Pierre Rousselot, Ambrose Gardeil, Maurice Blondel, and, curiously enough, John Henry Newman, who may yet be recognized as the most important theological influence of the Second Vatican Council.[4]

At the same time, through the intervention of a friend and former fellow seminarian John Crean, I made contact during the summer vacations with the extraordinary Catholic groups that flourished in the University of Chicago environment between the Second World War and the Korean war. They were veterans mostly, making it into the big-time academy on the strength of the GI Bill. Self-conscious intellectually because of their university experience and self-conscious religiously because of the YCS ferment on the Catholic undergraduate campuses of that time, these young men (and some young women) represented perhaps the most exciting Catholic presence that the University of Chicago was ever to know. Talking to them made it clear to me that the European theology was by no means irrelevant to the American situation. I remember standing on an "L" platform one night going home from Hyde Park and suddenly becoming aware that this was the first generation of Catholic intellectuals the United States had ever seen. There had been intellectuals before but never in such large numbers and never as committed to the Church as these people were. I remember saying to myself that the Church would never be the same again. (I discovered later that the Church was changed in the postwar years not merely by its first generation intelligentsia but also by the first generation of very successful upper middle-class professionals. Still, things changed even more rapidly than I thought.)

Sadly, most of those people dropped from sight. They

teach in colleges and universities around the country. They do not publish. One rarely hears of them. Somehow or other, the spark of the late 1940s went out.

By 1954, at ordination, I realized in a way that most of my classmates did not that we were going out into a world very different from the one we had left seven years before. It was not merely that television had appeared in the intervening years. There were new ideas sweeping the Church from the European universities and there were new people in the American Church filled with these ideas. In addition, while Monsignor Hillenbrand and his faculty had been removed from the seminary before my arrival, the Catholic Action movements that they had launched in the United States—Cana, Christian Family Movement, Young Christian Students, and comparable groups like Friendship House and the Catholic Labor Alliance —were appealing to a new generation of well-educated lay professionals who, while they may not have been University of Chicago type intellectuals, were still not like the people I knew at St. Angela.

So I knew the times were changing. We were not going to be just parish priests protecting the faith of the working-class imigrants in the comfortable parish enclaves like St. Angela. French sociologists (notably unencumbered by data, as it turned out) were already buzzing around the United States preaching that the old national parish was breaking up. (They did not add, and they might have, that it would engender a massive drift away from Catholicism.) They did not perceive (nor did I then) that the new neighborhoods that formed would become even more enthusiastically Catholic than the old.

So I was prepared, at least somewhat, for change. But I was not prepared for the two logical conclusions of the forces that I had observed beginning to work—Christ the King parish in Beverly and the Second Vatican Council.[5]

Beverly Hills—The Land of The Golden Gardens

The gardens didn't look golden to me as they did to the Chicago poet Gwendolyn Brooks. For me the principal color was the green of broad, carefully manicured lawns. The trees arching over the curving streets, shrubbery neatly arranged in front of each house—green everywhere, glistening in the warm summer sun as the newly ordained priest (me) set off down the street to take his first parish census (with the pastor's warning in his ears about staying away from drink). Georgian, Dutch colonial, early American, and an occasional imitation Frank Lloyd Wright home—comfortable, spacious, sometimes elegant; swarming activity on the basketball and volley-ball courts; unending streams of teen-agers pouring into the Hi Club as the Melody Knights beat out into the night what must have been primordial rock and roll; YCS meetings in the rectory basement, CFN groups gathered around the coffee table; the great white brick modern church; picnics at Potawatamee Park or in the Warren Dunes in Michigan; sophomores ambling down the street after school, college students pouring in at Christmas time, Gate 14 at the Notre Dame games, the annual Easter and Christmas plebicite when the size of the collection was taken as a sign of the parish's continuing approval of the pastor's work (a sign always doubted but always given), a blanket of snow turning the golden gardens white.

Without any doubt, the ten years I spent at Christ the King parish in the Beverly Hills district of Chicago were the most decisive experience in my adult life. I cannot even imagine who I would be or where I would be or what I'd be doing if July of 1954 had not found me riding with more than a little bit of awe down Hamilton Avenue (one of the most lovely streets in the City of Chicago) seeing the almost finished new Christ the King Church, at that time, beyond all doubt, the most modern in the diocese. In my wildest dreams I could not have expected a first assignment quite like the one I got. For many priests, the first assignment is something like a first love— something you get over, but you never quite get out of your system. For me, the impact was much stronger: I will never get over Christ the King. It is still my parish, still my neighborhood, and always will be. Much of this is personal and does not belong in the present sketch. It is sufficient to say merely that the parish's intellectual influence on me, which I propose to describe in this section, was only part of the story.

I knew theoretically that American Catholicism was

changing in 1954, that the immigrant years were receding into the past, but I was totally unprepared to find myself dropped into the middle of what quite obviously was the parish of the future. Beverly, as one priest with an Irish gift for turning a phrase commented, was the upper crust of the Irish middle class. It represented one of the three or four places in the city where the Irish had made it big not merely as individuals but as a group. It was one of the first of the college-educated parishes. In Beverly we were no longer the poor immigrant or the honest "cap and sweater" crowd (as one priest proudly said of his parish), or the hard-working laborers or the responsible clerks, salespeople, and high school teachers. Here were the professionals, the managers, the successful small businessmen, the stock brokers, the lawyers, the judges, the union leaders. Here it was not only possible for all the young people to go to college, it was unthinkable that they should not. Here the Americanization of the Catholic immigrant groups was entering its last phase. The Irish had arrived.

They were, I suppose, new-rich; but very few of them acted like it. While they were conscious of their wealth (or at least their large incomes), they were not ostentatious about it; if anything, they tended to live down instead of living it up.[6]

Contrary to all predictions, Americanization did not mean a decline in religious devotion. On the contrary, almost everybody in Christ the King parish went to church. I used to tell the young people that it was virtually impossible for them not to go to church, so strong were the cultural pressures. Religious loyalty, paradoxically enough, seemed to be more important in Beverly than it was in St. Angela's. Everyone went to Catholic schools, everyone went to Catholic high schools, almost everyone went to Catholic colleges. There were no fallen-aways to reclaim, no bad marriages to validate, no public school children to be instructed, and no alcoholics to be counseled at the rectory.[7] There were few mixed marriages (years would go by without one), everyone went to pre-Cana, almost no convert instruction took place, and there was no serious juvenile delinquency. There seemed little for a parish priest to do but go to wakes and weddings and funerals, count the Sunday collections, and mimeograph the weekly parish bulletin.

My surprise was twofold. Success in America meant higher rather than lower levels of religious devotion, and all the things I had been trained in the seminary to do were irrelevant. Will Herberg's *Protestant-Catholic-Jew* became a book of decisive importance for me (and Will, a lifelong friend). After reading it, I finally saw what was happening. Religion was more important as a means of identity and self-definition in American society once you had made it, because it gave you a base from which you could operate in the socially and culturally heterogeneous world of the manager and the professional. To use a phrase I later learned from Milton Gordon, in Beverly you may have become acculturated but you did not assimilate. You went out into the world of business and the professions and competed as an equal there, but at night you came back to your own community, which provided you with a pretty good idea of who you were and where you stood. I was not sure then and I am not sure now how long this final flowering of immigrant Catholicism might have lasted. My guess then was two, maybe three, generations, but I did not take into account the trauma of the Vatican Council. I would guess now one-and-a-half generations, maybe two.

I had no experience at all of working with adolescents and was wary of the assignment, but the teenagers were the only ones the pastor would trust a young priest with. I was warned by the older folks that the teenagers were "spoiled." Their parents, I was told, were trying to give them everything they (the parents) had lacked, and the result was selfish, inconsiderate, rude, and superficial young people.

This was calumny. They were poised, sophisticated, open, friendly, respectful to the clergy, polite, grateful for anything that was done for them. They were also, for the most part, very smart, very gifted, and, as it turned out, a very disturbed group.

But it took me a long time to realize just how disturbed they were. I quite correctly concluded that these young people were the hope for the future of the Church, that they would be the leaders of the community, the city, the Church, and perhaps the nation. If the Church could learn to minister to them and to those like them who would come along in many other parishes, then the final transition between the last stages of immigrant Catholicism and the first stages of a thoroughly American Catholicism would be covered rather smoothly. If not—well, the American Church would be in for hard times. We didn't have then (and I don't think now either, for that matter) a theory or a practice ("praxis" is the fashionable word today) for dealing with either the adults or the adolescents in Beverly. Everett Hughes, then chairman of the Sociology Department of the University of Chicago, confided to me at a social gathering after I had described my parish to him that what we did there was very important because it might shape the future of the American Church. He was certainly right.

While I was trying to figure out my parish and its people, I began to devour the work of David Riesman, who surely must be rated one of the most influential thinkers of our time. The problems of suburban leisure which concerned him in those days I had only to look out the rectory windows to see confounding the people of my parish. I don't know that either of us has ever figured out quite what the answer to those problems are, and more important things (or seemingly more important) have come down the pike. Later, I came to know David well. Like his Harvard colleague Robert Coles, Reisman is a secular saint, a man of immense personal concern and generosity with an unerring instinct for those who need his support and the invariable grace to offer it.

I began to draft memos for friends on suburban Catholicism and was called upon to give an occasional lecture at a priests' meeting or a summer study-week on the subject.[8] The lectures led to an article or two in Catholic magazines, a request for a book from Philip Sharper at Sheed & Ward, and my first two books, *The Church in the Suburbs* and *Strangers in the House*. Both raised the questions that were troubling me about the opportunities, challenges, and dangers in the new upper middle-class style of American Catholicism. Like most of the other things that have happened to me in my career, the magazine article and the subsequent books were incidental rather than planned. I did not think of myself as a writer and did not set out to be one. If anyone had told me at ordination time that I would write half a hundred books before my twentieth year in the priesthood, I would have thought them crazy.

In my work and in the writing that was coming out of it, I was relying more and more on sociological, psychological, and psychoanalytic writings. Karen Horney, C. Wright Mills, David Riesman, Erich Fromm were some of the people I devoured most eagerly because they seemed to be so pertinent to the work I was doing. I also became once more fascinated by American history and American Catholic history in particular, a subject I thought I had left behind in the minor seminary. If it was American my people were becoming, I had to figure out what that meant.

I also became one of the "Catholic action" clergy of the Archdiocese of Chicago.[9] John Egan and Bill Quinn, in particular, but also Leo Mahon, Walter Imbiorski, Jake Kilgallen, Jerry Weber, John Hayes, and, indirectly, Reynold Hillenbrand all had a profound influence on my thinking at this time. There was a meeting on Sunday evenings in Jake Kilgallen's room at Annunciation rectory from which flowed a steady stream of innovative projects in the diocese. I was the youngest member of the group and terribly flattered by the attention and the interest of the others. We had all said at the seminary that the Christian Family Movement was a great idea and it was too bad the pastors of the diocese would resist it. We could not have been more wrong, of course. By the time we were ordained, CFM had become a worldwide phenomenon. At Christ the King it was not necessary to talk the pastor into any organization. Cana, CFM, YCS, YCW—you name it, we had it. We also had bridge tournaments, a bowling league, and a wide variety of other things. The pastor believed (shrewdly) that you gave the people everything they wanted—just so long as the clergy were back in the rectory by eleven o'clock at night.

Those were very heady and exciting times. There were new ideas abroad in the Church. Through the Sunday night group I was tuned into these ideas almost as they were being produced. There were new organizations, new apostolic techniques developing in the parishes, and I was part of that too. It began to look like the challenge and the opportunity of the *"embour-geoisement"* of American Catholicism would be met easily. In retrospect our theories were dangerously shallow and our techniques naive. If we had had another generation, we might have been able to work it out, but that time was not given to us.

To add to my feelings of optimism, I had the vigorous support and confidence of the new cardinal, Albert Meyer. Shortly after his arrival, the cardinal invited me to visit him at the chancery office (discreetly sending word that the invitation was positive, not negative). He told me he had read what I had written, enjoyed it, thought it was excellent, and urged me to continue, assuring me that I had his complete and total support in what I was doing. He left it to me to decide what things he should see before they appeared—"either," as he put it, "because someone might raise trouble about them, or because it is something an archbishop can learn from." He quickly added that there were an awful lot of things archbishops had to learn.

I later found out that when he was preparing to leave Milwaukee, a delegation of older priests called upon him and urged him to "silence" me, expressing grave reservations about whether it was a good thing for a young priest to write—indeed for any priest to write. A witness to the conversation forwarded a characteristic response of Meyer, "I won't do that. It wouldn't be fair. I like what he writes. He should keep on writing." As Clete O'Donnell, Bishop of Madison, remarked to me after Meyer was dead, "He was a genius, he was honest, and he was a saint. Besides that he wasn't very spectacular." We shall not see his like again.

In retrospect I am appalled by my own audacity. John Egan, who may have had occasion many times since then to regret launching me into orbit, asked me to give a lecture to a study group of priests when I was ordained about a year and a half. I can't believe he asked me, and I can't believe I did it. Given the training I had received and the background I came from, I can't believe that I was writing "authoritative" books and articles long before I had completed my fourth year in the priesthood. It would be, I suppose, both the humble and appropriate thing to say that when I reread those books I am impressed with how naive, unsophisticated, and youthful their author was. But I won't say that at all. When I reread my books, my real reaction is that, damn it to hell, I was right!

After ten years at Christ the King, I left the parish a failure. My work with the adults and the young people of the parish had very little impact. Most of the great promise and talent of the teenagers was destroyed as they settled down to an overweight, mildly alcoholic middle-class respectability just like their parents. The personal reasons for this failure are beyond the scope of this sketch. In some ways John Hotchkin, who served with me for the last four years at Christ the King, and I were perhaps a half decade ahead of our time. If we had been in Beverly during and after the Vatican Council, we might have been somewhat more effective. But whatever personal mistakes there were (and there were many) and however unfortunate the timing may have been, the real problems were social and cultural. We had no theological or social science theory, no sophisticated "praxis" for responding to the challenge of urban Catholicism. The Sunday night group thought it had the answers. They didn't even know the questions. Before we had time to phrase them, the Council was upon us. Then, for a variety of reasons, it was too late.[10]

I conclude, therefore, that not merely my own ministry but the whole apostolate of the Church was a failure for the upper middle-class Catholic in the 1950s and 1960s. There were opportunities aplenty; we blew most of them.

What went wrong? We were terribly short of scholars; and those Catholic intellectuals (mostly journalists) who filled the vacuum created by the absence of scholars generally did not know what they were talking about. The American hierarchy went into a nosedive after the Council. It is not generally realized how much the composition of the hierarchy changed between 1964 and 1974. Between the death of Cardinal Meyer and the arrival of Archbishop Jadot, I am hard put to think of a single appointment to a major archepiscopal seat that was responsive to the rapidly changing situation in the American Church.

In the absence of scholars and a challenging hierarchical leadership, much of the burden of ministering to the new Catholics fell on the clergy. If the Council was a tremendous trauma for the clergy, even the liberals of the Sunday night group were rocked by its impact, however much they supported the changes intellectually. The Sunday night group collapsed. With a few exceptions its members seemed to enter a long period of personal deterioration. And they were the green wood. The American clergy turned in upon itself, became concerned with its own problems, its own identity, its own faith. The religious women, I fear, did much the same thing. Fads and fashions swept across the land. The college-educated parishes multiplied and we tried to serve them with a pastiche made up of the old and the new, with novenas and CFM, benediction and Pentecostal groups. But there was no time to think, no time to reflect, no time to really catch our breath and find out what was going on.

Finally, the people themselves were religiously cautious. They liked the new Church and found CFM much more satisfactory than the Legion of Mary. The trouble with the small "formation" groups was that you could be in them only so long, and then you would begin to understand what Christianity was really all about. You might perceive that it was a challenge to a life of excitement, of trust, openness, risk-taking and joy. Quite properly, the people were scared by that. People have been scared of that from the beginning. When the clergy seemed to lose their nerve, the laity breathed a sigh of relief, I think.

The young people, the ones I called so long ago "the new breed," were both more attracted and more tempted than their parents by the possibilities of the Christian life that were coming clearly into the open as the old forms of immigrant Catholicism began to dissolve. But the parent figure, external or internalized, was too much for most of them. The risks were too great. They were perfectly willing to be Catholic, but they didn't want to make a "big thing" of it.

So we lost. Indeed we lost far more than we had to. Eventually we will have to rediscover that which we needlessly threw away and frivolously let slip through our fingers. The Catholicism of Beverly Hills was limited (as are all cultural forms of Catholicism), but it was still damn good and capable of becoming much better. There was something there to build on, but we who were supposed to be the builders didn't know how to do it.

Jack Egan kept insisting about the need for competence, and a need for professional social science to provide the competence for both theory development and for practical application. So at Cardinal Meyer's word I went off to the University of Chicago to acquire that competence. By the time I had it, Meyer was dead, the Sunday night group was exhausted, and changes were upon us, and the kind of competence I had acquired no one, archbishop or clergy, was much interested in any more.

The Beverly Irish aren't much until you consider the alternative. Then they look very good indeed. A lot of them don't like me—partly that is their fault, partly mine, partly the fault of the pastor who felt it was best to minimize contact between his curates and adults in the parish. They thought, quite correctly, that I wrote my books about them. They also thought, quite incorrectly, that I wrote my books against them. The people of Beverly didn't read my books and they still don't. I am amused when occasionally someone will comment a propos of my column in the *Chicago Tribune* that I have changed a lot in twenty years. What they mean, of course, is the stereotype of what they thought I had written twenty years ago doesn't fit what stares out at them from the pages of the *Tribune*. So be it. As Peter Rossi used to say, "There are lots of ironies in the fire."

But, damn it, they are still my people; and if it was not for the vindictiveness of the present archbishop, I would be back working among them. Like I say, they may not be much, but I don't know anyone as good.

The University

No images here. How can anyone get poetic about the University of Chicago?

Nineteen sixty was a good time to show up at the University of Chicago. John XXIII was sitting on the banks of the Tiber and John Kennedy was running for the presidency of the

United States. To have a Catholic priest as a graduate student was a progressive, enlightened thing to do. ("Hell," said Peter Rossi, in an expansive mood, "we're so enlightened around here that we have a Catholic priest and a card-carrying Communist on the staff at the same time."[11] I asked Rossi later why many of those who had been so happy to have me as a graduate student became bitter enemies when the question of my being on the faculty arose. "That's easy," he replied. "In 1960 they thought you were going to convert. By 1964 they knew better."[12] It was an exciting time. Graduate studies turned out to be challenging, stimulating, and not all that difficult. So it was the university by day and Christ the King by night. Those were, I think, the best years of my life. If Hotchkin and I had not finally been swept out of Christ the King in 1964, I would have been happy to stay forever. Come to think of it, "forever" might well have been for only a couple of years, because trying to balance two fulltime jobs might have finished me off for good.

There were two great myths about the University of Chicago in the Catholic community. One saw it as a vehemently left-wing, radical, anti-Catholic institution. (Moscow Tech, we used to call it.) The other myth was of the Catholic liberal who saw the University as the quintessence of enlightened, liberal, dispassionate, impartial scholarship carried on by secular saints who were only interested in the careful and rigorous search for the truth. Both, as I learned rather early in the game, were false. The University of Chicago is probably one of the most conservative institutions in the country. Its best units —law, business, medicine, economics—are probably the most conservative of all. There were no assaults on Catholic faith. Being Catholic was no worse than being homosexual. It was something you wanted to do, and the University figured it was your business. There were and are genteel anti-Catholics in key positions at the University, but most of them do not even realize it. The University also is as much a victim of ineptitude, bureaucratic ambition, petty feuding, factionalism, and fakery as any other large corporate institution. It was disillusioning at first to find out that the University of Chicago was no more effectively run than the Church, but then it was also reassuring. I don't know what it is that makes Catholics feel they have a monopoly on organizational incompetence and stupidity.

So the University was neither a challenge to face nor a model of enlightened liberalism. It was, I guess, all a university should ever try to be: a place where some very able scholars plied their craft and passed on the arts and skills of their trade to a younger generation. Anyone who goes to the University of Chicago or any university to find greater morality or more profound vision or more intelligent human relations is kidding himself. Anyone who expects the university to preside over the reformation of human society may well be a dangerous madman. The university is for scholarship, and while not everyone there who pretends to be a scholar really is, there are enough scholars around a great university that if you really want to learn their skills, you can.

I am not sure that I am a scholar. I do scholarly things and publish scholarly articles (in the last ten years, more than any other sociologist in the department at the University of Chicago); but the life of a pure scholar is not for me. If to be a scholar you do nothing but scholarship, then I am not a scholar and have no desire to be one. But at least I went to the place where I could learn a lot of scholarly skills.

Most of the skills I acquired were absorbed at the National Opinion Research Center, an institution as much on the margins of the University as I was finding myself to be on the margins of the Church.[13] In the spring of 1961, I was looking for a set of data on which to do my doctoral dissertation. I had heard that Jim Davis—the best teacher I ever had—was doing a study of college graduates and their career plans. I wandered over to NORC to see whether he could use someone to analyze the influence of religion on career plans. I never left.

The NORC base was providential after Cardinal Meyer died. In addition to providing me with a base, it trained me in the logic of empirical research and in the skills and methods of national survey analysis. It was superb training—perhaps the best anyone could get anywhere in the world. You can learn, I think, such skills only by actually using them, first as an apprentice, then as a junior researcher, and then as a senior researcher learning the new skills the junior people are acquiring as the discipline develops. I had always been a pragmatic and empirical person. Perhaps that was the reason why I was attracted to NORC. The persistence and systematic search for evidence which is at the core of any scholarly training, particularly social scientific training, is a superb discipline. Too many of my colleagues in the priesthood wasted extraordinary talents precisely because they did not have the opportunity to learn the methods and the discipline of serious, systematic thought. Talent, insight, even genius will wither ultimately if it does not channel itself through the acquisition of disciplined method. Method isn't enough; it cannot teach you insight, give you flair, or enable you to produce with elegance; but without method those intuitive qualities can lead you away from truth rather than toward it.

What little respect I had left for the so-called Catholic intellectuals (of the *Commonweal* variety) went down the drain when they reacted with hostility to my doctoral dissertation. Catholics, it turned out, were going to graduate schools and were seeking academic careers. This ran so heavily against the conventional wisdom of the day that the *Commonweal* crowd decided that I was either an optimist or a conservative who was quite possibly angling to be a bishop. It was impossible to disagree with their conventional wisdom and be in good faith. It was also impossible to have empirical data that countervened their wisdom.

My dissertation had begun as an attempt to find out why Catholics weren't going to graduate school and were not choosing academic careers. As Bill McManus, then superintendent of schools in the Archdiocese of Chicago and now an auxiliary bishop, said to me when I asked what sort of helpful information I might get for the Church in my dissertation, "For the love of God find out why our kids aren't going to graduate school." The first run done on the data by religion turned up on my desk one morning with a notation in Jim Davis' neat handwriting: "Looks like Notre Dame beat Southern Methodist this year." Catholics were more likely to go to graduate school than Protestants. Eighteen hypotheses collapsed, so did a lot of conventional wisdom, and so, too, alas, did my image

with the self-proclaimed liberals of the Church. I learned a lot
that morning: Don't believe anything until you've got the data.

NORC is an unusual place. In the fourteen years I have
been there, there has never been a single factional feud among
the senior staff. When an occasional ill feeling erupts between
individuals, the whole staff rallies around to dampen it down.
This is not a matter of virtue on our parts, I think; it is rather a
functional necessity. We have no subsidy; we live by our wits.
We need each other's help. No individual person can possibly
have all the skills required to carry off large-scale survey research. We cooperate because we have to. Furthermore, we
deal our students in early as partners in the research enterprise
because we need their insight and their skills to carry off what
we're about. During the Cambodia Kent State demonstrations
at the University of Chicago, I walked into a room full of graduate students. "When are you guys going to close this place
down," I inquired, knowing full well that they wouldn't, because while the faculty would get salaries and students would
get grades, the research assistants wouldn't get anything. They
were all surprised by my challenge. One young woman commented, "Why should we close this place down? This is a nice
place." Another said, "We passed the word to SDS to leave
NORC alone. They better had, or they'll be in trouble with
us."

Before the educational reform movement of the late 1960s,
I was deeply involved in the attempt to combine liberal and de-
velopmental approaches to higher education.[14] It always
seemed to me that NORC, based on a colleagueship and ap-
prenticeship relationships, without subsidy, with contract dead-
lines to meet, with no time to be wasted on endless committee
meetings and departmental politics, was much more like what
a real university should be than most universities are. Small
wonder, then, we are on the margins of the University of Chicago.

At the end of my graduate training, Rossi asked me one
day what I had thought about the whole experience. I responded that it had been fun, that I had learned enough and was glad
I had come. "But what about your religion?" he asked. "Have
you had any religious problems since you have been here?" The

question stopped me. "Well, no," I admitted. "I guess I forgot that I was supposed to." For reasons that to this day escape me, Pete looked pleased. "I didn't think you would."[15]

Graduate education is designed to be an alienating process. In order that one might think for oneself, one must be torn away from the narrow, rigid perspectives of one's family background (unless one happens to be the child of a university scholar). To think means to be critical, and to be critical means to be critical of where one has come from. The university is designed to make it impossible for you to ever go home again. Only the deracinated, graduate school assumes, can think for themselves. Furthermore, those who are attracted to graduate school are probably alienation prone in many cases. They want to become deracinated so they have a pretext for not going home. To put the matter somewhat differently—and more cynically perhaps—you have to be desocialized from an old lifestyle and world-view in order that you might be resocialized into the ways of a practicing academic. Arts and sciences graduate school is no different than medical school or the religious novitiate. It is designed to make you over, not just to teach you certain ways of thinking but also certain things to think and certain ways to live.

Fortunately, no one told me this and I wasn't perceptive enough to catch on; so I was never alienated from anything by graduate school, had no problems with the faith, and received my Ph.D. from President George Wells Beadle totally unsocialized to the ways of a practicing academic. I didn't know what tenure was and cared less.

I was older than most graduate students. I had made my lifetime religious commitment long ago, continued to work full time in the very unacademic environment of Beverly Hills, and assumed I would end up in some kind of archdiocesan planning office. Why bother to learn the protocol of the academy, or to think, act, and talk like an academic when I wasn't going to need any of these things? Why experience alienation and resocialization when my stay in the university world was going to be such a brief one? By the time I discovered it would be a bit longer, it was too late to learn and I had already been typed as one of the rare failures of the socialization process. It didn't bother anyone at NORC, but it sure as hell bothered a lot of other people.

There were, however, two growth-producing experiences in the early years of my university stay. First of all, I discovered I could make it in the big world outside the Church on my own abilities. Most priests are never sure of this. They make it, if they make it at all, in the world of the Church largely because of built-in respect for the office. They don't really know what the extent of their skills and talents is because they never appear to be tested in the "real" world. I'm not sure that the world of graduate school is any more "real" than that of the Church, but at least it is defined as real by most people. If you can cope with the University of Chicago graduate school, you can cope with pretty much anything. I not only learned new skills, but I tested my abilities in an environment where results counted; I came away with considerably more self-confidence than I would ever have acquired as an assistant pastor in a church.

More important, I was able to think through my religious commitment in an environment where most people did not have the same commitment. Many Catholics of my era were profoundly shocked to discover the phenomenon of the "good pagan," a person with no religious faith who still leads a generous, sensitive, moral human life. The good pagans never bothered me much because I never had figured the Church had a monopoly on good human beings; but in an atmosphere shared mostly by good pagans, I had to think through much more explicitly than I would in a Catholic community the reasons behind my own religious position. I had to articulate more explicitly to myself what that position was. It was not a matter of doubt; I did not doubt, and never have, the graciousness of the Ultimate Reality, the love of God for each of us, the purposefulness of human existence, and the ultimate triumph of good over evil, life over death, love over hate, comedy over tragedy. But graduate school and my early years on the NORC staff provided an environment where these things had to become quite explicit not so much to answer questions of others (most of my colleagues were and are afraid to discuss religion —perhaps for fear that they would then have to think about ultimate things) but to answer my own. I was lucky; I was able to do it rather gradually before the Vatican Council forced many of my friends and colleagues in the priesthood to do it very abruptly and very traumatically. Reading the French theologians in the seminary and thinking through religious issues in graduate school gave me an almost unfair advance preparation for the post-Conciliar traumas.

My early efforts at NORC were in the area of the sociology of education because, as Rossi pointed out, "That's where the funds are." The parochial school study that he and I did in 1963 (which Bill McCready, Kathy McCourt, Shirley Saldanha and I are presently redoing) was the first national sample study of American Catholics. Its data are still being analyzed a decade later. The reaction to this study made it crystal clear to me that the skills I had acquired were not going to be of much use to the Church. The defenders of Catholic schools attacked the study on the grounds that it proved Catholic schools were not successful; the opponents of Catholic schools attacked the study on the grounds that it was a whitewash of the Catholic schools. Some people managed to attack it on both grounds. Professionally, *The Education of Catholic Americans* was a success. The hardback edition sold out, as did the paperback edition eventually. It was favorably reviewed in most professional journals and attacked in most Catholic papers. It still gets footnoted, and Pat Moynihan maintains it was the first in a long series of studies that produced similar findings about the effectiveness of education. I have the uncomfortable feeling that the replication of the study will receive a very similar reception.

I became a sociologist to serve the Church, but it became apparent that I had acquired the skills mostly in vain. The choice was clear: I could go on being a sociologist and become more and more excluded from the Church, or I could give up sociology and come in out of the cold. I said to hell with them.

In the meantime, however, two more fundamental sociological interests began to emerge. It didn't take me long to discover that what passed for sociology of religion was mostly the blindest kind of empiricism, which NORC had left behind at least ten years previously. Books like *Religion and Anti-Semi-*

tism by Charles Y. Glock and Rodney Stark were being hailed as great works in the field. They would not have won approval at NORC as a doctoral dissertation. Sociology of religion was not only a stepchild of the sociological discipline, it was an inept one. Yet Clifford Geertz's[16] notion of religion as a "culture system," which I had learned first from him personally when he taught in the anthropology department of the University of Chicago and later in his writings, especially *Islam Observed*, opened a whole new perspective in the social science approach to religion. Furthermore, Geertz's clear and elegant prose finally enabled me to understand Weber, Durkheim, Parsons, and the other greats of the sociological tradition. Reading other theorists like Peter Berger and Thomas Luckmann set me thinking along very different lines about both religion and the sociology of religion. From the Geertzian perspective I moved in two different directions. With Bill McCready I am attempting to develop operational measures of a person's ultimate values. If religion is a person's ultimate world view, his answer to the most basic questions a human can ask about life and death, then we should be able to find out what that world view is and how it influences the rest of his behavior. This is much more important than knowing what he thinks about doctrinal propositions or what denomination he is affiliated with, or how often he goes to Church.

Secondly, if one agrees with Geertz, as I do, that religion is a set of symbols that purport to give a unique explanation of reality, then the best way to approach the study of any religion is to find out what its symbols are and what they purport to say about reality. This insight enabled me to move ahead toward what was now developing into a clear statement of what I had vaguely begun in the early years of Christ the King: an attempt to synthesize theology and the social sciences into a new style of religious reflection, a new method of theological thought.

At the same time, I had become aware that ethnicity was a variable American sociologists had ignored for twenty years. I have not mentioned ethnicity before in this essay precisely because it was only at the University and at NORC in the middle 1960s that I became explicitly conscious of it as a variable in social research. You grow up in Chicago, you attend a multi-ethnic seminary, you work in a Chicago neighborhood, and you take ethnicity for granted. It is as obvious as the Illinois Central, the Prudential Building, or Michigan Avenue. The various ethnic groups have different styles and ways of doing things, different family structures. If you don't notice that, you're blind. But then when you arrive at the social sciences you discover they don't even ask questions about ethnicity in the survey questionnaires anymore. Pat Moynihan and Nathan Glazer write a book about ethnicity that sells over a half-million copies and they still don't ask questions about ethnicity in national surveys. Something is wrong.

Why ethnic questions were excluded and why the study of ethnicity was considered to be a dubious and suspicious enterprise are questions beyond the scope of this paper. Rossi and I pushed this through the middle 1960s, and finally in the early 1970s, the Ford Foundation took the lead in funding research and action in the ethnic area.[17] Our Center for the Study of American Pluralism was established within NORC. I do not know whether my recent book, *Ethnicity in the United States: A Preliminary Reconnaissance*, or our journal, *Ethnicity*, will legitimate this interest in the sociological discipline, but I do know that ethnicity is now just about the hottest area of research for graduate students in a number of fields. A lot of people are trying to discover their own identities.

In the study of ethnicity, three men have been particularly important in the shaping of my thinking. Arthur Mann, professor of history at the University of Chicago, has made it clear to me that ethnic diversity and pluralism has been part of the American way from the beginning. Indeed, it was the ethnic and religious pluralism in the country that generated its political pluralism. The 10th and 51st Federalist Papers of James Madison established America's pluralistic coalition politics not by inventing them but by articulating what was already going on. Such coalition politics are an affront to the political amateurs who periodically try to remake our system along neat, elegant, issue-oriented lines. I knew intuitively that these people were wrong from having grown up in the precincts of Chicago. The writing of James Wilson, Martin Meyerson, and, in his earlier manifestations, Edward Banfield confirmed this intuition of mine. But Mann's ideas and insights, as well as Gordon Wood's book, *Creation of the American Republic*, convinced me that ethnicity (which we define as nationality, regional, linguistic, racial, and religious diversity) has been important in this country from the beginning. To study ethnicity is to come to grips with the genius of American pluralism and to understand (and promote understanding) not only the various subgroups within the society but the protocols and procedures— largely implicit and even unconscious—by which this variegated, heterogeneous republic of ours manages to prevent itself from being torn apart. In so doing, of course, we also study what is happening to the Catholic ethnic groups in what I used to think of as the final stages of the acculturation process.

Ethnic diversity, it turns out, is not going away, although its operation in American society is becoming more complex and more subtle and hence more difficult to conceptualize and intellectualize. Social science is no more tolerant of people who go down strange back alleys than is the Church, but at least a handful of us who began research in ethnicity can be reasonably content that the next generation of scholars cannot possibly work in universities situated in the heart of great cities like New York, Boston, and Chicago and think that ethnic diversity has vanished in American society.

In addition to Arthur Mann and Peter Rossi (my first mentor at NORC), the other powerful influence on my ethnic thinking is perhaps the most unforgettable man I know. In 1962 (just after I got my degree), Pete dragged me off at the ASA meetings in Washington to a Trotskyite reunion in a room in the Shoreham Hotel. The whole crowd that went to Townshend Harris High School, CCNY, and then Columbia after the war were assembled there—Bell, Glazer, Lipset, etc. There was one face that clearly didn't belong. The face looked at my collar and said, "What are you doing here?" I looked at the face and said, "I might ask the same of you." The then Assistant Secretary and now Ambassador Moynihan and I knew we had each encountered one of our own kind. Pat is not the stage Irishman he sometimes permits the image-makers to portray him as. He is a sensitive, thoughtful, generous, haunted man with an almost incredible amount of integrity (in this respect much like my father). The Irish comedian business is a useful label to stick on if you cannot cope (the word used here advisedly) with his original, disturbing, penetrating, and complex mind. And if you are put off by his Irish wit and flair and elegance with language—which a lot of envious and inferior people seem to be—you will not appreciate a man whom historians of the future will no doubt conclude to be one of the two or three most important Americans of the era.

I never read a thing of Pat's that didn't have a strong intellectual influence on me. When the ethnicity business was uncertain and even risky, he was a tremendous intellectual and personal help.[18]

I went to the University of Chicago for two years and have been there fifteen and at NORC fourteen. My basic intellectual and religious interests have not changed, but the experience at NORC has deepened them, broadened them, developed them, given them, I hope, more rigor and discipline, more method and substance. Looking back on the years, I regret that the seemingly endless personal and organizational crises frequently made me anything but an effective witness to the religious world-view that grew deeper and richer because of what I was learning. Another way of saying the same thing is that I was probably my best at NORC and my best as a priest when my leprechaun strain was most in evidence. In retrospect, I fear that for months and perhaps years at a time, the leprechaun was nowhere to be seen. One more opportunity blown.

Grand Beach

White cabin cruisers moving in stately procession down the shore, swarms of freckled-faced Irish kids, waves pounding on the beach, water-skiers weaving and darting through the speedboat wakes, great dunes of ice in the wintertime, spring struggling to be born in early May, the fondue hat-trick on summer evenings, the blanket of stars late at night, the sun coming up through the trees, the village come alive on a Notre Dame football weekend, Lou Briody with the world's largest glass of sherry, little Nora and the cuckoo clock, big Nora searching for Liam . . .

Cardinal Meyer had intended for me to transfer to a university parish as a favor to make it easier for me to combine the two tasks of parish priest and scholar. But for reasons beyond the scope of this sketch it turned out not to be a favor, and I wrote him to tell him I could do one job but not both. His last official action before he died was to tell Clete O'Donnell to release me from parish work and to assign me full-time to the National Opinion Research Center.[19] O'Donnell told me that I could live wherever I wanted, indeed that it would not be necessary for me to seek a parish residence, though he thought it might be better if I did. I set out to find a place, and with dismay discovered that no one is much interested in a resident who might be counted against you as a resident (and thus make you ineligible for more help) but who couldn't guarantee his presence every weekend. I finally ended up with a single room in a windowless basement. It was the first hint I had (though there would be many more in the years ahead) that there wasn't much room in the Archdiocese of Chicago for someone who didn't fit the neat paradigm of pastor, curate, and resident.

I can work under almost any circumstances in the short run—airport waiting rooms, trains, buses, even standing in line waiting for a customs check; but I discovered the hard way that over the long haul my temperament and personality are such that physically drab and dreary (or dirty) surroundings slowly and subtly depress me. The house at Grand Beach was intended to be a place for thought, reflection, work, and recreation and an alternative to the basement with its glowering water pipes threading their way through the room.[20]

Grand Beach became more and more my "place," the spot where I felt most at home. It is the location for my most serious thought and reflection. Whether it is Twin Lakes reincarnate or not, as my sister suggests, it is a place that I think has a pervasive influence on my work. Anyone who is interested in the atmosphere in which a writer works must, I think, know about Grand Beach if he is to know about me.[21] At Grand Beach, particularly during the summertime when I bury myself in books (neglecting neither my sailing or water-skiing).

My drift toward some kind of synthesis of theology and

social science has continued. From John Hotchkin I learned about Paul Tillich and of the importance of religious experience if one is to understand religious symbols. (The work that McCready and I have done in the sociology of religion on ecstasy was substantially influenced by Hotchkin's suggestions.) John Shea helped me to understand more clearly the meaning of Tillich's method of correlation and how it could be translated into practical catechetics and homiletics. Gregory Baum's brilliant *Man Becoming* convinced me of the possibility of synthesizing social science and religion. Furthermore, it became evident to me that Gregory and I, coming from very different perspectives, were attempting fundamentally the same things. I continued to read Mircea Eliade, whose books had influenced me greatly in my days at Christ the King, and from whom I had had a course when I was in graduate school. If religion was a symbol system, then one had to understand more about the symbols of one's own religion. I devoured everything I could get my hands on of the new Scripture studies. Bultmann, Jeremias, Perrin, Fuller, Noth, Von Rad, Bronkaam, Raymond Brown, Dominic Crossen were all grist for my mill. The Protestant systematic theologians, particularly Knox, Pannenburg, and Langdon Gilkey, also made fascinating reading, and I profited greatly from books by Ramsey, Stenson, and Fawcett on religious language. At graduate school I avidly read Michael Polyani and became convinced by his description of how the scientific process works; the process he described had much more in common with what we were doing at NORC than did the textbook descriptions of scientific method. While social science didn't have any paradigms, Thomas Kuhn's description of the scientific revolution also seemed to fit the way we went about our work. David Tracy's brilliant new book, which I had an opportunity to read in manuscript, enabled me to put all of this together and develop a method of religious reflection that I hope links Eliade's history of religions, Geertz's sociological definition of religion, Tracy's concept of limit-experience, Ramsey's ideas on religious language, and Paul Ricoeur's approach to symbol interpretation. While I was in the process of working this method out, I read Merleau-Ponty and saw that the limit-experiences that we incarnate in religious experiences are essentially a restructuring of our perceptions at those times of acute existential need. Bill McCready and his wife were a substantial help in this process (though perhaps they did not know it), she by expressing religious experience in her poems that resonated with my own groping toward the meaning of Christian symbol, and he through his research attempts to get at ways of measuring the world-view that is communicated and articulated through basic religious symbols.

This method of religious reflection exists in an inchoate way in *The Jesus Myth*, in a more highly developed fashion in *The New Agenda*, and explicitly in *The Mary Myth*. What I tried to do in *The Mary Myth* may not be ultimately successful, and it almost certainly will receive little attention from priests and religious educators who are presently completely uninterested in theology, to say nothing of Mary. However, I am convinced that it is in this multidisciplinary direction that religious reflection must go in the years ahead. I am practically certain that whenever someone does get around to pasting together the bits and pieces of the Catholic theological tradition, the emphasis will be on symbol and experience.

At the same time I have become conscious that there are a number of people in the country who are trying in various disciplines and fields to reinterpret the meaning of being American and Catholic. They are doing so neither defensively nor apologetically but rather because they believe that in the American Catholic experience there are insights and techniques that should be useful to the whole of society. The neighborhood, the trade union, the urban political organization, the parochial school system, as Ralph Whitehead has pointed out to me repeatedly, all contain immensely important material for not only a self-understanding of American Catholics but also for building a better city and a better world in which to live. In addition to Ralph, the people who are in one way or another working in this area and who are shaping my thoughts there are Geno Baroni, Paul Asciola, Pastora San Juan Cafferty, Charles Shanabruch, and my NORC colleague William McCready. This attempt to develop what Whitehead calls "a Catholic ethic" or "a Catholic theory of society" is light years away, of course, from trying to adduce practical solutions from papal encyclicals. It is also light years away from the current dominant fashion in Catholic social science, influenced as it has been by the Berrigan mystique. For most contemporary current Catholic social actionists, the apostolate involved guilt, hatred of America, and the repetition of the most fashionable current liberal or radical clichés. The thought that there might be anything in the neighborhood or the urban political machine that could contribute to the solution of serious social problems seems to these people to be uproariously funny. To some Catholic observers of my generation, it also seems arrogant and reactionary. But I believe that this group is on the right track, and I am encouraged by the fact that John Egan, the greatest pragmatist of them all, resonates so well to what they are doing. In the next five or ten years, Catholic social thought will either go in their direction or simply won't exist anymore. I want to be on their side.

During the Grand Beach years, the critical influences on my thinking, indeed on my life, have come from people who are younger than I. Hotchkin, Shea, Tracy, the McCreadys, Ralph Whitehead, Paul Asciola, Jim Miller, Pastora Cafferty are mostly in their twenties and thirties. I can't figure out why I should be turning to the young thinkers, especially since the youth worship of the romantic liberalism of the last decade nauseates me. However, these are all very bright people, and I do not hold their age against them. It may also be that I have pretty much despaired of my own generation in the Church today. I feel that whatever is to be preserved of American Catholicism will be in the hands of those younger than I, who, unlike me, will probably live to see the promise of their work fulfilled. Always back a winner, my father used to say.

Since the Vatican Council, the Church has been swept by fads—Dutch Catechetics, Spanish spirituality (the cursillo movement), pop psychology, political radicalism (the demonstration type), Pentecostalism, fundamentalism, and now a return to traditional ascetic theology. In all these fashions there has been a desperate searching to recapture the lost certainties of years gone by. The new truths are repeated with the same apodictic enthusiasm with which American Dominicans quoted

Thomas Aquinas in the 1940s and 1950s and American Jesuits quoted Karl Rahner in the early 1960s.[22] I have resolutely argued against all of these fads not because there was not some truth in all of them and much truth in some of them, but because they were almost invariably presented with the simple-minded enthusiasm of those who must desperately find a panacea. I think that faddism will probably continue (Lord knows what comes next) until the actuarial tables take care of the problems of those who received their training and education before the Council.

The future belongs not to those who must have certainties but to those who can live with uncertainty, who can calmly and self-confidently explore the heritage of the past, the problems of the present, and the opportunities of the future without the crutch of rigid and doctrinaire ideology.

There are three principal intellectual concerns that occupy me at the present: ethnicity and pluralism in American society, the Catholic experience in the United States, and the coming together of religion and social science. As I prepared this sketch, it occurred to me that these three themes have occupied me in one way or another for more than thirty years. But my pursuit of these themes has been very unself-conscious. Indeed, I became aware of the continuities only as I worked on this paper. It would be pompous for me to refer to these three interests as "life projects." Others may well lay out systematic plans for the next several decades of their lives (like Jaroslav Pelikan's projected history of Christian thought); I have never done that and probably never will. My own intellectual style, I think, is much more empirical, pragmatic, intuitive. I move from problem to problem as the spirit moves me, "playing it by ear" (a phrase I first heard from Bill Quinn twenty years ago). If a subject or a book or an idea interests me, I pursue it without much thought whether it will fit into what I did last or what I may do next. If a project comes down the pike at NORC that seems intriguing, I get involved in it without much concern about whether it can be integrated into the other things I do. The three principal intellectual concerns that I have discovered only by sitting down to think about the things I am doing can hardly be called "projects." At best, they are, to lift a word from biblical scholars, "trajectories." I have no notion where these trajectories are going, and in fact I would resist the temptation to plot them. I much prefer to continue as I have in the past to do things because I want to and not because of any obligation to some ponderous "life project." Maybe that's because I'm a Catholic and not a Protestant.

Still, even before I began this paper, I did have the feeling that there is a convergence in my three lines of interest and thought. If there is such a convergence, however, it will take place in its own good time. I have no intention of trying to hasten the process by being self-conscious about it.[23]

So I usually laugh out loud when someone asks me what I will be doing in the next five years or even in the next year. The pertinent question might be, what am I going to be doing next week?

Whether this be a good or a bad way to think and live, I do not know. But as I watch the waves break against the wall at Grand Beach, I know it is the way I have lived and the way I propose to continue. I guess it affronts some people, but that's their problem.

Conclusion

"What do you mean you're a failure?" asked a friend of mine recently. "You write in the New York *Times*, both Op-Ed and *Magazine*; you get grants from the Ford Foundation; you traveled to India for the State Department; you are on the board of directors of *Concilium*; you have your own syndicated column; you lecture all over the country; *Time* magazine writes you up. Hell, you're even one of the eleven "most influential" Christian thinkers in the world.[24] You are the most successful American priest of your generation. Don't those things mean anything to you?"

The only thing I can answer to that is that mostly those things don't mean very much to me, for they would only be important if I had set out to do them, or if having done them, I took them very seriously. But I didn't set out to do any of those things, and I have never been able to work up much seriousness about them. They are things I do. They are, as Cardinal Meyer remarked of a Roman appointment of his, *"aliquid"* (something, but not very much). The things that really matter to me, things that are really important, things in which I really invested a good deal of my selfhood have all failed. But they have little to do with intellectual development and don't belong in this paper. Indeed I would have thought it uproariously funny two decades ago if I had been told anyone would want me to write such a sketch, for I never anticipated any theological development at all, much less one that anyone would deem interesting enough to put into a book. John Shea argues that Christians should prepare for death by developing a healthy capacity for surprise. If he's right, then maybe I am preparing well. My life since ordination has been nothing but surprises. The Lord, who is a comedian, and the Holy Spirit, who is a leprechaun, I'm sure have played a monumental joke on me. They haven't given me any of the things I wanted, but they have showered me with all kinds of things I could not have dreamed of.

Like I say, I don't believe in fighting the Holy Spirit, so I'm not complaining. I just say that I'm surprised.

If I can find any pattern at all, it is the same one in which my three intellectual trajectories have developed. My life, as well as my thought, has been empirical, pragmatic, ad hoc. I have thought and lived playing it by ear. When faced with a new opportunity or a new idea or a new project, I have for the most part said, why not? And when it was a question of speaking out or holding my tongue, over the last ten years I have rarely done the latter.

"Surely, Father," a pious clergyman once said to me, "you would say or write some things differently if you had it to do over again. Wouldn't you?" He continued, "On mature reflection I'm sure there's an awful lot you would want to change." My response was a mostly unconscious paraphrase of Frank Skeffington and James Michael Curley: "Not one damn thing!"

NOTES

¹In this case, the incredible "Diggy" Cunningham—major league baseball player, basketball star, school superintendent, Notre Dame superfan, and golf-course wizard. (Even now, fifty years a priest and living in retirement, he still cheers for the Fighting Irish and hits a mean golf ball.) The irrepressible "Diggy" is one of my favorite characters, and if I ever write a novel he will surely be in it, if only to batter permanently the stereotype of a dour authoritarian old Irish monsignor. A monsignor Diggy was, but dour and authoritarian he was not, and old he will never be. My father and he, incidentally, were friends from the "old neighborhood." He was, I think, the only one in the parish who dared call him "Diggy" to his face—much, I might add, to Diggy's delight.

²At Diggy's fiftieth anniversary, one of the speakers denounced explicitly a book of mine (much to Diggy's and my amusement). Ironically, that priest had been one of the heroes of my childhood, a man who encouraged me to write and to seek graduate-school training. There are sadnesses as well as joys in being from the neighborhood, but the description of these can be left to another occasion.

Incidentally, Diggy began his talk by thanking his old friends, "Dick and Sis" (Mayor and Mrs. Daley), for coming to the celebration. "I guess I've got to apologize to everybody," quothe Diggy. "You know, I said the prayer at his first inauguration and we've been stuck with him ever since."

³With the exception of two stimulating theology instructors, Thomas Motherway and Edward Brueggeman. The former demonstrated to me the meaning of real intellectual integrity, and the latter opened up for me the world of French theology.

⁴Yves Congar would later become a colleague on the international journal, *Concilium*. Unfortunately, the barrier of spoken language has made it impossible for me to communicate to him how much his *Jalons* meant in my intellectual development. In truth, I do not think that Père Congar understands Irish sociologists from Chicago.

⁵I left the seminary reluctantly, understanding perhaps how tough it would be to make the transition from that ivory tower to the real world. (I lost twenty pounds my first year of parish work despite the best rectory cook I have ever known), but I also was sorry not to have been asked to stay on to do doctoral work in theology. My reading of the French theologians had persuaded me that theological issues were critical, and I wanted to continue work I had done for my master's paper investigating the psychological and theological nature of faith. It turned out later that Tom Motherway had proposed to his colleagues just such a dissertation but he had been voted down. I'm not going to fight the Holy Spirit. Still, the issue of the changing nature of Catholicism, the relationship between social science and theology were issues that would remain with me for the next two decades.

⁶They were always very eager to learn what a new priest's father did so they could fit him neatly on the social ladder. Class consciousness was muted

but subtly present. It was made delicately clear to the priest, particularly if he was young, that he was welcome into the community because he was a priest, and the fact that his social background was not quite up to theirs was not to be counted against him. When I told them alternately that my father was a stockbroker or corporation executive I was greeted with looks of surprise and disbelief. How could it be that the priest came from their own social class? I don't think they really believed me. In retrospect, I would have been smarter to let them play their game, but even then, as now, I'd be damned if anybody would patronize me.

[7]Alcoholics there were plenty of; indeed, it was a contagious disease in Beverly. But unlike the old neighborhood, the upper middle-class alcoholic steered clear of his (or her—and there were loads of them) clergy.

[8]Ironically, Beverly is not legally a suburb. Technically, it is part of the nineteenth ward of the City of Chicago. Culturally, however, it was part of the post-World War II upper middle-class suburban expansion.

[9]I got along fine with the Catholic Action priests (about whom I wrote a chapter in my book *The Catholic Experience*), and always had a deep fondness for the late Pat Crowley. But I never did manage to make it into close relationship with the "liberal" lay types beyond my parish—mostly because I spent so much time with teenagers and because there was a doctrinaire liberalism required of "*Commonweal* Catholics" even in Chicago. The attempt of such nonideological people like Mike Schiltz and Ed Marciniak to transform the old Catholic Labor Alliance newspaper, *Work*, into an authentically Chicago liberal journal unfortunately came to naught—although Ed and Mike are first-rate thinkers and doers whose importance has never been fully appreciated either nationally or in Chicago.

As a result of not being part of the "liberal" establishment, I found myself drifting into the orbit of the Thomas More Association. Dan Herr, the impressario of this group, was also an outcast from the ranks of Chicago's official liberals because Thomas More was in direct competition with "their" bookstore, St. Benet's. A number of my books emerged from his direct suggestions, and several more came out of dialogue with him. There are few observers of the American Catholic situation who are so acute and perceptive. His frequently acid comments on the "state of things" are almost always right—save when he has the temerity to disagree with me. The impact of the Thomas More operation in general and Dan in particular on the American Church is not adequately estimated, I think, because he has never followed party lines in a Church which in the present state of its development requires rigid adherence to them.

[10]As the Council was beginning, I happened to read Hans Küng's famous *The Council, Reunion and Reform*. Like most American Catholics of the time who paid any attention to it, I did not expect much from the Council. Küng opened my eyes to the possibilities. In retrospect, it is almost as though he wrote the script for what would happen—perhaps to his own surprise. His later books on the Church were a help in clarifying my own

theological thinking. Hans would become a good friend when I went on the board of *Concilium*. I have never been able to understand the animosity against him in Rome and among many of his colleagues. His writings are often controversial—as are those of any good theologian—but his concern for the Church, his strong Catholic faith, and his fundamentally conservative approach to the importance of the Church as institution ought to have made him immune from the vicious and persistent sniping that has plagued him for years. My own hunch is that envy of success and popularity have a lot to do with the persecution of Hans Küng.

[11]A Yugoslavian postdoctoral student who became a good friend of mine. He wasn't much of a Communist.

[12]The year I was informed that the then chairman of the sociology department had referred to me as "He's nothing but a loud-mouthed Irish priest." Rossi said later that he had left out one adjective. "Which one?" I asked. "Smart-assed," was the reply.

[13]John Wilson, the provost of the University of Chicago, informed a number of its staff some time ago that NORC was of no more importance to the University than the American Meat Institute—a comment that reflects how out of touch with social science Mr. Wilson has become.

[14]See the Hazen Foundation Report, *The Student in Higher Education*, which I drafted.

[15]Rossi's description of his own religious situation is characteristic and insightful. "One day I woke up and discovered I was a Catholic. I hadn't changed at all. Without my noticing it, the Church had moved its boundaries out so far that I was inside again. The least they could do is warn you."

[16]The official sociologists of religion still seem unaware of Geertz's existence. A recent collection of his essays, *The Interpretation of Culture*, is garnering all kinds of prizes but was subjected to a patronizing and infantile review in the *Journal for the Scientific Study of Religion*.

[17]I doubt that Ford would ever have got involved in this if they did not have an extraordinary vice-president, Mitchell Sviridoff. He did not graduate from high school (his wife claims he could pick up a diploma now because he has enough courses finally, but he prefers to remain ungraduated); he was a UAW local representative at twenty-five, and he is the most untypical foundation executive I can imagine. Sviridoff has "street feel" instead of a doctorate, and it enables him to know that ethnic diversity is important in American society even when all the Ph.D's were saying it wasn't. There is no reason, of course, why you can't have both street feel and a doctorate, but that would require a major change in the way we train graduate students. I should add, by the way, that MacBundy of the Ford Foundation proved himself a good and loyal friend when things got rough at the University of Chicago. If it hadn't been for the personal and organizational support the Ford Foundation provided, our research enterprise would have been out of business and I would have been walking hat in hand to the chancery office. God forbid!

[18] In my personal memoir of Moynihan which I shall write someday, I shall certainly include his wife Liz, who is as admirable and fascinating a person as her husband. One story: McCready and I were staying overnight at the Moynihan house after an ethnic conference at Harvard. Another well known Boston Irish intellectual type was present. Sensing in McCready a new and young audience, the two master storytellers took us on a guided tour of the Celtic twilight of New York City in the 1930s and 1940s. It got more and more Celtic and more and more twilight as the evening wore on. Finally, when the other Irishman headed none too steadily for his car and the drive through the snows of Boston to home, Liz whispered in my ear, "I don't know whether I believe in such things anymore, but give that man conditional absolution before he goes."

[19] I intended to continue direct pastoral work with an experimental "small group parish." This effort went on in some fashion for six years and then slowly dwindled away (for reasons I discuss indirectly in my book *The Friendship Game*). It was only in 1973 that it finally dawned on me that I was no longer engaged in pastoral work. I promptly sought out a place where I could at least engage in some weekend parish activities, but the archbishop vetoed the plan.

[20] I suppose a word must be said here about money, since many people find the subject of my income of obsessive importance and interest (mostly, I fear, because of a lamentably overblown notion of book royalties). Anyone who grew up in the Great Depression, at least anyone whose family was stricken by it, will adopt one of two possible attitudes toward money. He will either be concerned about it all the time, or he will be rather indifferent to it. I chose the latter long ago. I didn't set out to make a lot of money, and I didn't want to have a lot of it. It was and is a subject that doesn't interest me much (to the dismay of accountants, insurance men, and investment advisors). For two years I refused all salary at NORC, and then Rossi insisted that I accept one because there was no other way my overhead expenses could be charged to clients. I have never sought a raise and repeatedly tried to turn them down. Most recently, I suggested to Jim Davis (the present director of NORC) that he give my increase to someone else. He responded that I had to be budgeted for what it would take to replace me should I leave; so, like it or not, I was going to get the raise. When NORC first began to pay me a salary, I offered to turn it over to Cardinal Meyer. He declined. "It's your stewardship and your responsibility, not mine," he said. I do my best to exercise that stewardship wisely. I am appalled that it makes so much difference to so many priests. In any event, how I exercise my stewardship is a matter between me, the Deity, and the Internal Revenue Service. It is no one else's damn business.

[21] Professor Rodger Van Allen has recently suggested that my self-image as a marginal man is merely an "ego trip." I'm sure he and perhaps others will consider this whole essay an ego trip in principle. I don't have any other word than "marginal" to use, and I must come to grips with that fact that

anyone who does and says and writes the things I do will inevitably be an outsider in the Church today. I guess I also face the fact that I have been an outsider all my life. I don't like that particularly, but I don't think I could pay the price required to come inside. Or, as my colleague Norman Bradburn remarked once, "You don't like being marginal, but you do like doing the things that make someone marginal."

[22]My friend and colleague Rahner would be appalled, I think, to know all the things he is supposed to have written. It just goes to show that even a heavy Teutonic academic style does not make you immune to the ravages of the instant popularizers.

[23]John Kotre, a student of mine, is currently engaged in writing an "intellectual biography" of me (for reasons he can explain because I can't). I am mildly curious to see if my trajectories harmonize with John's. To be the subject of such a work is a harrowing experience, by the way. After John interviewed me for two solid days last summer, I managed to fall off the sea wall and bang myself up—a Freudian would have a picnic with that feat!

[24]Any list that includes Billy Graham and Rosemary Reuther on it is not one I'm so sure I want to be on.

Journey

ANTHONY T. PADOVANO

Kentucky is a long way from New Jersey when you're uncertain as to why you've come. The distance is more than geographical. The railroad track seemed singularly exposed to anyone who might happen to walk across it. One didn't get that close to tracks back home, I thought. At least a protective guardrail or gate should have been provided. But, no matter . . .

The first time I visited the abbey at Gethsemane I was a high-school student and *The Seven Storey Mountain* had recently been published. The contemplative life attracted me as did the conversion experience of Thomas Merton. I couldn't realize then that I had encountered the center of my life rather than the beginning of an uncertain journey. There in a desolate region of Kentucky, farther from the New York area than miles could measure, lived a monk I was never to meet, leading a style of life I longed to follow. Both of us had been shaped by New York City, its culture and dynamism, its raw secularity and its surprising sentimentality, its style and class, its sense of having arrived at wherever it was going and yet its strange way of not knowing this.

New York is a city where words count, where the articulate inherit the earth and the literate people the kingdom of the saved. It is a place for publishers and authors, magazines and media, the *New York Times* and Damon Runyon, the unemotional speechmaking of the United Nations and the excited shouts of Wall Street. Jewish delicatessens with all their chatter are more native to its environment than quiet Oriental restaurants where conversation is kept to a minimum. New York is the town people mean when they speak of "the talk of the town." It is a bizarre location for theology, a seemingly uncongenial environment for conversions. Burning bushes would hardly get a start in the Bowery. They would either be ignored, attributed to an arsonist, or extinguished undramatically by the New York Fire Department. New York takes less kindly to pilgrims than reliable moneymakers; it favors those who arrive at its shores with no further journeys required.

Or so it seems. It is also a city for mystics, not European mystics but American mystics. No monastic cell is more confining than the turnstiles and crowded subways where poverty-stricken contemplatives still manage a vision or two. No one can understand the brand of spirituality New York gives rise to except Americans. There are probably more heroic experiments and heartbreaking ventures that begin in New York than anywhere else in the world. Contemplatives in this city are either on the move or pushed or occasionally mugged. Mugging has a way of keeping mystics real. This is the city of Babylon for those who find its awful accent impossible to decipher and not worth the effort.

But we are now in Kentucky, the season is summer, and there are not enough years in life to help one interpret his present experience. It is a place where things ought to be more sharply defined, where good and evil are less gray, where rural values and less complicated systems of thought allow quicker certitudes. Kentucky is the old home one comes to, a state more like England than most others in America. It is not as easy to begin a conversion there as it is in New York because the extremes are not as painful.

Birmingham, England, is not a city one would easily choose for residence. Like Kentucky, it has less extremes than New York. It has inherited the defects of the Industrial Revolution and the aberrations of large city life in a singularly un-British manner. Birmingham is what many people would expect New York to be. Unlike New York, it is a place one goes to after conversion.

John Henry Newman came here and remained. He was already a convert and one day to become a cardinal. He wrote

English prose as well as anyone ever did. He created theological works to rival Origen or Augustine or Aquinas. Like Thomas Merton, he knew the violence of conversion and the pacifism of faith. He was a man of the city.

Cardinal Newman was once as absurd an impossibility for the young Anglican preacher as Father Louis would be for the New Yorker who considered communism and made erotic sketches. I lived for a while in Birmingham, celebrated the liturgy in the room where Newman wrote and prayed and died. He was the conscience of the twentieth century, living a hundred years too early, as most prophets do. Merton would capture the spirit of the twentieth century better than Newman did, the self-conscious secularity, the need to become a restless hermit, the melding of Oriental and Western mysticism. But there would have been no Merton without Newman. Both of them were drawn into the maelstrom of theological modernism; both created from their radically altered former convictions a subtlety so elusive that some would question the validity of their theology, in the one case, or where this new spirituality was taking them, in the other.

Newman struggled with his conscience in a Catholic environment that made too much of authority. He tried to define an identity for himself and for the new world Marx and Darwin and Freud would create. He knew he could not do this reliably unless he remained a Catholic throughout the process. He fought the English establishment of his day, academic as well as ecclesiastical, questioned the infallibility of the Pope, trusted the indefectibility of the Church, and sought a grammar by which the language of his loyalty and assent might be read properly by those who favored clearer sentences.

Newman was often as unpredictable a theologian as Merton was an unsettled monk. Newman was not a theologian who would perform yeoman service for the *magisterium* anymore than Merton could be counted on to write books about why people ought to become priests or cloistered religious or even devout Catholics. Like the nineteenth century which his life encompassed, Newman lived long enough to die with a sense of having completed an important work. Merton, however, embodied the ambiguity of the twentieth century and died in Asia.

The metaphor of his death was replete with his fascination with an unfamiliar faith, an absurd accident, and the beginnings of a mysticism that would need another century to develop. He too was a hundred years too early with his belief in Buddhism as an adequate way of becoming a Catholic.

No one appeared to be more startled than Angelo Roncalli at the ridiculous idea of his being Pope. The night of his election, they could not find a white cassock to fit his rotundity. Since Leo XIII, popes had managed to be frail and to look somewhat undernourished. I remember standing in the Piazza of St. Peter's that evening disappointed at the prospect that anyone other than Pius XII had a right to be Pope.

John was somehow wrong on every count. He came with intuitions to a Church that had favored rational certitudes since Pius IX. He called a Council that had nothing to define in a Church that had equated councils with definitions, and in an environment that led to three major dogmatic proclamations in a century, more dogma than at any other time since the sixteenth century. As the modern age made the Church more insecure, it responded with clearer statements of infallible papal prerogatives and strict Marian doctrine. Nothing made Roman Catholicism more distinct from the rest of the Christian world and the uncertain twentieth century than its official positions on Mary and its absolute claims for the papacy. John had the wrong age, the wrong figure, the wrong name, and the wrong theology for the papacy. He was as out of place in his station as Merton was in Kentucky and Newman after he left Oxford. Yet John's Council finally made Newman respectable, a safe theological influence. The same Council sent Merton on his journey to the East and made creative religious life a hallmark of the latter quarter of this century.

A soothsayer would have earned his reputation had he predicted the priesthood for Merton, the cardinalate for Newman, the papacy for Roncalli. Even when they exercised these functions they handled them in so unorthodox a manner that one has difficulty considering them churchmen or clerics. They are not easily categorized. Literature and theology both respect Newman. *Development of Doctrine* and *Grammar of Assent* are written for Catholics, although the former precedes Darwin and the latter, Freud, whom Catholics almost universally distrusted. Merton is respected by Buddhists and Christians, by those who seek contemplation and by those who admire his literary criticism and poetry, his pacifism and staunch defense of civil rights in America. Merton's writings fit well in *Cistercian Studies* and *Commonweal*. John is the only pope since the Reformation whom a majority of Protestants might willingly elect, the first pope to talk with communists and send birthday greetings to a soviet premier.

The three men belonged to far more than their own constituencies and would require more than their own century for an adequate evaluation of their lives. One man re-did theology, the other the spiritual life, the third the papacy and the structured Church. In Newman I began to see the possibilities of aligning literature and theology and learned to admire his subtle and creative blending of modern thought and traditional values. Merton was a living symbol of a venturing, questing spirit who helped his readers appreciate the new forms contemplation might assume. From John I learned the power of freedom, the reliability of intuition, and the value of spontaneity in a structured Church.

The three men functioned on the level of charism rather than reason. Newman had no system, Merton no consistent development, John no predecessors. They demythologized their respective vocations. Newman never rejected the substantive *magisterium* but he emphasized conscience as a bold and absolutely necessary counterforce. Merton died while learning from non-Christians how a monk might pray. John, in less than five years, called for a reform of the Church, world economy, his own papal office, and a radical approach to peace on earth. The very richness of their respective lives impoverished them. Newman lost most of his friends; Merton died alone; John's passing was received with a sigh of relief by a number of influential Catholics who felt the Church could not survive another year of his papacy.

Although Kentucky is a long way from New Jersey, New York is a lot closer. I might not have known why I went to

Kentucky, what I hoped to see, but I knew why I was driving into New York. I had an appointment. I had been in Denver a year before and a young editor at Sheed and Ward had listened to my intermittent interventions at a theological convention. It was another of those East-West meetings, but not as dramatic as Merton's since New York, where the East begins in the United States, is not as different from Denver, where the West begins, as Americans might like to think.

There is a romance of the word that editors and writers fall in love with more easily than others. Eastern Americans may be especially susceptible since the New Yorker lives by volubility as much as the cowboy once survived because of his taciturnity. I was being asked to write, to go into print, although, except for a dissertation on Newman, I had published nothing before, not even an article. I was pleased although I was not comfortable with the idea I had anything to say or convinced that a firm I admired as much as Sheed and Ward would consider it.

Frank Sheed and Maisie Ward were institutions in their own right, lay pioneers in a Church that believed that by and large publishing and theology belonged to the clergy. They were rooted in England, transplanted to New York, and lived by *choice*, unbelievable as it may seem, in Jersey City, New Jersey. Woody Allen once commented that God's Being permeates everywhere except certain parts of New Jersey. Frank Sheed and Maisie Ward managed to live in those very places. Together they transformed Catholic publishing in the United States. There was something slightly absurd and premature about them in the sense we have been considering.

What kind of a book did I want to write? Where was theology going now that the Council was complete? The year was 1965; the outcome of this unsettled decade was far from clear. How does one write theology in an age that remembered John XXIII, heard Merton denounce Vietnam, and rediscovered Newman? What shape does the theological enterprise take in a Church no longer terrified of pluralism?

Pluralism makes people concrete. This has been the story of America. The only philosophy the American people have bought is pragmatism. This is because the nation struggled with pluralism, although it never succeeded with it. Success belongs to the homogeneous. The ends never fit right, the lines do not go where they ought when people try to align diversities. There is something perennially messy about pluralism. Success is not the only experience that belongs to the homogeneous. They also own metaphysics. Abstract theology occurs when the Church is settled; it flourishes most easily in an environment where differences are minimized and systems are required. This may explain why metaphysics has been so elusive since the Reformation or the Renaissance or the Industrial Revolution. America does not produce metaphysics easily. It is highly unlikely it will create a core of theologians who will be effective with abstract thinking.

New York is a metaphor for the entire continent we call the United States. As I came through the Holland Tunnel, I realized that this was not a city for philosophers. New York is probably America's way of keeping the culture sufficiently Jewish. More Jews live in New York City than in Tel Aviv. They have engendered a healthy distrust of the Puritan idealism that once almost made this country homogeneous. Jonathan Edwards managed some pretty good metaphysical theology and Edward Taylor wrote a theological epic that was a wilderness attempt to rival Dante or Milton or any one of those poets who needed theology and metaphysics for their verse. But Americans read pragmatic Franklin for their early prose rather than Edwards and secular Walt Whitman as their epic rather than Taylor.

Puritan Boston was even farther from New York than Kentucky, although cartographers would never suspect as much. New York was more like Israel than Plymouth Plantation, and New York spoke to the nation, although the nation resented its awful accent. New York, like America, is more Hebraic than Hellenic. It is better at making things and finding its way than at metaphysics or philosophy. There is something vaguely Jewish about American theology, something distinctively urban (the Jews hated the desert), and unmistakably biblical. The Bible is so pluralistic that it becomes downright contradictory at times. It is the nightmare experience of people who try to interpret it in consistent and coherent categories. This may be why American religion has often revolved around the Bible, howsoever ill-conceived. The Bible is an urban book that dreams of a new Jerusalem, a city to which all may one day repair (not, of course, without becoming properly Jewish or patriotically American as the case may be). It is the only sacred book in world religion that is so radically pluralistic that it includes the writings of two faiths that have tried to have as little as possible to do with each other. It is a book written by the persecuted in both testaments for those who are unsettled in every age. At least the Bible is concrete. Moses tells stories and Jesus, parables. Both lead people to something like New York. Moses takes the Jews out of the desert and Jesus goes to Jerusalem for his resurrection.

Americans are better at existing than at researching it. They speak pragmatically from their experience rather than ideologically from their heads. American theology is best when it is concrete. Perhaps that is why I admired Merton and Newman and John. Newman wrote theology not from a system but when it was necessary. *Development of Dogma* came from his need to settle an issue in his mind for his conversion; *Apologia pro Vita Sua*, from the contemporary climate in England and a critic's attack; *Grammar of Assent*, from a lifelong interest in the process of affirmation to religious truths. Merton's books were occasioned by the mood in America, John's papacy was a nonideological response to the desperate longing for less restrictive barriers as the modern age unfolded.

How could Frank Sheed and Maisie Ward decide to leave England for Jersey City? Why did the Pilgrims leave Europe for Boston? What made John upset a Church that seemed reasonably content and successful? It was like sending the Church into Jersey City. Why would anyone want to do that?

Pluralism makes strange bedfellows of us all. Americans don't think before they act. They act and consider a philosophy to explain it later. Sometimes Europe becomes paralyzed with its own brilliance, hemmed in by the precision of its metaphysical systems and the consistency of its own ideology. But America is pragmatic at its best, opportunistic at its worst. It is Jewish, concrete, Hebraic, urban, pluralistic, superficial to those who favor philosophy, graceless to those who prefer tradition to immediacy.

New barriers. That was what I was thinking as I rode through Greenwich Village to Sheed and Ward. I wished I were back in Kentucky where I could think this out more carefully. But Jersey City or New York, Birmingham and Rome, have never been great places for thinking. Or so it seems. Tolerance is more necessary in the city than in the desert. Maybe that is the direction theology must take.

The Jews had a persistent problem with promiscuity. They never remained as pure about their system as the Greeks did. They frequently ran after strange gods because they became so unsure of their own. He did not seem pragmatic or useful enough at times. He demanded passion rather than certitude and passion is more unreliable. He kept losing wars for the Jews all through the Bible. Whenever people wanted a city to sack in the Bible, they sacked a Jewish city. America had the same problem. It put things together that everyone said did not belong and took apart previously unquestioned unities. The secular and the sacred should have been kept distinct. Religion and State should have been formally joined. A culture that began with a rural ideal should not have allowed New York the influence it achieved. A wilderness settlement should not have sustained a revolution as enduring as the American experiment. We were told that democratic government could not achieve stability and that a secular society would bring about the death of all religious institutions. We were told these things, and without reasoning to a conclusion, we discovered pragmatically that many ideological impossibilities operate quite comfortably.

Newman would have been a better cardinal, Merton a safer monk, John a less controversial Pope if they had functioned more conventionally, less pragmatically, and with a somewhat diminished regard for styles of life not their own.

I looked up and saw Sheed & Ward's offices. I was certain now that theology ought to operate in a concrete, existential, pragmatic framework. Right next to Sheed & Ward, there was a Jewish delicatessen. This had to be a good publisher.

Greek drama concerned itself with the vices our virtues create. Excessive talents have a way of intruding on other lives. Nothing so painfully manifests the limitations of the human condition as the poverty of our own success.

Catholic education in the United States had a way of going too far with its virtues. I thought of this one evening on a long drive back to Darlington Seminary. Seminaries have a way of being far from everything, even when highways and suburban settlements surround them. I had never seen a seminary until the day I entered one, never taught a class until that morning in September of 1962 when I returned to the seminary where I had once been a student to begin a ministry of teaching theology. But Catholic education in its broadest implications was on my mind that day as I wandered through the dark roads that led to Darlington.

Catholic teachers were effective, I thought, and then realized that the "they" was now "we." We were good at teaching people a distrust of secular salvation. The twentieth century has lived painfully with the shattered dreams of its secular hopes. The economic miracle of America has not brought the country peace. The nihilism of our national literature after World War I was filled with the cries of a generation that thought it could build unsinkable ships, make the world safe for democracy, and create a paradise of scientific splendor. Eden isn't built so easily. Towers of Babel keep getting in the way of our fruit trees and improved agricultural methods. Forbidden apples continue to bloom despite our advanced fertilizers.

This century has hurt our pride and bruised our hearts. It has crucified us in polyester dreams and drip-dry visions. I wouldn't want to do without any of it. That was where Catholic education made some of its mistakes, I reasoned. I wondered who would be around to talk to as I got back to the seminary. Nothing is so desperately alone as a seminary building with hundreds of people in it and no one to talk to. Of course it would be midnight before I returned. I couldn't expect an entire institution to remain alert so that someone might watch me finish a sandwich and hear my latest revelations of the state of the world.

Catholic education had a healthy way of creating some unhealthy consequences. America needed a good dose of secular realism. It had to overcome the hopeless effort to make Eden happen here. Nathaniel Hawthorne used to talk of the sadness the Puritans felt when they had to build a cemetery and a jail in their New Jerusalem communities. Catholics in America have built some of the best cemeteries in the world. That's one thing Catholics have been good at—we have helped people see those tombstones they keep overlooking. You know, Darlington has a cemetery on its property. The Puritans would not have liked that.

Catholic education had a healthy distrust of secular kingdoms and projects. Sometimes it was too healthy and tended to keep us out of the mainstream. Our virtues keep making vices we can't eliminate. But no matter. There was a new spirit in the air. The Council had been a success, more brilliant and hopeful, more stunning and significant than anyone could have imagined. One of the things we would have to avoid would be the temptation to make the Council a secular endeavor and to believe that the Church could be reformed by success rather than failure.

It was that night, on my way home, that I thought of writing an article on the theology of failure for a new book I was completing on who Christ is. Seminary education over the next five or six years was destined to live out the mystery of failure in a manner none of us could have predicted then. Our buildings would empty; our definitions of ministry falter; our philosophy of education waver. In fact, Catholic education in this country would be shaken to its foundations. It too would learn the lesson of its own teaching: secular splendor and success is no guarantee of immortality or even bigger buildings, of salvation or even federal aid.

The other thing I realized about Catholic education . . . I stopped for gas. American gas was so much cheaper than the prices I paid in Europe. Gasoline was thirty cents a gallon then. I paid $1.20 a gallon in Rome. The rich get richer and the poor get poorer.

But the other thing I realized about Catholic education was the awe or reverence it communicated. No one really knows what it is to be human until he trembles a bit in wonder. Sometimes they, "we," made them tremble in fear. I even had some teachers whose specialty was trembling; either they were all aflutter themselves or they managed to keep us quaking. America could use a little trembling. Especially now when there is so much despair in its heart—over Vietnam, riots in the city, disruption on the campuses, assassinations. But it has always been that way in America. We were never a settled nation. When people get bleak about the country, I would like to remind them of what it must have been like to live through the Civil War, the assassination of Lincoln, the impeachment of Johnson, the corruption of the Grant administration—all in rapid succession.

The virtue of Catholic education, its capacity for wonder, became at times a vice as the sense of awe was attached to people who held certain offices in the Church. Sometimes we became so happy with the Church we had built that we forgot what it was for. I wonder if I could get that into my lecture to the seminarians tomorrow. We did a lot of good things, beautiful things. We can't forget that. But a sense of awe—how can we get people to feel reverence for themselves, their own worth, the sheer goodness of God, the power this Church still has for love and mercy. Maybe it's hard to realize the Providence of God when gasoline is $1.20 a gallon in poorer countries. We have too much in America. Maybe you can't become filled with wonder until you are poor. That fellow in the Gospel who stuffed his barns with wheat probably never noticed how beautiful wheat can be before it is cut.

Catholic education may have to be cut down in poverty before it releases its enormous potential for wonder and leads us to experience awe not for officers in the Church in particular but for the heart of man as such. It can do this but it may need a little crucifying before it can see the fullness of the empty tomb.

I always liked the Catholic emphasis on personal sacrifice. Sometimes that too got to be a bit much. Calls for personal sacrifice bring out not only the heroes who hate to die but the masochists who revel in punishment and the sadists who are eager to torment a person or two in the name of God. We were not as sharp as we might have been in making these distinctions. But we mustn't forget the heroes we managed and still produce. A lot of good people who loved their comfort laid down their lives for their brothers and sisters.

I realized as I turned onto the Revolutionary War highway which winds past the seminary that secular education was emphasized in America as the only means to enlightenment. I wondered if this were not a new effort at equating education with salvation. The Puritans built Harvard while a wilderness existed around it. Ever since then Americans have spent more money on education than any other nation on earth. We still do. And woe to those who do not receive the sacramental signs of academic degrees. They shall be forever on the left hand of God or commerce and spend their days with goats and other disorderly creatures.

In the next few years, Catholic education would experience the dilemma of its own success. It would see its secular power collapse and question even its capacity for reverence and the value of making personal sacrifices for an uncertain future.

I passed the new college due to open its doors about a mile from the seminary. Its superstructure was strung with lights. It would be a good place, I was told—innovative, interdisciplinary, tutorial centered. A state college and a seminary—secular and sacred, at least by formal definition—civil and ecclesiastical education—indistinguishable at times by right or by default. Education was important—Christ was a teacher—isn't that what "rabbi" means? They, it was "they" now, wanted me to teach literature and religious studies there. Sounded like a great idea—Newman revisited, prose and theology, novels and councils. It would be fascinating to help begin a new college. They didn't even have grass there yet. But they were trying to make something beautiful and important happen. They didn't have a name for the college yet, just an idea and a superstructure. I wonder . . . Theology needs another influence than the formal Church if it wishes to communicate. A priest is someone who ministers to those who require his presence and find hope in his words. Life grows not where we intend for it to flourish; before it's even named, it comes on the scene wherever it has a chance to become itself.

It was dark and quiet at the seminary. A theology of failure never works until you have felt the failure and the poverty in your bones, until you have witnessed the heartsinking end of dreams and visions. There's no getting around the cross if you have any regard for Easter. We have the principles. All we need now is the pain—and the belief that God saves us even when we make the mistake of succeeding all the way.

It was midnight; the combination of darkness and the sense of a mighty body of water on all sides was exhilarating and reflective. That afternoon I had received a phone call.

"Could you come to Pittsburgh this evening?"

"Yes, I think so. I guess it's important that it be immediate."

"It is. There will be five bishops here for a meeting. We are going to write a national pastoral letter and think you might be able to help us."

"I'll be there this evening."

"Call me back when you have arranged for a flight. Someone will meet you at the airport."

It sounded dramatic. Wonder why I was called. I hadn't published enough to be prominent or been around long enough for anyone, including myself, to be sure of the shape of my theology or its priorities.

Now that I think of it, it could have been dangerous to be wandering around a riverbank at midnight in a large American city. For some reason that didn't occur to me then. The Hilton Hotel where I would remain for the next month was close to the meeting point of the three rivers at Pittsburgh. We had worked for hours that evening and I wanted some fresh air and some time to sort things out.

The Allegheny and the Monongahela became the Ohio at Pittsburgh. Pittsburgh was once the beginning of the West, a frontier Fort Duquesne, an Alpha and Omega place one might say, a juncture where endings and beginnings happened so quickly that one could not easily distinguish them.

The lights of the hotel nearby were warm and inviting in the deep darkness of the first hours of a new day. The Council had been concluded but months before and a **post-conciliar** era of immense magnitude and peril had begun. The Council was like a raft, sturdy enough for a journey down the Ohio but not so self-sufficient that it could operate independently of the currents and the winds, not protected enough from the elements to minimize the darkness or the cold dampness. But it was an exhilerating, pilgrim, tentative, probing time. Something that the American Church had lived with for a long, long time was coming to an end, although none of us at the meeting that evening was able to perceive how decisive the end would be and how radically altered the future would become.

It was a good time. And the pastoral letter was begun in hope. There was an eagerness to bring the Council home, to redeem its promise, implement its program, give a record to the future of what it meant to live now, why we had reached this point, how alive we felt at this moment, and what we experienced as we absorbed the shock and promise of a remarkable meeting point of divergent historical opportunities.

The flow of the rivers at Pittsburgh is rapid. Things don't remain fixed very long. The riverbanks are like the railroad track in Kentucky. One gets so close to the water that he begins to feel somewhat hesitant. Beauty and danger trade places with such facility.

There would be another pastoral letter after this one. But the mood would be different. The next letter would be even more liberal and open. It would encourage theological dissent and try to define its legitimacy, criticize the Vietnam war, the arms race, support selective conscientious objection, a volunteer army, and the role of conscience in the structure of moral decisions. Both letters would quote Newman, reflect Merton, and give shape to John's Council. A new era had dawned and we were privileged to see its first light. But it was a time of rising expectations in the American Church. A tide of inflated anticipation would engulf some of the tender hope and fragile willingness of these early attempts. Lines were beginning to harden. The birth-control debate dominated the composition of the second letter. That letter was also written in Pittsburgh, but now the endings and beginnings had shifted. *Humanae Vitae* signalled the end of a major post-conciliar phase and began a different era.

But all this was a year away. For the moment, things were more fluid than they would be again for a long time. They were, well, like the three rivers at my feet that still had an opportunity to take any shape and flow at any speed. It was autumn and the last life of summer was beautiful in its dying. It was a good time for bishops and theologians, for young priests and older men, for John's Council and Paul's papacy. It was a second spring as Newman would have said. Things would pass quickly. I started back to the hotel and walked through the park and across the street. Where was the Spirit leading us? The letter was completed in the winter and released to the American Church a few weeks before the beginning of spring.

The closer we get to our dreams the more quickly they pass us by. Like the rivers. They flow more slowly and assume different shapes at a distance. Yet it was good to have dreamed. And somehow nothing is lost. Hope needs only life, not success. The Allegheny and Monongahela become the mighty Ohio although both must die in the process.

The word is a long journey. Like any important journey, it is not direct. Words are best when they say more than they declare, when they send people on oblique paths and expect them back at points that have not been predetermined. Words are the most effective ministry. They require symbols to give them flesh, but they are the very stuff out of which human reality is made.

A theologian deals with words. In this sense, he is always a teacher and literature is part of his total identity. American theology is most effective when it is concrete rather than abstract, Hebraic rather than Hellenic, urban rather than rural, present-oriented and existential rather than traditional or futuristic. America does not become as concretely involved with the shape of the future as Europe does. We are not as prone to elaborate categories for future behavior as those devised by Auguste Comte or Karl Marx or, for that matter, Plato's *Republic* or Thomas More's *Utopia*. America moves toward the future with both feet planted in the present.

As he deals with words, a theologian realizes that the success of a theological undertaking is in direct proportion to the reality words evoke rather than explain. In this sense, poetry and theology are akin and parables get the point across on more effective levels than syllogisms. A theologian encounters mystery by the very force of his faith. Logic can destroy his work with a precision more congenial to reason than revelation. The religious potential of the modern age is reflected in its fascination with what James Joyce called the epiphany moments of enlightenment rather than arduously reasoned conclusions. Newman once wrote in *Arians of the Fourth Century* that Aristotelian logic and Euclidean geometry led the Arians to their heresy. Christ is not perceived adequately by rational constructs or mathematical formulas. Neither faith nor theology, poetry nor literature yield easily or rightfully to clarity.

The unifying elements in theological elaboration are a love for words, ministry, and teaching. Theology is impoverished when the theologian uses words only to declare his concepts rather than to evoke a response in others on a preconceptional or transconceptional level. Theology is not only a craft but an art, not a product we produce but an experience to be communicated. A theologian must be a teacher, not exclusively in the Western tradition of reaching others rationally, but in the Oriental sense of initiating others in a mystery larger than teacher and disciple, a mystery both experience together in awe. Contemplation, poetry, and theology converge and support one another.

The end result of theological words is ministry. Theology is a way of caring for people. Concrete pastoral practice is sometimes a more reliable guide for the theological enterprise than research or abstract reflection. Theology becomes ineffective the more a theologian withdraws from life. Newman and Merton were so involved in the life of their times that they were open to criticism on a hundred different levels. They reached people profoundly because they did not know how to do without them. John XXIII created the most stimulating environment for theology which the Church had experienced for centuries. It was not his use of words or his charism for teaching but the character of his ministry that created its own theological era in the Church. His theology was concrete. He made the abstract work of many classical theologians obsolete by the very nature of the care he demanded that others be given in Church.

Words, teaching, and ministry are effective in direct proportion to the sensitivity of the person who identifies himself by them. The insensitive do not know what to say to people. They feel no attraction to ministry and cannot function as teachers. Sensitivity and fragility are the prerequisites of the theological enterprise.

The point of discrimination for the value of words, teaching, or ministry is the relationships they engender. Before the Council, there was. a tendency to define the Catholic norm by which relationships would be judged adequate or not. Since the Council, there is more attention given to the validity of relationships in their own right as an influence on the definition of Catholic reality. These relationships include not only personal encounters but ecumenical and interfaith endeavors, as well as the dialectic of the sacred and the secular and the dialogue between atheism and belief.

The most fundamental ministry of the Church is the ministry of the word. On this level, all legitimate ministry continues and endures. Preaching and Scripture, theology and teaching, even sacrament and symbol are manifold manifestations of the central mystery of the word that binds us together as human, creates our faith, confesses our orthodoxy, and indicates to us where God may be found.

The word is a long journey. It leads to the human heart. In my case, the journey led me to Kentucky and Birmingham, to Rome and New York, to Darlington and Pittsburgh. It is a long journey to learn what to say and how to say it so that one speaks in such a manner that he verbalizes the spiritual striving, the intellectual groping, the emotional yearning of his age and brings people the serenity of shared understanding, mutual faith, common hope, and concrete love. The right word is our act of mercy to one another as well as the most telling theology we can write. It is a long journey and the pilgrim is still far from home.

As I looked down on Seattle from the air, I was impressed as seldom I have been with how beautiful a city can be. Seattle is one of those cities that seems to be a long way from everywhere. It also has a right to be. People will come to it even if it is out of their way. It comes at the end of continental America and is a gateway to Alaska.

Seattle is as open as a city can be geographically. It has more ways out of it and into it than any other city in America. Washington is a good state for world fairs, national parks, and realities as American as apples and Indian names like Seattle or Yakima. It is the only American state named after a president.

Seattle is more akin to New York than one might imagine, in that strange way in which opposites are similar. Both cities suggest infinite possibilities: New York with its concrete canyons and the pace of its life; Seattle with its forests and mountains, its rivers and numberless islands. Seattle has preserved something vaguely nostalgic in its unabashed newness. It is the embodiment of the American myth of paradise, a waterway into the frontier fascination and wilderness romance Americans find exciting. The topography of the state makes it seem even more vast than its actual size. Seattle is America before the Fall, the western outpost that takes us as far from our problems as we are likely to go, a place made for the airplane more remarkably than any other city in America.

I had come here to lecture in a program of speakers and to teach a graduate course to university students. The fact of lecturing as far from New Jersey as Seattle was now a familiar feature of my life. I had last flown over Seattle on my way to deliver a series of lectures in the Orient. I felt free here and at home. I had probably made more friends in Seattle than anywhere else in America outside my native environment. Seattle was a little less severe on the loneliness of the lecture circuit than other cities. Few places are as crowded and forsaken in America as its airports. Even the railroads, for all their decay, have kept a sense of warmth. I don't know why, but disgruntled train conductors seem more human than airline hostesses with their smiles and courtesy. The real is more attractive than the artificial even when it's bad.

The jet has shaped American theology. No theologian publishes today as a hermit. We have produced a generation of contemplatives who have left their cells and choir stalls for the greater confinements of airplane cabins and seat belts. No monk remains at home if he chooses to write. Contemplation, therefore, has to happen on the run. A lot of theological writing is done now on airplanes rather than in libraries.

I never realized in Kentucky that writing and contemplation are the same art. Neither happens unless you know what it is to be lonely and unless you care to overcome it. A theologian is never any good at what he does unless he contemplates. The better he becomes at theology the more easily he turns to writing. But even when it's easier, it's not easy. The anomaly of it all is summarized in the fact that the theologian quickly becomes a celebrity in America today. His loneliness creates an audience. Perhaps the process is something like the hermits centuries ago who kept becoming founders of religious communities because people sought them out so often.

It is a frightening responsibility, being listened to. Even when you write your heart out with every book you compose it in pain. Giving oneself is never an indication that what is given is what the world needs, even if it wants it. It is a lonely endeavor, this effort to say what one is and to speak his faith in the marketplace. I wonder how lonely St. Paul must have been. There isn't much room for anyone else in the baskets in which they keep lowering him over city walls. Lightning kept hitting him on the road to Damascus and missing everyone else. He was always on a journey trying to put together the Christ he formerly persecuted. Once he went to the desert alone to put himself together. Tentmaking may have been the earlier version of airport loneliness. I never saw a tentmaker work with anyone else. They call Paul the first theologian in the Church, don't they?

What does the lecture circuit teach the American theologian? In the beginning, it initiates him into the American myth of mobility. If he is not careful, he can mistake movement for progress. Since we often measure our worth in terms of how many miles from home-base we are invited to address an audience, we can equate distance with depth. But the lecture circuit also reminded me of how painful it is to journey from familiar surroundings and of how much a theologian is expected to do this. A theologian is expected to be creative even when he deals with the past. He begins his work with the conviction that good theology can heal people and bring them hope more directly than any other human endeavor. And he tries in a thousand different attempts to say it better, to think it better than he did before, because someone else who heard nothing until now may listen and become settled. But the theologian himself has to be restless to accomplish this for others.

Seattle is anything but settled. It is congenial to the airplane because it is so open a city. A military expert would find it an easy city to invade. It is vulnerable at so many points. The airplane is an effective symbol for the city. Boeing aircraft and the Space Needle both belong here.

Vulnerability and loneliness are manifestations of the same reality. I remembered John XXIII that night on the balcony of St. Peter's and I thought of how lonely he appeared. The whole world was looking at him and he had no face to focus on. He blinked and seemed bewildered at the lights, at this strange basilica that was to be his home, at this frightening office he had been elected to at the end of his life. I remember seeing his face that morning in the Basilica of St. Peter's when he celebrated his coronation. He walked to the end of the center aisle. As he was elevated in the chair to begin the long march to the papal altar, he became pale and frightened. I wondered what he was thinking that moment. John would have liked Seattle. He would know all about airports and the fragility one senses in himself when others look to him for strength.

Something about an audience reveals the vulnerability of the speaker. Like preaching in a marketplace, it demands distance from others for its accomplishment. Thomas Merton died alone. He would have had companions had he never written. He was on a long journey when it happened, fragile, vulnerable, isolated. It is such a paradox. Loneliness is necessary for writing; writing overcomes aloneness; writing creates distances. Newman once preached on the parting of friends. He became a good theologian, but no one knew how to keep him from the loneliness he often mentioned.

Regardless of the statistics, Americans feel more vulnerable in airplanes than anywhere else. Nor will reassuring statistics ever convince them otherwise. The sense of insecurity comes from the fact that air is not our native environment as humans and that placing our lives in the control of someone else is not a congenial atmosphere for self-reliant Americans. As we landed in Seattle, I became ready to trade the insecurity of air travel for the supposed security of lecturing to an audience. The common denominator was the fragility necessary for both endeavors to succeed.

Perhaps this is why Seattle is an effective metaphor for the theological enterprise. Seattle comes at the end of a long journey. Theologians from New York don't get invited that far until they have gone through miles of fragility and paid the price of loneliness for their accomplishment. Seattle is unsettling and convinces us of our insecurity. It is open and, although beautiful, lacks the protectiveness of a city slum or a New York ghetto. It forever raises mountains to let you know how small you are and leads you at every turn to water which is the only element, after air, that makes us uncertain. A theologian who spends a lot of time in airplanes begins to distrust the control he has over his own life and the influence of his own theology.

The lecture circuit is a prolonged paradox. Fragility creates courage; courage assembles an audience; an audience convinces us of our weakness. A theologian is never any good at his work until he realizes how unimportant it is and how dispensable he may be. One's disposability makes him courageous, less frightened to risk himself, convinced that God counteracts foolishness and the wisdom of the community will not allow mistakes to flourish. Courage never comes from a conviction of strength but from an awareness of weakness. Trust has the same source. Airplanes may be the technological equivalent of Old Testament boils and frogs. The Egyptians learned how vulnerable they were from the plagues they suffered. The lecture circuit convinces everyone except the obtuse of the necessity of grace for all theological work.

The routine was now familiar. There were people at the gate to greet me, friends whose faces I knew, baggage to wait for, familiar questions to ask, chatter about the distance to our destination, the size of the audience, the quality of the acoustics, the time allotted for prepared remarks and audience response, the possibility of newspaper interviews. It was Seattle, but every once in a while I was sure I was back in Kentucky. My vocation as a contemplative was intact so long as I experienced the loneliness and the need for people, the fragility and the agony to communicate, the awareness that God prevails even despite the theologians and that his grace and love are the only hope men have for the future. It was Gethsemane and Kentucky once again and Seattle had become a seven storey mountain.

We were trained as Aristotelians. We were taught to be rational, systematic, logical, nonpersonal, abstract, conceptual. And it was good. The human mind is sometimes as evasive as the weather. It needs an anchor, a center of sorts, definable poles, discernible limits. But the world is no longer Aristotelian. Aristotelian thinking is as alien to the twentieth century as the Ptolemaic cosmology Aristotle inspired.

It is difficult to write about oneself because there are so many pitfalls. One might become confessional, self-serving, ego-oriented. Emotional restraint and intellectual discipline must accompany autobiography if it is to be serviceable in the theological enterprise. Nonetheless, our personal histories must be explored. Those who study our books have a claim on the interpretation of our minds and the analysis of our motives.

And so I tried to write, personally and yet not so subjectively that others could make no use of my thoughts for their own lives. I wanted this essay to be an example of the very theology I believe is indispensable for the modern world. I wanted to write theology as a piece of literature, subtle, subdued, and nonovert in its intentions.

The last century and a half has heightened our awareness of evolution and psychoanalysis, existential philosophy and process thinking. We can no longer do theology as faithful Aristotelians. The world has become a symbol to be questioned and pondered rather than a design with logical connections, functional parts, and no excess pieces. Not everything fits. The fact that it does not fit is not due to our not knowing its reason.

It is due to the exuberance of life which operates in nonrational categories. Everything has a purpose if God is conceived of as a supreme rationalist, an omniscient thinker, an omnipotent planner. But God is very emotional as Jews and Christians understand him. He is not an Aristotelian deity, a Platonic ideal or an Enlightenment Geometer. He is a symbol-maker, a superbly literary craftsman, absolutely enthralled with metaphors. God is a poet. The best of all books about God is the Bible. And the Bible is poetry. It has little place for syllogisms and no love for the God of the philosophers or the Supreme Being of the Greek thinkers or the *Ipsum Esse Subsistens* of theologians who feared to look into their hearts when they searched for God. *Cor ad cor loquitur* was Newman's way of saying it, heart speaks to heart. Not only theology but even God must be demystified and demythologized of the rational and intellectual pretensions with which we endowed them. Western civilization and our own personal interests often lead us to an affirmation of conceptual knowledge as a way of escaping and repressing subjective experience.

And so I thought I would write an essay about a journey and I tried to unify the images in a metaphor. The essay begins with the scene of a young boy standing alone by railroad tracks in rural Kentucky. Every image that follows is one of movement: a journey to Birmingham and a road to Rome, an automobile ride into frenetic New York, a return along the back roads to Darlington, the rush of rivers at Pittsburgh, an aircraft that circles the city of Seattle and the waterways that lead into the wilderness.

There is no easy way to understand what led me to this manner of thinking. Perhaps it was the encounter with so many experiences that made sense even though they did not fit. It was the intuition of Newman who did theology with his heart, the contemplative Merton who preferred submission to assertion, the unpredictable John XXIII who reformed the Church by his spirit rather than with his intellect. Most of all it was the people I met and the vague hunger in them that seemed satisfied when I wrote and reasoned with symbols. The most direct route to the human spirit is oblique language. The symbol evokes resonances and stirs the depths as no concept can. This is why Jesus is remembered for his parables and his stories of wheat, for his love of flowers and his lessons with fish, for his symbols and imagery rather than for his concepts and rational system. John the Evangelist realized this more effectively than any other New Testament writer.

I have met many people who reasoned well but who were not free. I never met someone who created symbols in constraint. Without inner freedom, life is logical rather than metaphysical, theology becomes a system rather than a symbol, Christianity is reduced from experience to ideology. The freedom of God is most clearly demonstrated in the symbols of the universe and in the figurative preaching of Jesus.

And so I wanted this essay to be a testimony to freedom. I needed episodes and process to make it work, a journey motif and a series of vignettes. I had to move its structure from cause-and-effect associations to wholistic and integrative experience. The relationship between the parts had to be sure but not obvious. I needed connections that would appeal to the spirit rather than logically satisfying junctures. And I wrote it all down. Everything I can understand about my life is in these few pages but none of it is direct. There is a paradox in the tight structure of this fluid essay. Everything fits because it has no reason to be there except for the fact that it happened. The essay is an effort at poetry without verse, an epic with no rhythm. It is the way I believe theology must be done in this era.

I was once asked to write a book about freedom and faith, about commitment and options. I was asked to do this with photographs and drawings, with a free style of writing and with passion. I wrote *Free to Be Faithful* as a symbol for those who needed symbols to sense their aliveness. In that book, I left forever the Ptolemaic universe and I ended my acceptance of Aristotle as the norm for my thinking. I had no regrets for the passage or the parting nor any remorse for the former association. But I required a freedom not from my past thinking but for my future work. I wanted to bring Aristotle and Newman together, to blend the supreme conceptualist with the master of intuitive theology. I know I am not adequate for so massive a task but I needed to sacrifice myself in the attempt.

Fidelity to this task demanded the freedom to make symbols as the rational universe collapsed and to express hope as the Church I once knew died a long overdue death. It was time for the twentieth century to dawn and to enlighten a new Church with its grace. It was time for the Church to go on a journey, with meager means and provisional priorities. It was time to abandon rigidity and to make symbols in the pale light of a new age. It was a tentative Pentecost but one so overwhelming that the very suggestion of the new Spirit was irresistible. It was an hour for freedom and the theological community was summoned by the Spirit to bring poetry back into the Church, to make metaphors with language and life, to create symbols for a starved community, to cry for freedom in the darkness. There is little logic, let this never again be forgotten, there is little logic in freedom or fidelity, in faith or the building of the future. But a symbol inspires these realities for reasons no one knows. No logic could lead Jesus to the cross or bring him back to life in Easter. But the mystery that created these events in his life is best expressed by symbols that make everything whole by the connections and visions they inspire.

People, Places, and Metaphors

GABRIEL MORAN

All writing to the extent that it comes from one person's pen has an element of autobiography to it. Religious writing probably has a higher degree of the autobiographical than most kinds of literature. Occasionally the personal element is flaunted in religious writing when a believer in some faith gives testimony of what God has done in his or her life. More often, however, the biographical influence is minimized because the writer is intent on stating the "objective truth" of some sect, system, or sacred book.

I suspect, however, that there is another reason besides objectivity for religious writers veiling the autobiographical. Even those of us who use "experience" as our fundamental category may shy away from our own personal experiences. There is resistance to revealing the experiences of our lives that have been determinative of our thinking and imagery. I think that the reason for this veil is a quite simple one, namely, that we are embarrassed to admit that the base of our own experience is so narrow. The impulse within religious statements is toward some universal truth. Even the most modestly formulated statement about religious matters still makes claim to the All or the ultimate. In contrast to the presumptions of religious writing most people seem to live ordinary and provincial lives. How can such grand conclusions issue from the undramatic lives that most of us lead?

To this question there is an answer, that in religious matters depth, quality, and simplicity count for more than breadth, quantity, and pyrotechnics. This answer has been arrived at by many people in their own undramatic ways. Of course, that

236

fact can lead to the charge that this answer is induced out of necessity and is simply delusionary. Nonetheless, the conviction for many people stands firm of the "greatness of small actions" (Pasternak) and the "goodness of minute particulars" (Blake).

To understand the religious a person need not travel around the world, speak a dozen languages, and have read the literature of East and West. One needs only to have experienced the ordinary in unordinary ways. This principle is not an anti-intellectual one because it has been arrived at by, among others, people who have made intellectual journeys. Religious inquiry pushed to the limits brings us back home again to the simplicities of our beginning.

The principle stated above does provide face-saving possibilities for writers, though it is not specially designed for them. What the principle should do for writers is make them realize that ordinary lives, including their own, may contain important untapped riches for religious reflection. Only on the basis of this conviction do I presume to offer the following ordinary life as worthwhile material for religious study.

Before I had ever begun to reflect on my own religious history I had come to think that the two most important religious influences in life are: 1) one's community, that is, the people who are most closely related to a person; and 2) the place or places where someone has lived. These two things happen to be the main themes around which my personal history can be woven. Obviously, the two themes themselves intertwine, but I wish to distinguish them for the purpose of this description.

I wish to emphasize the significance of using place as one of my themes. The theme of community is obvious enough. Christian writing has probably overdone its concern with personal influence, family upbringing, church fellowship, etc. But not only has place been underdeveloped as a theme, it has from early in Christianity been considered a dangerous if not negative influence. Christianity's rather presumptuous claim to be the vehicle for all of God's children led to a rejection of tribe and turf. The availability of a final answer in verbal form undercut the diversity of local custom. The ideal of a universal

Church easily translated into the demand for a homogeneous Church without roots anywhere in the earth.

When I first read Mircea Eliade's work fifteen years ago I thought I had found why Christianity is right and everybody else is wrong. Today from the same data I draw almost the opposite conclusion, namely, that to the extent Christianity disregards what everyone else considers important then Christianity must be deficient. I refer here specifically to a concern for one's own place, for the nonhuman elements of the earth, and for the symbolism of center.

The outline for my material is quite simple. Under the heading of community I will cite three strong influences: 1) early family experience, especially two of my sisters; 2) the religious organization of brothers with which I have been associated for twenty years; 3) one person who has taught me the meaning of the word interpersonal. Under the heading of place I will comment on two influences: New Hampshire and New York City. Although I have lived in a number of other places, my religious imagery is conveniently describable as New Hampshire childhood and New York adulthood.

If one is a fourth child born in the first six years of the depression, it sets one to thinking about what might have been had one's parents not been devout Irish-Catholics. I would think that there had to be some tinge of mixed feelings at the arrival of another mouth to feed, but if that was the case the feelings were extraordinarily well concealed. In fact, as I remember my childhood, the picture seems too good to be true. Perhaps psychoanalysis could uncover repressed memories of what was bad, but I would still think that it was an unusually good family situation.

My parents were (and are) devoted to each other and to the welfare of their children. Family life was calm, ordered, and stable. I cannot recall a single incident of unfair or unkind treatment by either parent. I was generally aware of the difficulties of our economic situation, but money was never placed first. My parents have always lived by the conviction that if something was worth doing they would manage it financially; amazingly enough they always did seem to manage.

When my mother became angry or upset the problem would come flowing out in words. When my father became angry he would get very quiet, a trait that I have since discovered is not a healthy way to get angry. I always looked upon my father as intelligent, strong, successful and, most of all, gentle. I never saw in him any of the vulgar traits that I have come to take as standard equipment in the American male. It was presumably a good image of fatherhood on which to base a notion of God.

My mother worked with incredible devotion to children, Church, and kitchen. It was the kind of devotion and commitment that hardly seems possible anymore. As the oldest in her own family my mother had to go to work in the city's garment mills when she had finished the eighth grade. She would have loved to go further in school and she was determined to give each of the five children every educational opportunity possible. The children in their turn never had the slightest doubt that they would succeed. That presumption could have been disastrous if one of us had lacked the equipment. Fortunately, it was an unbroken line of top students, a feat that was accomplished without any seeming pressure or great exertion.

Until my parents developed some sickness in old age no one in the family was ever sick or went to the hospital, let alone died. I took that for granted when I was growing up, but it must be a remarkable family medical record. I presumed health just as I expected fidelity, love, and consistency. I have already admitted that the picture is too idyllic to be perfectly accurate, but the point of this description is that this is the world that impressed itself on me. There was a time, of course, when I was about eighteen years old, when I thought my parents could have done things much better, but as the years went by that feeling melted away into simple gratitude for all that they did do.

I said above that two of my sisters had a strong influence upon me, a sister who is six years older and a sister who is six years younger. It was to my older sister that I could turn for a combination of maturity and sisterliness. I suppose for my younger sister the same relation existed with a reversal of roles. To this day I would trust them with any problem I have and be confident of an intelligent and sympathetic understanding. Both of them not only proved that they could fend for themselves in the man's professional world, but that they could also be loving wives and devoted mothers. Neither of them describes herself as a feminist, but both are examples of women who combine traditional roles of women and an independent identity of their own. My mother sometimes asks in fearful tones how she could have produced such a free-thinking lot of children. We try to convince her that she should consider the accomplishment a success, but she still has her doubts.

The second communal influence upon my life is the religious organization that presumes to call itself the Christian Brothers. My feeling toward this group of men is unreservedly positive. In the early days there were a lot of crazy rules, but even then the people always surpassed them. I walked into this organization not having the faintest idea of what I was doing or why. From a later perspective I can only guess that my joining the organization was equal parts of attempt at heroism and an attempt to escape from life's problems. The surprising thing is that I never had a moment's regret or a thought of leaving after I had become a member.

The organization of brothers provided personal friendship and professional support. The educational opportunities were almost unlimited. In 1960 the man who was head of the province asked me if I would like to study religious education. I was not very enthusiastic about the field, but he thought I would be good at it. I was willing to give it a try. He told me to go anywhere in the world I wanted and to take as many years as I needed but to become expert in the field. That kind of offer was not the standard fare in the brothers, but neither was it entirely unique. My opportunities have been better than most of the men, but I still know of few men who, on leaving the organization, have had negative or bitter feelings about their experience. I make that comment with some confidence because as executive head of the province my job included reading what former members had to say about leaving the brothers.

The esprit de corps of years past was in part created by our peculiar position in the Church. The Roman Catholic

Church in practice has only three forms of membership: priest, nun, layman. We were not any of those things, which was confusing in years past but has been a blessing lately. The Roman Catholic Church mostly ignored us while we in turn tried to prove that we were the best teachers in the Catholic Church. There was great friendliness with individual priests combined with a strong anticlericalism. We relied upon one another and trusted our own mystique because that was all we had.

I realize now that it was an extraordinary group experience we had before most people had ever heard of group experience. However, the whole way of life was in a process of change more rapid than any of us could have imagined. When Catholic schools ran into trouble and the Church started questioning everything, the precarious balance of our lives was upset. The breakdown of the tight little world of brothers' school/brothers' house seemed to be a liberation and in some ways it was. However, without the old base of operations many individuals drifted away, and the pitch for recruiting new members became confused and unsure.

In the history of our organization, especially throughout these later years, the bond of continuity has been a sense of brotherhood. Most of the paraphernalia was expendable, but an organization of brothers makes more sense to me today than it did twenty years ago. Society at large is only beginning to suspect that its great need (in addition to sisterhood) is brotherhood, that is, the freeing of males from hierarchical systems and the forming of communities. It remains to be seen whether those of us who have had a share of the word brother can recreate an organization from what is left of the past. Whatever happens to our organization in the future, the experience of brotherhood has established itself at the center of my religious thinking.

The third communal influence that has deeply affected my life is a person I met in the mid-1960s. This experience transformed all of my previous experience and became a permanent influence in my life. I could write a book or two on this relationship, but for present purposes I think a few brief comments will be most appropriate.

In the early part of the 1960s I had studied and written about personal relationships. I had used the words revelation, mutuality, I-thou encounter, trust, and love. All of those words suddenly took on immeasurably more meaning with the entrance of one person into my life. She taught me to laugh and play, to feel happy and sad at the same time and to see the world with eyes afresh. It was the discovery of the meaning of person: my person, her person, everybody's person. The first months and years of this relationship were a time of postponed adolescence. Feeling like an adolescent when one is already an adult can be a silly and embarrassing experience. Nevertheless, the delay can heighten the experience and make one appreciate it more. One begins to think that it is tragic that adolescent love is wasted on adolescents.

With the passage of the years we found out what millions of humans before us had discovered, namely, that the road of human love is not a smooth one. All of the romantic comedies we are fed from birth do not prepare us for the difficulty of meshing personal love and social form. If two persons are going to become independent human beings while they also become freely dependent on each other, they need the support of surroundings, the maneuverability of space, and the leisure of time. Unfortunately, what many of us experience is an intolerable pressure upon the thin membrane of personal love. Everything shouts at us "to solve the problem immediately," as if a human being were a machine with a blown fuse. I am more convinced than ever that the mutuality of persons is the ideal worth striving for, but I now glimpse how complicated is the reality to which the word mutuality refers.

The paradox of human love is the paradox of finite and infinite. To love intensely is to become aware of the precariousness of life and the limits under which each of us lives. One cannot love another without becoming aware that that person is going to die and that some day the world is going to become almost unbearably lonely. In a myth of the Blackfoot Indians, Old Man and Old Woman debate whether people should die. Said Old Man: "We shall die for four days and then come to life again." "Oh, no," said Old Woman, "it will be better to die forever, so that we shall be sorry for each other."

Without taking back any of the reality of death, the experience of love is the intimation of immortality and infinitude. Immortality is obviously the wrong word, but it is the one we are saddled with in trying to speak of death and more than death. Love is the affirmation of being in the face of death. Love is a fragile instrument with which to overcome death, but love's power is to change the meaning of power. C. S. Lewis, grieving at the death of his friend Charles Williams, wrote: "When my idea of death met my idea of Williams, it was my idea of death that changed."

There are many attacks today upon the desire for immortality; it is said that the wish to preserve one's ego is selfish and narrow-minded. But John Baillie correctly noted that this attack fails to understand the relation of love and death. To love is already to leave one's ego, and the drive for life beyond death comes most strongly from the affirmation of the other. The question of immortality finally comes down to whether the unique qualities we love in another are useless sports in a cruel and impersonal world, or whether the beauty we recognize in another is a genuine and lasting contribution to a more than personal universe.

For the past ten years my chief religious category has been experience. Because of the narrow meaning of the word experience in modern Western European thought, it is a struggle to maintain the open and comprehensive meaning of the term. However, I know of no other word in the American-English language to refer to the total matrix of human and nonhuman relationships. There is another reason for the fact that it is a struggle to accept a comprehensive meaning of experience. The more comprehensively one sees the world, the more obvious become the absurdity, chaos, and sufferings of the world. In recent years no writers have affected me so deeply as Albert Camus and Samuel Beckett. Despite all the good things that have happened to me—or could it be because of them—I have always been aware of the encroaching darkness of depression and despair. The love of one person in my life has been enough to delay the twilight but not to dissolve it. More than that one cannot ask of a single human being, and for the gift of herself I am grateful beyond words.

In conclusion to the first part of this essay I wish to note that all three of the communal influences come together in the feminist movement. Since the late 1960s I have been acutely aware that the women's movement is the key to both the deficiencies of Christian theology and the kind of imagery and language needed in future religious bodies.

The first and third influences that I cited are fairly obvious in their implication of feminism. The impact of strong and healthy women in my life has been central to experience. But the influence of the brothers' organization may seem not to fit here at all. At the most obvious level it is a life segregated from women. Nonetheless, life in a community of brothers has not been a bad preparation for understanding the women's movement. Our experience has been an unusual one for American men because we have not played the role of dominant male toward women, toward each other, or toward the Church organization. Within the Roman Catholic Church our organization had a feminine role without the ambiguous advantage of sexual favors to bestow. That experience does not necessarily produce sexually liberated people, but it can give men an interesting perspective on the women's movement. Brotherhood is not far removed from sisterhood in the struggle for a fully human race.

The second major theme that I wish to develop is that of place. People live somewhere and that somewhere is more determinative of attitudes, imagery, and speech than they are usually aware. If some people seem to live between places in their automobiles and airplanes that fact is significant. To have no place of one's own is to have a very specific relation to place. Of course, people who travel much may still have a strong sense of place and have a rich variety of spatial imagery available to them.

The danger of increased travel in the modern world is the homogenization of place. Gertrude Stein described the city of her origin by saying: "There's no there there." The ability to get there quicker will not be progress if there is no there to get to. I sometimes feel that I live inside a machine whose shape keeps changing from train to plane to bus. Fortunately, however, I have had two places in life that have functioned as centers of space for me. The two are in sharp contrast, but each brought something rich to my life and thinking.

New Hampshire is a place that has only recently come into fame as a desirable place to live. Until the late 1960s when I would tell people where I was from they would look at me sadly as if to say: poor, underprivileged child. In recent years their eyes light up and they say: wow, terrific, why did you ever leave? I think that the second reaction is as inaccurate as the first. I do not regret having spent my early life in New Hampshire, but I distrust the idealization of it that is now emerging among nostalgic, antiurban people.

What first comes to mind about the place I grew up in is quiet and orderliness. There were clear rules to live by. People knew the rules or if they did not that was their fault. Rules got broken and things sometimes went badly, but the important thing was the feeling that the world made sense. Especially after World War II there was an expectation of normalcy. Children were expected to grow up, marry, settle down, and watch the next generation of children grow. At that time the state with the longest life expectancy was New Hampshire.

I was hardly aware that there were big cities with severe problems. Boston was the only metropolis I ever saw, and that only to visit for a day or two each year. Until I was thirteen we had no automobile, I had never been on a plane or train, and television did not exist. The world was the magnificent scenery of the immediate environment and the undifferentiated population of the small town.

The adjectives "magnificent" and "undifferentiated" are ones I apply only in retrospect. I could not then appreciate how incomparable was the mixture of mountains, lakes, streams, seashore, rolling hills, and brilliant foliage. But I can still feel the soft summer grass under bare feet and smell the burning leaves of autumn. Nothing catches better the sense of the place than the stone walls that ran in straight lines for mile after mile. They stood for more than a century, though nothing held the stones in place except the hands that originally placed them there.

We always assumed that a running stream was pure enough to drink. The woods existed for children's play and tree-top houses. We also had to recognize that the animals had rights of prior possession to the land. Hunting was a sport mainly for the "flatlanders," that is, anybody from south of the state border. In short, life was neither primitive nor idyllic; it was a simple existence with a restricted outlook, but also with some homey virtues that most people then did not even know were virtues.

The undifferentiated population is a more questionable matter. At the last census New Hampshire was 99.4 percent white. That figure must represent an influx of nonwhites since my childhood. People did not think of themselves as white because there was no other color for comparison. Variety within the whites was also limited. Throughout my childhood I thought that there were three kinds of people: Irish-Catholics, French-Catholics, and Yankees. There were in the neighborhood one Jewish family and one Albanian family, but they represented peculiar deviations from what everybody was supposed to be.

I realize now that there was a large amount of racial and national bigotry. It was not personal hatred of known people so much as a fear of their existence and the fact of difference at all. Thus, the order and simplicity of the place were bought at a considerable price. The family seashore resort was one of the last total prohibition towns in the country. It also had an unwritten law excluding Jews. Obviously we had chosen the right way because the contrasting situation could be seen across the bridge in the Massachusetts beach town. I don't think it ever occurred to us that our attitudes, laws, and exclusivity were part of the problems elsewhere.

The narrowness carried into religion. The city of Manchester was 65 percent Roman Catholic. More children were in the Catholic school system than in the public schools. There was no conflict between Church and state; in fact, there was a stretching of the law to give every help possible to the Church. Anyone who dared to object was obviously an atheistic agitator. The newspaper publisher who has since become a national index of intolerance was putting out the only news in town. What the newspaper recommended every Saturday was to go to the Church of your choice; what it implied every day was that God is a right-wing American of unspecified Christian denomination.

All of the children in the family had at least twelve years of Catholic school. Catholics who went to the public school were thought to be a semi-lapsed variety. Each of my three sisters received four years at the local Catholic college for women. Following the lead of my brother I decided to go to the state university. I can still see the high school principal calling me out of class and berating me for choosing to go to an atheistic school. The only worse place imaginable would have been Dartmouth.

I do not know whether the elementary and secondary schools were good or bad. I just know that I found the whole thing unutterably boring. The teachers were probably underprepared and overworked. They took us through the traditional curriculum with earnest devotion. I never gave anyone any trouble and I got the highest marks, so no one ever inquired whether I was learning anything; and I was not about to disturb the agreement. I cannot remember anything interesting ever happening in school, but there was always after school time, weekends, and summer vacations. The best thing about high school was that it finished at 1:00 P.M. each day—until some reformer decided to improve our education by extending the school day.

The most boring thing in school was religion class. I always assumed it was intended to be boring so that one would appreciate by contrast the other elements of religious practice. No one, including the teachers, seemed interested in religion as a course of study. But religion as a way of life was a deadly serious business. The purpose of the course in school was to memorize fine points of law and doctrine. A round of devotional practices stabilized the day, the week, and the year. It was a comforting world to grow up in because one had been fortunate enough to have been born into the one true religion. The attitude toward non-Catholic friends was not so much intolerance as sadness and hope for conversion. The Catholicism was not an ideology rigidly held but a symbolic system imbibed with mother's milk and quietly but persistently followed throughout all of life.

It could have been a fairly healthy religious life except for the sexual repression. I doubt that there was any sexual control system that could equal small town Irish-Catholicism reinforced by New England Puritanism. The Ten Commandments came down in practice to one, and we knew what confession and retreats were really for. While the preachers and teachers kept saying that it was dangerous even to think about the topic, an atmosphere was generated in which teen-agers could hardly think about anything else. I am happy that, whatever the ambiguous success of the current sexual revolution, young people can no longer experience the kind of oppressive sexual control that was common a few decades ago.

I grew up with the good and bad sides of the environment and both of them left permanent traces in my attitudes. It is possible to broaden one's vision if it has been narrow, but it is more difficult to change one's emotional life. Each of the children in our family had to leave home to find his or her way in the world. The exodus of all the children to other cities was not the usual pattern of the time. Despite the mixed feelings of our parents they gave us the means and the encouragement to make our journeys. In later years our parents became seasoned travelers by visiting all the places that the children lived. I think that New Hampshire was not so bad a place to be born and I might even want to die there, but for the present I love it at a distance.

My first experiences of New York City were terrifying. It offered the strongest possible contrast to everything that I took to be normal. Many people never get past the first shock of New York even if they return many times. I think that New York is a nice place to live but I wouldn't want to visit it. New York can be a frightening place for anybody, but for those of us hooked on it, fear is not the first emotion to arise. "The city" (as New Yorkers chauvinistically call their home) is simply a microcosm of everything that is good and bad about the human race. I have seen more ugliness here than anywhere else in the world but also more beauty. One thing sure is that it is never boring. Just when you think you have seen the limit, something else happens. In this respect New York is a very religious place, a place that calls into question ordinary existence and immerses one into ecstasy and pathos, anxiety and grief, joy and sorrow.

There is plenty of the religious in the city but it is hard times for the churches. When I first met New Yorkers I was fascinated by the fact that they would identify where they came from by their parish. I doubt that that still holds true with the growing generation. I describe the Catholic church across the street as looking like bombed-out Berlin of 1945. All of the men seemed to have died in some war and what is left are old women and little children. I have the feeling that the pastor comes out every Sunday morning with the faint hope that the Irish have returned. Instead, there is the French Mass for Haitians, the Spanish Mass for Puerto Ricans, and the English Mass for the incredible diversity of black, yellow, and white. I do not mock the pastor who has kept trying for thirty years in his own earthy style. The Church here does not function well, but other institutions (e.g., post office, bank, supermarket) look even worse. Gary Wills ridiculed the Woodstock Jesuits for failing to transform the neighborhood, but 50,000 Jesuits here would not make a dent. One does not convert the city or make it look nice according to plans. If one lives by the city's rhythms one might eventually find some way to contribute. Anybody who comes with a "mission" to set things straight gets beaten into the pavement. I hardly need say that my image of God is no longer a white, male, middle-aged, Irish-American Roman Catholic.

What the city particularly did for me was to transform the meaning of order and control. When Wallace Stevens wrote that a great disorder is order he might have been referring to the neighborhood. In contrast to my previous conceptions of order in which all the rules are obeyed, I discovered that there was another kind of order that emerges from the give and take of diverse elements. The contacts of body and body, humans and machines, develop their own patterns of order. Of course, once order is viewed this way then large numbers of people and noisy activity are healthy signs. A massive flow of life creates its own ordering system and can sustain itself despite chaos and suffering.

For the individual, however, living in New York is like living in a hospital. People have to grow shells because if one were to feel everything one could not bear it. The first impression one gets of the residents is callousness, but if you scratch the shell you will very likely find extraordinary tenderness and vulnerability. Great wells of sympathy and compassion are always just below the surface.

As in a hospital, too, one sees people die here. In most of the country we successfully hide the fact of death, but in a place where 600 people die daily it becomes impossible to hide them all. Death becomes a fact of life and one becomes aware of how precarious all of life is. Death makes some sense here because it is in the midst of life. Even a lonely individual does not die alone when the flow of diverse human activity is death's context.

The above point is illustrated in a passage from the writing of Loren Eiseley. In this poignant description Eiseley reflects upon the old people in Grand Central Station, some of whom are waiting for trains and the rest of whom are waiting to die. After reading this passage I could never walk through the station without seeing what Eiseley describes. Later I realized that the passage is a description of the whole city and explains why so many of us live here.

The old ones cling to their seats as though these were symbolic and could not be given up. Now and then they sleep, their gray old heads resting with painful awkwardness on the backs of benches. . . . Once in a while one of the sleepers will not awake. Like the brown wasps, he will have had his wish to die in the great droning center of the hive rather than in some lonely room. It is not so bad here with the shuffle of footsteps and the knowledge that there are others who share the bad luck of the world. There are also the whistles and sounds of everyone, everyone in the world, starting on journeys. Amidst so many journeys somebody is bound to come out right. Somebody.

The city is less the cause of human problems than the receptacle for them, but its capacity to absorb troubles has reached the breaking point. State and federal governments continue to steal the city's billions while basic services are left to deteriorate. The drug problem, in large part artificially induced from outside the city, has devastating effects upon the population. The amazing thing is not that the city functions well but that it functions at all.

New York's reputation suffers from a crime myth generated by news media and exploited by the movies. Of course, there are many crimes here because there are many people, and street crime is possible because there are people on the street. Wherever I go in the country people ask of New York: Is it true that everyone is afraid to walk on the streets? To which I usually reply: As far as I know it is almost the only place where people do walk on the streets.

Statistics indicate that New York is one of the safer places to live in this country, which is not to say that it is safe. We are an incredibly violent people in this country, but the FBI's crime statistics distract us from the bigger questions of violence. The great danger on the streets of New York is not muggings but automobiles. I run into a crime only several times a month, but I hear or see an automobile accident almost daily. The unconscionable slaughter of people goes on every day in this country but hardly anyone seems capable of believing the statistics. Almost nothing is being done to stop the slaughter that obviously could be stopped. In New York two-thirds of the people killed in car accidents are pedestrians. Perhaps little is done to protect pedestrians from cars because 80 percent of pedestrians killed in the U.S. are either under four or over sixty-five.

My friends think I have a peculiar obsession in my lifelong hatred of the automobile, but I refuse to be the one who is classified as crazy. If there has ever been invented the perfect symbol of human self-destruction, the automobile is it. To feel the force of that statement it helps to have heard the screams of a child whose mother has just been run over, or to encounter incidents like the following:

1) I am crossing Broadway to get the paper at 5:00 P.M. As I wait on the west side of the street, an old man takes a step

off the island in the middle. At the same time a car takes the inside lane at about 40 m.p.h. The car lifts the old man into the air about 30 feet and his body hits the pavement as the brakes screech and a few muffled screams are audible. What seems most horrible to me is that the man himself never made a sound. Someone picks up his cane and dozens of people try to help him. Contrary to the myth, there are usually too many people trying to assist. Our excellent ambulance service arrives within 10 minutes and takes away the old man. I have lost my appetite for dinner.

2) I am in my room at 10:00 A.M. I hear no brakes (long screeches of brakes are usually a good sign) but only the scream of a woman. I look out the window and see the woman lying motionless in the middle of the street. Everyone else in the scene looks like they are posing for a still photo. The deliverymen and mothers on the sidewalk say nothing; the addicts on the benches keep staring ahead. In the deadly silence the first voice I hear is a child saying: Mommy, why is that lady lying on the floor? It is a good question but only children seem to ask.

The neighborhood is perhaps the only industrial population that knows it is in a life-and-death struggle with the automobile; it is an issue of daily survival. Nothing mobilizes the inhabitants like the fight against the interstate. It is not a very fair fight and the people are likely to lose this battle, but it is the kind of war that must be fought for the emergence of a post-industrial civilization.

Living in New York thus forces one to be aware of the unity of life and death, the relation of person to nonhuman environment, and the fact that each of us is part of some unimaginably large drama of the universe. Monica Furlong, in her book *End of Our Exploring*, suggests that the modern religious journey is not so much tragic or romantic but ironic. Our tragedies are like millions of other human tragedies and we must not take ourselves too earnestly or too solemnly. One must come to appreciate absurdity and the millions of peculiarities of human beings. Human beings are a messy sort who don't package well, but I think that their straightening-out ought to be resisted.

My choice for the most exploitive film of recent years is *Godspell*. It was the suburbanite dream of New York with all those beautiful buildings and no people. If the producers had chosen to shoot the movie in Vermont, the music and scenery could have made a good movie. The choice to use New York but exclude people required a miracle of technical skill, but it was a morally corrupt decision. In that context the sentiments of the song lyrics are ludicrous and abominable. If the Christian Church or any other religious body wishes to reestablish itself where people live it has to dissociate itself from this kind of exploitation.

* * * * * *

In recent years my religious interest has continued to grow, but I am no longer able to call myself a Christian theologian. Not that I became some other kind of theologian or that I joined some other religion. I am Roman Catholic to the marrow and even if I wished to "leave the Church" (which I don't) it would take decades of work to do so. Nonetheless, I consider the word theology to be etymologically and historically unsalvageable. I am interested these days in the metaphors, symbolism, imagery, and words that people use in trying to be religious. I find it neither necessary nor helpful to introduce the word theology into the discussion. Many people find my position arbitrary if not unintelligible, but I see no way to explore today's religious questions within the restrictions of Christian theology.

My choice in recent years has been to work with the term religious education. Of course, that term is considered less promising than theology in most Christian circles. I have some confidence, nevertheless, that logically, etymologically, and institutionally I am on the right road. I have not been successful so far in opening up the term religious education for people coming from a Christian past, but I intend to keep on trying. The exploring of the religious within an educational setting does constitute a threat to ecclesiastical institutions, but I have no interest at all in attacking Churches or Church officials. My intention is to offer educated criticism and avoid both personal attacks and anti-institutional tirades.

What we all need are some space in which to maneuver

and some other people to accompany us on our journeys. My own journey recounted in these pages is not very dramatic, but I have had the good fortune to be helped by the people and places that accompanied me.

Into the Political Kingdom

RICHARD P. McBRIEN

> "Nobody likes to be found out . . . Any autobiographer, therefore, at least between the lines, spars with his reader and potential judge."
>
> *Erik Erikson*

There are no Heideggers, no Harnacks, no Bultmanns, no Rahners, no Congars, not even a Schillebeeckx, a Küng, or a Lonergan in my academic history. My doctoral dissertation director and a few of my seminary professors were reasonably competent and unfailingly encouraging, but none was a theological giant and no conventional master-disciple relationships were to develop. I am essentially a self-made theologian.

Neither are there any holocausts, midnight flights from Nazi persecution, wartime concentration camps, or labyrinthine conversions to Roman Catholicism under the shadow of John Harvard's statue in my personal history. Born a Catholic in Hartford, Connecticut, I was to spend my early years in a manner that one must describe as ordinary for a young man of my particular intellectual ability, interests, and vocational orientation.

Neither are there any grandfathers occupying distinguished chairs of theology or Church history; a father walking the corridors of power in university or government; relatives and family friends leading lively drawing-room discussions on philosophy, ethics, and public policy. Three of my grandparents were immigrants, one from Ireland and two from Italy; my father was a policeman and a guard, my mother, a registered nurse; and our relatives and friends were people of modest means and opportunities.

I am a theologian today only because I am a priest. Had I decided as a boy to pursue some other vocational course, I should not now be holding a professorship in a university theology department nor the directorship of a religious education institute. Even though laywomen and laymen have entered the field of religious studies in larger and larger numbers, I am reasonably certain that I would never have gone into theology had I not been oriented, from the earliest years of my conscious existence, to the Catholic priesthood.

Why I am this kind of theologian, why I have focused on one set of issues (ecclesiology) rather than others, and why I have treated such issues with a particular emphasis are the kind of questions I intend to pose in this essay.

1. This *interest in ecclesiology* emerged from my very early preoccupation with politics. In high school I was an attentive reader of American history and was particularly fascinated by the biographies of U.S. Presidents. Although I do clearly remember the election of 1948 (I was twelve at the time), I didn't really cut my teeth on the quadrennial sweepstakes until the Eisenhower-Stevenson race in 1952. Thereafter, the political process itself became an object of consuming attention, with my range of study gradually broadening from absorption with electoral politics to a concentration on more fundamental questions of philosophy.

In the major seminary I would, on my own initiative, devote many hours to Jacques Maritain's *Man and the State, True Humanism, Philosophy of History*, and similar works of his, as well as those of Christopher Dawson and Walter Lippmann. It was a relatively logical passage from there to a formal concern with the Church's social doctrine. The textbooks of Father John Cronin, S.S., especially his *Catholic Social Principles*, and the writings of other recognized scholars in the field, including Oswald Nell-Breuning, Joseph Messner, H. A. Rommen, Paul Hanley Furfey, and even Cardinal Suhard, dotted my independent reading list. I reread the social encyclicals of Popes Leo XIII and Pius XI with a newly critical eye, and did my best to construct a coherent social doctrine from Pius

XII's assorted pronouncements (to midwives, jurists, streets-weepers, and occasional assemblies of the College of Cardinals). *Commonweal, The Catholic Messenger* of Davenport, Iowa (edited at the time by Donald McDonald), and the now defunct *Social Order* provided weekly or monthly reading fare.

These various sources confirmed, rather than initiated, a way of thinking. My readings and reflections in the field of politics had already alerted me to the impact of institutions and structures upon the quality of human life, and had persuaded me of the importance of choosing the most effective means of changing those institutions and structures which function to oppress rather than liberate humankind. Chronologically, I was a liberal Democrat before I was a Catholic social actionist, and I was both before I was old enough to vote.

Like some other Catholic liberals of the 1950s, I used the papal documents in much the same fashion as a traditionalist Catholic does today: as an arsenal of proof-texts with which to confound and overwhelm the opposition. It was only after my philosophical and initial theological studies in the seminary that the abiding values of that social teaching became more fully apparent and intrinsically persuasive.

One of the key elements of papal social doctrine that would make a decisive impact upon my later ecclesiological studies was the principle of subsidiarity: nothing is to be done by a higher agency that can be done better, or at least as well, by a lower agency. On the surface, it is a manifestly conservative principle: decentralization of government, and all that. But situations change. Yesterday's liberals become today's conservatives, and vice versa. Progressives rather than conservatives now appeal to the principle of subsidiarity as a major basis for the institutional reform of the Catholic Church: Rome should not control all appointments to the hierarchy; Rome ought not to decide how priests are to be trained in precise detail for every nation and culture; Rome should not determine how every marriage problem is to be resolved. Matters like these are best settled at a lower level, closer to the scene.

If an antecedent interest in politics cleared a path into social action, then this subsequent interest in social action edged me, in its turn, into liturgy. Under the influence of Father Shawn Sheehan, a past president of the North American Liturgical Conference and a Church history professor of mine at St. John Seminary in Brighton, Massachusetts, I began to see how the social aspect of Christian faith could be incorporated, and indeed was incorporated, into the whole of Christian systematic theology. The ecclesial image of the "Body of Christ" and the Pauline concept of the "restoration of all things in Christ" were among the significant points of intersection. Moreover, it was Sheehan who used to insist that the doctrine of the Church was itself a kind of synthesis of all other doctrines.

The combination of liturgy and social action provided a sturdy framework for the academic study of theology. My first year of formal studies included, as it always has for most Catholic seminarians, a major course on the Church. Although the course itself wasn't memorable (apart from the eccentricities of the professor), the subject matter intrigued me. This surprised and amused one or two of my friends in the priesthood, because the field was, at this time, still dominated—literally and figuratively—by the massive presence of the late Monsignor Joseph Clifford Fenton, of the Catholic University of America. He had given the tract *De Ecclesia* a bit of a bad name, although he had just as surely bequeathed to the Catholic clergy a treasure trove of outrageously funny anecdotes about his classes. In any event, my readings in political philosophy and the philosophy of history continued in high gear, and this new ecclesiological focus launched me on a theological exploration that hasn't yet ended.

2. My *preliminary ecclesiological perspective* (i.e., pregraduate work) was fashioned principally by my private study of Yves Congar. Indeed, Congar influenced me more than any other theologian during those seminary years: his *Lay People in the Church; Christ, Our Lady and the Church; Vraie et fausse réforme dans l'Eglise; After Nine Hundred Years; The Mystery of the Temple*; and especially his classic article on "Théologie" in the DTC *(Dictionnaire de Théologie Catholique)*. I remember returning eagerly to my room each evening, after supper and recreation, to continue my work on that piece. Consequently, I was excited in November 1963 when I had an

opportunity to meet Congar in person at the University of St. Thomas (the Angelicum) in Rome and chat with him for an hour or more about my theological interests and a possible dissertation topic.

His *Lay People in the Church* made the greatest and most sustained impact. Congar challenged what most of my regular seminary courses (with the gratifying exception of Sheehan's theologically wide-ranging lectures on the liturgy) had not even questioned: the clericalistic, monastic, and monarchical concept of Church mission and Christian life. Congar's major theses seem conventional by today's standards, but in the late 1950s they raised the consciousness of one young theological student: the Church is composed of lay people, some of whom are ordained; ecclesiology itself, as a specific tract within the total theological enterprise, is the product of reactionary forces: reactions against conciliarism in the first instance, against Protestantism in the second, and against the new wave of nineteenth-century Liberalism in the third; so-called worldly ("lay") realities are good in themselves, and not simply as occasions of contact with, or propulsion toward, the spiritual and the divine; the mission of the Church, therefore, includes the transformation of the earth (in the spirit of Teilhard); this world is destined to participate in the final glory of the Kingdom (over against Louis Bouyer and others of a more negative orientation); the laity must share in the missionary apostolate of the whole Church (although Congar's notion here reflected the "Catholic Action" mentality then in vogue during Pius XII's pontificate); the Church is People of God, not simply, nor even primarily, a hierarchical institution.

Congar's *Christ, Our Lady, and the Church*, although a relatively tiny book, had a similarly lasting impact upon me. It demonstrated the method and practical effect of systematic theological thought. The mysteries of Christian faith are radically interconnected. Thus, a review of the major Christological heresies, particularly those that emphasized the divinity of Christ at the apparent expense of his humanity (Nestorianism, Monophysitism, etc.), should alert us to the risks of comparable distortions in our theology of the Church. Congar insisted on a balanced incarnational ecclesiology. The Church consists not only of the invisible divine reality within, but of the whole visible institutional structure as well.

His *Vraie et fausse réforme dans l'Eglise*, a book withdrawn from circulation soon after it was published in the early 1950s, pursued the same theme, although more explicitly. Congar's critique of Reformation ecclesiology seems severe by present ecumenical standards, but what entangled him in the Vatican's inquisitional web was his very practical, pointed, and hard-hitting conclusions directed against French Integralism. The Integralists were comparable to the Catholic traditionalists of our own day, represented by *The Wanderer, Our Sunday Visitor*, the *National Catholic Register*, Catholics United for the Faith, and like-minded organs and organizations. With customary historical acumen, Congar challenged certain conventional assumptions about ecclesiastical authority. While he insisted that the Protestants had not gone about reform in the right way or according to the right principles, he nevertheless argued that there was much unfinished reform to undertake and a right principle by which to achieve it. That lesson was not lost upon me. Nor did I miss the lesson implied in the manner by which Congar himself was officially treated!

And finally, there was the DTC article on "Théologie," to which I have previously referred. Although I have engaged in relatively little direct historical research, I have never failed to be stimulated by works of history that are competently done (including one of Congar's latest, *L'Eglise de saint Augustin à l'époque moderne*). Congar's histories of ecclesiology have always relativized for me the Romano-Scholastic ecclesiologies that, until very recently, have passed for the "tradition of the Church." And his history of theology itself had the same effect, although over a much broader spectrum of issues. I have returned again and again to my exceedingly detailed notes on that DTC essay. Indeed, I made extensive use of them in the first course I taught at Pope John XXIII National Seminary in 1965, fundamental theology.

3. My *early formal ecclesiology* (graduate studies, 1963-65, and immediately thereafter) was enriched by such slim non-academic volumes as Congar's *The Wide World, My Parish*, wherein he argued that the Church is a minority in the service

of a majority; by Oscar Cullmann's scholarly and exegetically detailed *Christology of the New Testament*, especially his chapter on "The Suffering Servant," which I found immediately pertinent to the Church, an application I drew out in one of my first published articles, "The Church as the Servant of God" (*Clergy Review*, July 1963); by Dietrich Bonhoeffer's *Letters and Papers from Prison*, which was given to me as a diaconate ordination gift by Peter Berger and Joseph Duffey; by Berger's own *The Noise of Solemn Assemblies*, wherein it is argued that involvement in the institutional reform of the Church is itself a Christian vocation; and, of course, by the Second Vatican Council, which was in its second and third sessions during my time of graduate work in Rome.

The Bonhoeffer volume was especially influential, although its implications were not immediately apparent to me. Anyone who has read my *Do We Need the Church?* or some of my weekly columns in the Catholic press will know at once how Bonhoeffer's basic insights permeated my own thought: his view of the Church as being in and for the world, of Jesus as the "man for others" and of the Christian community as a community for others, of the call of the Church to reform for the sake of mission, and so forth.

Berger, of course, has influenced many academic people, and in areas well beyond the ecclesiological. I, too, have profited from his many writings—on the discipline of sociology, on the sociology of knowledge, on the meaning and function of religion, etc.—but his *The Noise of Solemn Assemblies* and *The Precarious Vision*, both published in the early 1960s, have made the strongest impact. Berger was at the Hartford Theological Seminary in those days—my home town. He went from there to the New School for Social Research in New York City, and then to Rutgers. In early 1975 he was much in the news for his co-chairing of a conference of moderately conservative theologians on contemporary trends in religious thought, particularly as they imply a rejection or diminution of transcendence. Duffey, on the other hand, is best known for his vigorous, albeit losing, campaign for the U.S. Senate in 1970. He now serves as executive director of the American Association of University Professors. Both Duffey and Berger reinforced my growing appreciation of the wider socio-political mission of the Church, calling my attention to such newly developing fields as urban ethics and to some of the earliest popular treatises on Christian *diakonia* (over and above Bonhoeffer's), such as Arnold Come's *Agents of Reconciliation*. The vision and perspective of Peter Berger is captured by the quotation from the Book of Amos which serves to set the tone of his first monograph, *The Noise of Solemn Assemblies: Christian Commitment and the Religious Establishment in America*:

I hate, I despise your feasts, and I take no delight in your solemn assemblies.

Even though you offer me your burnt offerings and cereal offerings, I will not accept them, and the peace offerings of your fatted beasts I will not look upon.

Take away from me the noise of your songs; to the melody of your harps I will not listen.

But let justice roll down like waters, and righteousness like an ever-flowing stream (5:21-24, RSV).

For Berger the social relevance of the Christian community is not a political imperative but an imperative only of the Christian faith. "It is the nature of the Christian faith, not the nature of society, which calls for the prophetic mission of the Christian community. Christians are called to be the salt of the earth. If they cease to be that, they risk betraying the very purpose of the Church of Jesus Christ." He lists four major possibilities of social engagement in the world: (1) Christian diaconate, which is "the helping outreach of the Christian community to individuals in distress—those suffering from illness, poverty, or other personal difficulties"; (2) Christian action, which is "any attempt not only to deal with individuals but also to try to modify the social structure itself"; (3) Christian presence, which may be defined as "the erection of Christian signs in the world" such as was envisaged by Charles de Foucauld in founding the Little Brothers of Jesus; and (4) Christian dialogue, which is "the attempt to engage the Christian faith in conversation with the world."

The Church will be able to engage in these areas of secular mission only to the extent that she can free herself from the bondage of the taken-for-granted religious establishment. Here the distinction between "religion" and authentic Christian faith as proposed by Bonhoeffer is central to Berger's argument. "Religion," he contends, "functions sociologically to represent the integration of the society. Religion may then function psychologically as a 'socializing agency,' that is, to assist the individual to adjust to this society and to be happy in the process." Religion, therefore, serves as a major obstacle to authenticity. It prevents the person from seeing himself objectively, apart from the routines of his everyday life. In fact, "it ratifies the routines, sanctifies the values by which the social roles are rationalized, comforts the individual if personal crises threaten his social adjustment." Thus, *the social irrelevance of the religious establishment is its functionality.*

The main thrust of Berger's thesis is carried through in his second book, *The Precarious Vision: A Sociologist Looks at Social Fictions and Christian Faith*, wherein he reasserts his conviction "that the preponderant tendency of religion is to be socially functional rather than disfunctional. That is, religion will tend to provide integrating symbols rather than symbols of revolution. Religion will tend to legitimate power rather than to put it in question. Religion will tend to find rationalizations for social inequalities (both among the beneficiaries and the injured in these arrangements) rather than to seek their removal." Religion ratifies what he calls the "okay world," and in doing so religion contributes to bad faith because in reality man does not live in an "okay world" at all. Accepting Bonhoeffer's anti-religious critique and his analysis of the "world come of age," Berger synthesizes his own position in this way:

The natural inclinations of man lead him to take society for granted, to identify himself fully with the social roles assigned to him, and to develop ideologies which will organize and dispose of any doubts that might possibly arise. There is an instructive affinity between Christian faith and the analytical enterprise of the social sciences in that both serve to disturb this happy state of affairs. The Christian faith, in its prophetic mission, confronts man with a truth of such force that the precarious pretensions of his social existence disintegrate before it. The debunking effect of social-scientific analysis is far from contradictory to this prophetic mission. Indeed, it might be called its profane auxiliary. The smashing of idols, with whatever hammers, is the underside of prophecy. (p. 204)

I went to Rome in September 1963 where I was exposed to essentially the same Scholastic theology that I had learned in the major seminary. To be sure, the Gregorian University version was more highly sophisticated and its faculty more academically productive. But the most pressing challenge to a new graduate student was linguistic, not intellectual: the lectures, textbooks, and examinations were in Latin. Translating Hebrew into Latin was especially awkward, and taking Latin orals was a particularly embarrassing ordeal. I felt like a runner being asked to shift from dirt track to molasses. Even Churchill would have sounded tongue-tied under such circumstances.

As many others who have done graduate work in Rome would verify, the best part about studying in Rome is studying in Rome. It can be as intellectually arid as it is culturally enriching. Those who, out of some self-interest, wish to sustain the conventional myths about Rome will tell a different story: of how Lonergan alone made it all worthwhile (without prejudice to his achievements, he did not), and of how one professor or another was clearly the leading scholar in his field (they usually were not). Indeed, I was as stunned as I was amused to hear Congar say in 1963 that he had never heard of Lonergan. That may have said more about Congar than about Lonergan, but it said something about the Gregorian's range of influence, too. It wasn't what the American Church's *pauci electi* liked to think in their more triumphalistic moments.

The most important shift in my ecclesiological pursuits occurred while in Rome. Originally I had intended to do my doctoral work on the meaning and theological distinctiveness of ordained ministry. Then, after my conversation with Congar at the Angelicum, I shifted to "The Relationship between Community and Ministry in the Writings of St. Augustine." But the longer I stayed in Rome, the more evident it became that such a project was too ambitious and hence impractical, given the condition of the libraries and (for an American) the peculiar restrictions placed upon their use. They were about as functional as ice-skates in the Sahara.

I had done a special seminar on Christian apologetics in my first semester at the Gregorian and decided, during a Christmas trip to London, to do my seminar paper on John A. T. Robinson's *Honest to God*, a book that had just appeared the previous March and that had immediately made an extraordinary international splash. That modest seminar project was to develop into a doctoral dissertation on Robinson's total ecclesiology, and an early ticket back to the United States.

My work on Robinson proved crucial to my understanding of the Church, and indeed of all theology. In an essay written in 1954, "Kingdom, Church and Ministry," Robinson had argued that our doctrine of the Church, and indeed of ministry as well, has to be fashioned in an eschatological context. Ministry makes sense only in subordination to Church, and Church only in subordination to the Kingdom of God.

His is the most typical spirit of Anglicanism: the spirit of comprehensiveness. He has been critical of both Anglo-Catholics and Liberals, particularly with regard to the debate on Church unity in which they were both engaged between the two world wars. The Anglo-Catholics, he has suggested, placed far too much emphasis on the ministry and apostolic succession: no bishop, no Church! Any doctrine of the Kingdom, i.e., of God's universal rule in history, was subordinated to his design for his Church, and issues in the contemporary world did not sufficiently concern them. The Liberals, on the other hand, appeared to emphasize the *Kingdom* rather than the Kingdom *of God*. They maintained too low a doctrine of the Church, subordinating it to the Social Gospel or the religious experience of the individual; and so, too, was their doctrine of the ministry inadequate. The views of the Anglo-Catholics prevailed, aided partly by the strength of their principles and partly by the direction of world events. Thus, the question of the Church of South India, for example, was debated almost entirely on the Anglo-Catholic priority: "The Church must be judged by the Ministry, and the Kingdom by the Church."

"In this rather depressing situation," he wrote, "the most significant new factor has been the revival in biblical theology, of which in this field the Bishop of Durham's *The Gospel and the Catholic Church* was the harbinger. The result of this revival has been to confirm the position of neither party. Its most immediate and obvious consequence was to confound the Liberals. It convicted them of having pitched their doctrine alike of the Kingdom, the Church, and the Ministry too low. . . . But of greater significance in the long run will perhaps be the question that this biblical theology has put against the whole Anglo-Catholic sequence of priorities.

"The renewed interest in the theology of the New Testament has revealed indeed that nothing less than the highest doctrine of the ministry is compatible with the teaching and practice of Apostolic Christianity . . . providing always our doctrine of the Church is higher. But it does not stop there. For as the ministry is a function of the Church, so the Church is a function of the Kingdom, of the universal Lordship of God in Christ."

In Roman Catholic ecclesiology the Kingdom of God had been understood traditionally as a synonym for the Church. Catholic preachers automatically transposed the parables of the Kingdom into parables of the Church. And many still do. I concluded that this was Roman Catholicism's most serious ecclesiological deficiency: its tendency to identify Church and Kingdom. (The council, too, recognized this problem, at least implicitly, by the addition of article 5 to its Dogmatic Constitution on the Church.) As I would argue in later books, especially *Do We Need the Church?* (1969), the identification of Church and Kingdom is responsible for most, if not all, of our institutional aberrations and for our distorted, or at least incomplete, understanding of mission.

The Church-Kingdom relationship has been a controlling element in all of my writings in theology. It is there in my first published book, *The Church in the Thought of Bishop John Robinson* (Westminster Press, 1966), in Cardinal Richard Cushing's pastoral letter, *The Servant Church* (Advent 1966), which I coauthored, in my *Do We Need the Church?* (Harper & Row, 1969), in my *Church: The Continuing Quest* (Newman

Press, 1970), and in many of my articles and weekly columns
directed to a nonspecialist audience. My personal work, therefore, has generally been ahead of, rather than behind, those
recent developments in theology that move in an explicitly eschatological direction: the theology of hope (Moltmann, Pan-
nenberg, *et al.*), liberation theology (Gutierrez, *et al.*), political
theology (Metz, *et al.*), etc.

Robinson has often been scorned by his colleagues for his
readiness to popularize serious scholarship, although they give
him proper credit for his earlier exegetical and theological
studies, particularly concerning the Johannine literature. Some
of the disfavor has its origin in that durable human passion,
envy. But some of the negative criticism is justified. Robinson
tends to oversimplify in his eagerness to construct syntheses,
and his writings are frequently laden with undigested quotations. However, I shall always be indebted to him for that fundamental insight regarding the Kingdom of God and the
Church.

4. In the last few years I have moved even more explicitly
into the interdisciplinary area of *ecclesiastical reform*. In a
sense, my book *The Remaking of the Church: An Agenda for
Reform* (Harper & Row, 1973) brought my ecclesiological
studies full circle: from theological reflections on the nature
and mission of the Church, to an application of the theological
principles upon the life and structure of the Church herself. For
this reason, I find it impossible to separate my work as a
theologian in the service of the Church from the contemporary
process of institutional change within the Body of Christ. Unlike most of my colleagues in the theological community, my
area of research, lecturing, and writing brings me inevitably
and sometimes forcefully in contact, if not in confrontation,
with the ecclesiastical leadership and the whole structural network of the Church.

In the spring of 1972, my professional life as a theologian
and my identity as an institutional person began to crisscross
with some unpleasant effects. My professional career was pro-
gressing at a reasonably rapid pace. In 1970, at age thirty-four,
I was given a tenured position at Boston College and elected to
the board of directors of the Catholic Theological Society of

America. Two years later I would be promoted to full professor at the university, chairman of its joint doctoral program, and vice-president of the CTSA, succeeding to the presidency in June 1973.

But while my professional life prospered, my more strictly ecclesiastical connections began to fray at the edges. Two events in March of 1972 may have done more to effect this change than any other factors. First, I keynoted the annual convention of the National Federation of Priests' Councils in Denver. I was pilloried on the front page of *The Wanderer* for my assorted heresies, and worse. The conservative-to-reactionary wing of the Catholic Church was alerted to my presence in a dramatically new way. From that point on, I was regularly flogged in their journals and papers. And their assorted pressures, no doubt, have deterred several dioceses and religious communities from inviting me to lecture. Lawyers call this a "chilling effect."

The second event was my signing of an international theological statement, drafted principally by Hans Küng, on the present state of reform in the Catholic Church. I thought it to be an essentially positive and constructive document. Even its title reflected a fundamentally pastoral concern, "Against Discouragement in the Church." But it was perceived very differently by extreme conservatives, and even some moderates. My name and face were prominently displayed in nationally syndicated news stories about the manifesto. *The National Catholic Reporter* gave it major coverage, and *The New York Times* devoted relatively prominent attention to the Vatican's sharply negative reaction. CBS's Rome correspondent, Winston Burdett, announced with trembling voice that the Pope was gravely disturbed by this bold assault upon his authority.

Although my book *The Remaking of the Church* has proved a steady seller for Harper & Row since it first appeared in November of 1973, it has not provoked the kind of controversy I had hoped (but did not expect). I recall confiding to my closest friends, just as the book was ready to appear, that the attention it received would tell me much about the state of American Catholicism. I predicted then that the book would not generate a great amount of controversy (as, for example, Mary Perkins Ryan's *Are Parochial Schools the Answer?* had done more than a decade earlier). And the reason would be, I argued, that interest in reform was dying out, that the reformers had grown discouraged, disinterested, and worse. And I knew, too, that the custodians of power in the Catholic Church would studiously ignore the book. One of my friends with an exquisite sense of imagery had said that this book could have the effect of someone's "driving a motorcycle into a hotel lobby." That may have been so, but instead of confronting the cyclist or calling the police, the proprietors merely sealed off the lobby and resumed operations at another entrance. They cannot refute the arguments for reform, so they follow the next best course: they pretend the arguments do not exist. Their allies are apathy and ennui. But out of such cynical alliances as these can emerge only short-term victories. In the long run, the whole unreformed institutional apparatus that the conservative bureaucrat cherishes faces the near certainty of major transformation. Shall it be a process we shape, or not?

In the summer of 1974 I was appointed Director of Boston College's Institute for the Study of Religious Education and Service, the largest institute of its kind in the United States. I assumed active responsibility for the program in January 1975, after a semester's sabbatical. That sabbatical signaled a turn in my academic research. I followed a systematic reading program in modern political philosophy, from Machiavelli to the present (Hobbes, Locke, Spinoza, Hume, Kant, Marx, Weber, *et al.*). I had hoped thereby to deepen my philosophical foundation and to broaden my theological perceptions, especially as they pertain to the mission of the Church and the socio-political dimensions of the Kingdom of God. I have since been appointed the first Visiting Fellow at the John Fitzgerald Kennedy School of Government, Harvard University.

Undoubtedly, my longstanding interest in politics and political philosophy has nourished and sustained my academic and pastoral concern for ecclesiastical reform. If I had an opportunity now to become something other than a theologian, I should probably choose to be a United States senator, a college president, a constitutional lawyer, and a nationally syndicated political columnist, roughly in that order—or any combination thereof.

Such dispositions of soul may be explained in part by the fact that I have an analytical mind, which gets me quickly to the heart of issues, and a pragmatic sense, which heightens my awareness of their practical implications. I popularize, at some professional risk, because I want to influence people beyond the confines of specialized groups. I want to contribute to the process of reshaping those institutions, including the Church, which affect the quality of human life so directly and so profoundly. That is why I have done a weekly column (which John Macquarrie encouraged me to pursue, in spite of the risks), written four of my eight books for a strictly nonprofessional audience, and delivered hundreds of lectures to priests, religious, and laity in all parts of the United States and Canada.

I have been assured that my writing is clear and orderly, and my lectures, lucid and forceful. I am as confounded as anyone else by the ponderous rhetoric and grammatical gymnastics of some of my more distinguished colleagues (Karl Rahner, for one, as well as the whole Lonergan school), and I am impatient with the cautiousness of some of my friends in the discipline who recoil from drawing too many specific, concrete conclusions (Avery Dulles, and a multitude of others). I do not accept the argument (implied particularly by those in biblical studies) that theology is all a matter of history, texts, and *status quaestionis*. Theology is not paleography, although a few contemporary New Testament scholars might leave us that impression. Neither is it a mere cataloguing, however thorough and sophisticated, of previously expressed positions. What the theologian—and the systematic theologian in particular—requires is insight, judgment, and decisiveness. The sooner he or she is liberated from the sheer mechanisms of bibliographic exploration, the sooner he or she can do theology. For too long we have celebrated the mechanics (those with wide command of languages and even wider chunks of privacy and free time), and deplored our thinkers. And since the mechanics draw a practical conclusion about as regularly as a stone draws a breath, they retain a reasonably good reputation within the ecclesiastical bureaucracy. The systematic thinker, on the other hand, probes, criticizes, diagnoses, and prescribes. And the bureaucracy marginalizes him. He is infrequently invited these days to conduct clergy workshops, never asked to address the body of bishops, and excluded from most national projects and committees.

If this situation perdures, the Catholic Church will continue to forfeit the services of some of its most creative people. Some day, of course, the lines of communication between critical theology and pastoral leadership may be reopened. Anyone seriously committed to the advance of theology and the fruitfulness of the Church's mission can only hope that this day is near at hand.